AF780149

Advances in
MATHEMATICAL ECONOMICS

Aims and Scope. The project is to publish *Advances in Mathematical Economics* once a year under the auspices of the Research Center for Mathematical Economics. It is designed to bring together those mathematicians who are seriously interested in obtaining new challenging stimuli from economic theories and those economists who are seeking effective mathematical tools for their research.

The scope of *Advances in Mathematical Economics* includes, but is not limited to, the following fields:

- Economic theories in various fields based on rigorous mathematical reasoning.
- Mathematical methods (e.g., analysis, algebra, geometry, probability) motivated by economic theories.
- Mathematical results of potential relevance to economic theory.
- Historical study of mathematical economics.

Authors are asked to develop their original results as fully as possible and also to give a clear-cut expository overview of the problem under discussion. Consequently, we will also invite articles which might be considered too long for publication in journals.

S. Kusuoka, A. Yamazaki (Eds.)

Advances in Mathematical Economics

Volume 9

Springer

Shigeo Kusuoka
Professor
Graduate School of Mathematical Sciences
University of Tokyo
3-8-1 Komaba, Meguro-ku
Tokyo, 153-0041 Japan

Akira Yamazaki
Professor
Department of Economics
Meisei University
Hino
Tokyo, 191-8506 Japan

ISBN 978-4-431-99817-4 e-ISBN 978-4-431-34342-4

Printed on acid-free paper
Springer is a part of Springer Science+Business Media
springer.com

Printed in Japan

Camera-ready copy prepared from the authors' LaTeXfiles.

Table of Contents

Adv. Math. Econ. 9, 1–23 (2006)

Advances in
MATHEMATICAL
ECONOMICS

Option on a unit-type closed-end investment fund

Takashi Adachi*

Fukushima Medical University, Fukushima City, Fukushima 960-1295, Japan
(e-mail: ada@fmu.ac.jp)

Received: October 26, 2004
Revised: November 30, 2005

JEL classification: C61, G13

Mathematics Subject Classification (2000): 49L20, 60H30, 93E20

Abstract. In this paper we study options on a unit-type closed-end investment fund. These options are included among the exotic options, because the underlying asset of the options is the value process of the investment fund and therefore depends on a fund manager (= an option writer)'s action. We prove that a fair price of such option is represented as the value function of the associated stochastic exit time control problem. Using Hajek's mean comparison theorem, we find an explicit form of the fair option premium in the case of a constant volatility. We also characterize the fair option premium as a limit of a sequence of classical solutions to the associated Hamilton-Jacobi-Bellman equations with a classical Dirichlet boundary condition in the case of a diffusion market model.

Key words: capital guaranteed fund, stochastic exit time control, fair option premium, dynamic programming principle

1. Introduction

There are a considerable number of capital guaranteed funds in a financial market. One of them is a unit-type closed-end investment fund with a guarantee of refunding at least a set percentage of a principal at a redemption date. Such guarantee can be regarded as an option which is written on the investment fund and gives its holder the right to receive the difference between the set percentage of the principal and the value of the investment fund when the value of the investment fund is less than the set percentage of the principal (see Example 2.1). However the study of such options has been strangely neglected by

* I would like to express my gratitude to the anonymous referee for valuable comments and suggestions on this paper.

students in the field of the mathematical finance to the best of my knowledge. In this study, therefore, we investigate the options on the unit-type closed-end investment fund in the framework of the mathematical finance.

The feature that differentiates the options on the investment fund from the typical contingent claims is that a price fluctuation of the underlying asset (= the investment fund) depends on a trading strategy of an option writer (= a fund manager). This feature gives rise to the stochastic control problem and we will show that a fair price of the option on the investment fund is given by the value function of the associated stochastic control problem. Another option that the price fluctuation of the underlying asset depends on an action of the parties (= the option writer and/or holder) concerned about an option trading is the passport option which has been studied by Ahn *et al.* [2], Delbaen and Yor [7], Henderson [11], Henderson and Hobson [12], Hyer *et al.* [13], Nagayama [21], Shreve and Večeř [22] and the author [1]. For the case that the option holder does not have the right to redeem before maturity, we can directly apply their methods for analyzing the passport option to making an estimate of the fair price of the option on the investment fund. In particular, in §4.2 we will use the methods of Shreve and Večeř [22] to obtain an explicit form of the fair option premium in the case of a constant volatility.

We also treat the case that the option holder has the right to redeem before maturity. In this study, a criterion of an option holder's decision to redeem before maturity is set up at a purchase date of the option, and we define a redemption date as an exit time of the value process of the investment fund from some region (see (2.6)). Then we will be in need of the Dynamic Programming Principle (DPP, for short) for the stochastic exit time control problem to determine the fair option premium. In our model, although both a drift coefficient and diffusion coefficient of a controlled process depend on a control which takes value in an unbounded set, each of them is *linearly* dependent on the control. Therefore, under some conditions (see Assumption 3.1), we can adapt the arguments in §5.6 of Karatzas and Shreve [17] to our stochastic control problem in order to obtain the DPP. We will establish the DPP in §5. (We remark that we can not directly utilize the existent results for the DPP in Borkar [5] and Lions [19], because Borkar [5] was studied for only the case where the diffusion coefficient was independent of the control and it is difficult to check that the standing assumption of Lions [19, (A.2)] is satisfied with the exception of several examples.) In the dynamic programming approach to the stochastic control problem, one of most important aspects is to approximate the value function by classical solutions of the associated Hamilton-Jacobi-Bellman (HJB, for short) equations. In §4.3 we also study our control problem in this line.

This paper is organized as follows. In the next section, we specify the market model and the options on the investment fund. The main result is given in

§3. §4.2 and §4.3 present the probabilistic approach and the partial differential equational approach to the estimates of the fair option premium, respectively. The proofs of these claims are given in §5.

2. Option on investment fund

2.1 Market

Let us deal with the following model for a frictionless financial market where $N+1$ assets are traded continuously up to some fixed time horizon T. One of them is non-risky and has a price $P_0(t) = \exp\left(\int_0^t r(s)\,ds\right)$, $0 \le t \le T$. The remaining N assets are risky; their price processes $\{\widehat{P}_i(\cdot)\}_{1\le i\le N}$ are modelled by the linear stochastic differential equations

$$\frac{d\widehat{P}_i(t)}{\widehat{P}_i(t)} = \mu_i(t)\,dt + \sigma_i(t)^\top d\widehat{B}(t), \qquad 0 \le t \le T, \qquad \widehat{P}_i(0) = p_i > 0,$$

and their dividend rates are given by non-negative processes $\{\widehat{d}_i(\cdot)\}_{1\le i\le N}$. Here $\top$ denotes the transpose operation and $\widehat{B}(\cdot) = (\widehat{B}_1(\cdot),\ldots,\widehat{B}_N(\cdot))^\top$ is a standard N-dimensional Brownian motion on a complete probability space $(\Omega,\mathcal{F},\widehat{\mathbb{P}})$, endowed with a filtration $\mathbb{F} = \{\mathcal{F}_t\}_{0\le t\le T}$ which is the $\widehat{\mathbb{P}}$-augmentation of the filtration generated by the Brownian motion $\widehat{B}$. We assume that the risk-free rate process $r(\cdot)$, the dividend rate process $\widehat{d}(\cdot) := (\widehat{d}_1(\cdot),\ldots,\widehat{d}_N(\cdot))^\top$, the mean earning rate process $\mu(\cdot) := (\mu_1(\cdot),\ldots,\mu_N(\cdot))^\top$ and the $\mathbf{R}^N \otimes \mathbf{R}^N$-valued volatility process $\sigma(\cdot) := (\sigma_1(\cdot),\ldots,\sigma_N(\cdot))$ are $\mathbb{F}$-progressively measurable and satisfy the mild condition

$$\int_0^T \left[|r(t)| + \sum_{i=1}^N \{\widehat{d}_i(t) + |\mu_i(t)| + |\sigma_i(t)|^2\}\right] dt < \infty \qquad a.s.$$

We shall denote by $\mathcal{P}$ the set of all $\mathbf{R}^N$-valued $\mathbb{F}$-progressively measurable processes $p(\cdot)$ such that $\int_0^T |\sigma(t)p(t)|^2 dt < \infty$ *a.s.*

Furthermore we assume that the market is standard and complete.[1] Then $\sigma(t,\omega)$ is non-singular for *a.e.* $(t,\omega) \in [0,T] \times \Omega$, the process $\theta_0(\cdot) := \sigma(\cdot)^{-1}(\mu(\cdot)+\widehat{d}(\cdot)-r(\cdot)\mathbf{1}_N)$ satisfies $\int_0^T |\theta_0(s)|^2 ds < \infty$ *a.s.*, and the process

$$Z_0(t) := \exp\left[-\int_0^t \theta_0(s)^\top d\widehat{B}(s) - \frac{1}{2}\int_0^t |\theta_0(s)|^2\,ds\right], \qquad 0 \le t \le T,$$

[1] For the definition of the standard and complete market, we can refer to Chapter 1 in Karatzas and Shreve [17].

is a $(\widehat{\mathbb{P}}, \mathbb{F})$-martingale, where $\mathbf{1}_N := (1, \ldots, 1)^\top \in \mathbf{R}^N$. Thanks to Girsanov's theorem,[2] therefore, the market has the risk-neutral equivalent martingale measure $\mathbb{P}$ defined by $\mathbb{P}(A) := \int_A Z_0(T, \omega)\widehat{\mathbb{P}}(d\omega)$, $A \in \mathcal{F}_T$, and $B(t) := \widehat{B}(t) + \int_0^t \theta_0(s)\, ds$, $0 \le t \le T$, is a standard N-dimensional Brownian motion on $(\Omega, \mathcal{F}_T, \mathbb{P}, \mathbb{F})$.

Let $\pi(t) = (\pi_1(t), \ldots, \pi_N(t))^\top$ be the amount of money invested in corresponding assets at time t. If we denote by $\widehat{W}^{w,\pi}(t)$ the wealth of a small investor at time t, the self-financed wealth process $\widehat{W}^{w,\pi}(\cdot)$ obeys the equation

$$d\widehat{W}(t) = \sum_{i=1}^N \pi_i(t) \left\{ \widehat{d}_i(t)\, dt + \frac{d\widehat{P}_i(t)}{\widehat{P}_i(t)} \right\} + \left\{ \widehat{W}(t) - \sum_{i=1}^N \pi_i(t) \right\} \frac{dP_0(t)}{P_0(t)}, \quad (2.1)$$

$0 \le t \le T$, with an initial wealth $\widehat{W}(0) = w$. And hence, if $\pi(\cdot) \in \mathcal{P}$, the discounted self-financed wealth process $W^{w,\pi}(\cdot) := \widehat{W}^{w,\pi}(\cdot)/P_0(\cdot)$ is given by

$$W^{w,\pi}(t) = w + \int_0^t \frac{(\sigma(s)\pi(s))^\top}{P_0(s)}\, dB(s), \qquad 0 \le t \le T. \quad (2.2)$$

Also the discounted price processes $\{P_i(\cdot) := \widehat{P}_i(\cdot)/P_0(\cdot)\}_{1 \le i \le N}$ satisfy the equations

$$\frac{dP_i(t)}{P_i(t)} = -\widehat{d}_i(t)\, dt + \sigma_i(t)^\top dB(t), \qquad 0 \le t \le T, \qquad P_i(0) = p_i > 0.$$

We set $P(\cdot) := (P_0(\cdot), P_1(\cdot), \ldots, P_N(\cdot))^\top$.

2.2 Investment fund

We consider a unit-type closed-end investment fund. Let $\widehat{X}_1(t)$ be the value of the investment fund, $q(t) = (q_1(t), \ldots, q_N(t))^\top$ be the proportions of $\widehat{X}_1(t)$ invested in corresponding assets, and $\delta(t)\widehat{X}_1(t)$ be the distribution of gains from investment at time t. Then, as in (2.1), the process $\widehat{X}_1(\cdot)$ obeys the equation

$$\frac{d\widehat{X}_1(t)}{\widehat{X}_1(t)} = \sum_{i=1}^N q_i(t) \left\{ \widehat{d}_i(t)\, dt + \frac{d\widehat{P}_i(t)}{\widehat{P}_i(t)} \right\} + \left\{ 1 - \sum_{i=1}^N q_i(t) - \delta(t) \right\} \frac{dP_0(t)}{P_0(t)},$$

$0 \le t \le T$, with an initial capital $\widehat{X}_1(0) = x > 0$. Hence if we denote by $\mathcal{D}$ the class of all $\mathbb{F}$-progressively measurable processes $\delta(\cdot)$ such that $0 \le \delta(\cdot) < 1$

[2] See Theorem 3.5.1 of Karatzas and Shreve [16].

a.e., and if $u(\cdot) = (\delta(\cdot), q(\cdot)) \in \mathcal{D} \times \mathcal{P}$, then the discounted value process $X_1^{x,u}(\cdot) := \widehat{X}_1^{x,u}(\cdot)/P_0(\cdot)$ of the investment fund satisfies the equation

$$\frac{dX_1(t)}{X_1(t)} = -\delta(t)\,dt + (\sigma(t)q(t))^\top dB(t), \quad 0 \le t \le T, \quad X_1(0) = x, \quad (2.3)$$

and $X_1^{x,u}(\cdot) > 0$ *a.e.* We assume that the fund manager can choose the strategy $u(\cdot) = (\delta(\cdot), q(\cdot))$ from among some class $\mathcal{U} \subset \mathcal{D} \times \mathcal{P}$.

2.3 Option

Let us consider the following options. A financial institution is planning to sell the investment fund $\mathcal{U}$ with an *option* whose holder has the right to receive the payment

$$P_0(\tau_0) f(\tau_0, X_0^u(\tau_0), X_1^{x,u}(\tau_0), P(\tau_0)) \qquad \text{at time } \tau_0 \in [0,T], \qquad (2.4)$$

where f is a nonnegative continuous function on $[0,T] \times [0,\infty) \times (0,\infty)^{N+2}$ with the properties $f(t,\cdot,x_1,p)$ (resp. $f(t,x_0,\cdot,p)$) is non-increasing for each $(t,x_1,p) \in [0,T] \times (0,\infty)^{N+2}$ (resp. $(t,x_0,p) \in [0,T] \times [0,\infty) \times (0,\infty)^{N+1}$),

$$X_0^u(t) := \int_0^t \delta(s) X_1^{x,u}(s) l_0(P_0(s))\,ds,$$

l_0 is a nonnegative continuous function on $(0,\infty)$, a call date $\tau_0 = \tau_0^{x,p,u}$ before maturity T is

$$\tau_0 := \inf\{t \ge 0 : (X_0^u(t), X_1^{x,u}(t), P(t)) \notin O\} \wedge T,$$

and O is an open subset of $\mathbf{R}^{N+3}$.

Example 2.1 (Capital Guaranteed Funds). The discounted payoff function corresponding to the capital guaranteed funds is represented as

$$\begin{aligned} &f(t, X_0^u(t), X_1^{x_1,u}(t), P(t)) \\ &\quad = \frac{1}{l_1(P_0(t))} \left(a x_1 - \{X_0^u(t) + l_1(P_0(t)) X_1^{x_1,u}(t)\}\right)^+ \end{aligned} \qquad (2.5)$$

for some constant $a > 0$ and a positive function $l_1 \in C(0,\infty)$. In §4 we will study for the following cases:

(A) In the case $l_0(\cdot) \equiv 0$ and $l_1(\cdot) \equiv 1$ (resp. $l_1(p_0) = p_0$), the investment fund with the option (2.5) guarantees to refund at least $100a\%$ of the *real* (resp. *nominal*) value of the principal x_1, since

$$\max\{a x_1, X_1^{x_1,u}(t)\} = X_1^{x_1,u}(t) + (a x_1 - X_1^{x_1,u}(t))^+.$$

(B) In the case $l_0(\cdot) = l_1(\cdot) \equiv 1$ (resp. $l_0(p_0) = l_1(p_0) = p_0$), the investment fund with the option (2.5) guarantees that the sum of the redemption value and the total distribution of gains from investment is not less than ax_1 in *real* (resp. *nominal*) terms.

In relation to the examples above, we are interested in the following call date:

$$\tau_0 := \inf\{t \geq 0 : Y^u(t) := X_0^u(t) + l_1(P_0(t))X_1^{x_1,u}(t) \leq bx_1\} \wedge T \quad (2.6)$$

for $0 \leq b < a \wedge 1$. In §4 we will estimate the fair option premium for such cases by making use of Hajek's mean comparison theorem and the standard theory of the partial differential equations (PDEs, for short).

3. Fair price

Our purpose is to estimate the fair price of the option (2.4). The objective of the option writer is to find a pair of strategies (π, u) such that

$$W^{w,\pi}(\tau_0) \geq f\big(\tau_0, X_0^u(\tau_0), X_1^{x,u}(\tau_0), P(\tau_0)\big) \qquad a.s., \quad (3.1)$$

where w is the amount that the writer receives from the holder at time $t = 0$. The inequality (3.1) says that the writer's wealth starting with the initial wealth w will have grown by the call date τ_0 enough to cover the payment $P_0(\tau_0)f\big(\tau_0, X_0^u(\tau_0), X_1^{x,u}(\tau_0), P(\tau_0)\big)$ which he has to provide the holder at τ_0. We remark that the aim of replicating the option does not conflict with an obligation to seek to increase the value of investment fund because $f(t, \cdot, x_1, p)$ and $f(t, x_0, \cdot, p)$ are non-increasing. Therefore the *upper hedging price*, which is the least initial amount w that enables the writer to achieve (3.1), is denoted by

$$h_{up}(x, p) = \inf\{w \in H_{up}(x, p)\}$$

for each $(x, p) \in (0, \infty)^{N+2}$, where

$$H_{up}(x,p) = \left\{ w \geq 0 \;\middle|\; \begin{array}{l} \exists(\pi, u) \in \mathcal{P} \times \mathcal{U} \quad s.t. \\ \text{(i) } \exists\beta \in \mathbf{R} \ s.t.\ \mathbb{P}\{W^{0,\pi}(t) \geq \beta,\ t \in [0,T]\} = 1. \\ \text{(ii) (3.1) is achieved.} \end{array} \right\}$$

On the other hands, the option holder desires to find a portfolio strategy π^u, which is chosen according to a strategy u making up the investment fund, such that

$$W^{-w,\pi^u}(\tau_0) + f\big(\tau_0, X_0^u(\tau_0), X_1^{x,u}(\tau_0), P(\tau_0)\big) \geq 0 \qquad a.s., \quad (3.2)$$

where $-w$ is the debt that he incurred at time $t = 0$ by purchasing the option. The inequality (3.2) means that if he adopts the strategy π^u then the payment

$P_0(\tau_0)f\big(\tau_0, X_0^u(\tau_0), X_1^{x,u}(\tau_0), P(\tau_0)\big)$ at the call date τ_0 make it possible for him to cover the debt $-w$. Therefore the *lower hedging price*, which is the largest amount w that enables the holder to achieve (3.2), is denoted by

$$h_{low}(x,p) = \sup\{w \in H_{low}(x,p)\}$$

for each $(x,p) \in (0,\infty)^{N+2}$, where

$$H_{low}(x,p) = \left\{ w \geq 0 \;\middle|\; \begin{array}{l} \forall u \in \mathcal{U}, \quad \exists \pi^u \in \mathcal{P} \quad s.t. \\ \text{(i)}\;\; W^{0,\pi^u}(\cdot) \text{ is a } (\mathbb{P},\mathbb{F})\text{-supermartingale.} \\ \text{(ii)}\;\; (3.2) \text{ is achieved.} \end{array} \right\}.$$

To ensure $h_{up} = h_{low}$, we are now in a position to make some conditions.

Assumption 3.1.

(i) *For each $u \in \mathcal{U}$, there exists $m > 1$ such that*

$$\mathbb{E}\left[\sup_{0\leq t\leq T} f(t, X_0^u(t), X_1^{x,u}(t), P(t))^m\right] < \infty.$$

(ii) *There exists a sequence $\{f_n\}_{n=1}^{\infty}$ of $C^{1,1,2}([0,T]\times[0,\infty)\times(0,\infty)^{N+2})$ such that*

$$\lim_{n\to\infty} \|f - f_n\|_\infty = 0 \qquad \textit{and} \qquad \mathbb{E}\left[\int_0^T |G^u f_n(t)|\, dt\right] < \infty$$

for each $u \in \mathcal{U}$ and $n \geq 1$, where $\int_0^{\bullet} G^u f_n(t)\, dt$ is the finite variation process in the canonical decomposition of the semimartingale $f_n\big(\cdot, X_0^u(\cdot), X_1^{x,u}(\cdot), P(\cdot)\big)$.

Then we have the main result:

Theorem 3.2. *Under Assumption 3.1, $h_{up}(x,p) = h_{low}(x,p) = V(x,p)$ for each $(x,p) \in (0,\infty)^{N+2}$, namely, the fair price of the option* (2.4) *is given by $V(x,p)$, where*

$$V(x,p) = \inf_{u\in\mathcal{U}} \mathbb{E}\big[f\big(\tau_0, X_0^u(\tau_0), X_1^{x,u}(\tau_0), P^p(\tau_0)\big)\big]. \tag{3.3}$$

4. Estimates for Example 2.1

In this section, we confine our attention to the problem of estimating the fair price of the option (2.5) with the call date (2.6). In order to begin addressing this problem, we make sure that the process $Y^{x_1,u}(\cdot) = X_0^u(\cdot) + l_1(P_0(\cdot))X_1^{x_1,u}(\cdot)$ obeys the equations:

$$\text{In the case (A): } \frac{dY(t)}{Y(t)} = \big(-\delta(t) + l_1'(P_0(t))r(t)\big)\,dt + \big(\sigma(t)q(t)\big)^\top dB(t), \tag{4.1}$$

$$\text{In the case (B): } \frac{dY(t)}{l_1(P_0(t))X_1(t)} = l_1'(P_0(t))r(t)\,dt + \big(\sigma(t)q(t)\big)^\top dB(t),$$

respectively.

4.1 Zero-premium option

To start with, we consider for the case $u_0 \equiv 0 \in \mathcal{U}$. We first see that

$$V(x_1, p) = x_1(a-1)^+, \qquad (x_1, p) \in (0, \infty)^{N+2}$$

for the case $l_1(\cdot) \equiv 1$. Indeed, since $Y^{x_1,u}(\cdot)$ is a $(\mathbb{P}, \mathbb{F})$-supermartingale, Jensen's inequality gives

$$\mathbb{E}\Big[\big(ax_1 - Y^{x_1,u}(\tau_0^u)\big)^+\Big] \geq x_1(a-1)^+ = \mathbb{E}\Big[\big(ax_1 - Y^{x_1,u_0}(\tau_0^{u_0})\big)^+\Big]$$

for all $u \in \mathcal{U}$.

Further, we suppose that $T^{-1}\log a \leq r(t)$ *a.s.* for every $t \in [0, T]$. Then, for the case $l_1(p_0) = p_0$, we obtain $V(x_1, p) = 0$ because $Y^{x_1,u_0}(T) = x_1 P_0(T) \geq a\, x_1$.

Consequently, we have the fact: *If* $0 \in \mathcal{U}, 0 < a \leq 1$ *and the risk-free rate* $r(\cdot)$ *is non-negative, then the fair price of the option* (2.5) *with the call date* (2.6) *is equal to zero.*

Remark 4.1. The condition $0 \in \mathcal{U}$ enables the fund manager to invest all the funds in risk-less asset. And then he may invest all the funds in risk-less asset to avoid the advanced redemption, even if he knows that it may be against the beneficiary's own interests. For reasons mentioned above, it seems reasonable to assume that $0 \notin \mathcal{U}$. In §4.3, therefore, we will develop the arguments under the condition $0 \notin \mathcal{U}$.

4.2 Constant volatility

Next we consider for the case $l_0(\cdot) \equiv 0$ and $l_1(\cdot) \equiv 1$, i.e.,

$$f\big(t, X_0^u(t), X_1^{x_1,u}(t), P(t)\big) = \big(ax_1 - X_1^{x_1,u}(t)\big)^+,$$
$$\tau_0 = \inf\big\{t \geq 0 : X_1^{x_1,u}(t) \leq bx_1\big\} \wedge T$$

in the market with a constant volatility matrix $\sigma(\cdot) \equiv \sigma \in \mathbf{R}^N \otimes \mathbf{R}^N$. We also assume that

$$\mathcal{U} = \big\{(0,q(\cdot)) \in \{0\} \times \mathcal{P} : q(t,\omega) \in Q \quad \text{for } \textit{a.e.} \ (t,\omega) \in [0,T] \times \Omega\big\}$$

for some compact subset Q of $\mathbf{R}^N$. Then Hajek's mean comparison theorem[3] gives

$$V(x_1,p) = \mathbb{E}\Big[\big(ax_1 - X_1^{x_1,u_*}(\tau_0)\big)^+\Big] = x_1\varphi(a,b,T\colon u_*) \tag{4.2}$$

where $u_*(\cdot) \equiv (0,q_*)$, $q_* := \arg\min_{q\in Q} |\sigma q|^2$,

$$\varphi(a,b,T\colon q_*)$$
$$:= \begin{cases} (a-1)^+ & \text{if } q_* = 0 \\ \int_{\mathbf{R}} \big(a - e^{|\sigma q_*|x - \frac{1}{2}|\sigma q_*|^2 T}\big)^+ \, \mathbb{P}\{\widetilde{\mathbf{w}}(T) \in dx\} & \text{if } q_* \neq 0,\ b = 0\ , \\ \psi(a,b,T\colon q_*) & \text{if } q_* \neq 0,\ b > 0 \end{cases}$$

$$\psi(a,b,T\colon q_*) := \frac{(a-b)}{\sqrt{b}} \int_0^T e^{-\frac{1}{8}|\sigma q_*|^2 t} \mathbb{P}\{T_{\widehat{b}} \in dt\}$$
$$+ \int_0^{\widehat{b}} \int_{-\infty}^{y} e^{\frac{1}{2}|\sigma q_*|x - \frac{1}{8}|\sigma q_*|^2 T} \big(a - e^{-|\sigma q_*|x}\big)^+ \, \mathbb{P}\big\{\widetilde{\mathbf{w}}(T) \in dx,\ \widetilde{\mathbf{w}}^*(T) \in dy\big\},$$

$\widetilde{\mathbf{w}}^*(\cdot)$ is the running maximum of a standard 1-dimensional Brownian motion $\widetilde{\mathbf{w}}(\cdot)$ and $T_{\widehat{b}}$ is the passage time of $\widetilde{\mathbf{w}}(\cdot)$ to the level $\widehat{b} = (-\log b)/|\sigma q_*|$. For the distributions of $\widetilde{\mathbf{w}}^*(\cdot)$ and $T_{\widehat{b}}$, we can refer to §2.8 in Karatzas and Shreve [16]. Although the claim (4.2) is similar to that of Shreve and Večeř [22] for the passport options, we give its proof for the interested reader in §5.2.

Moreover, for the case $a < 1$ and $q_* \neq 0$, there exists a $\gamma \in (0,1)$ such that

$$\gamma \cdot \varphi\Big(\frac{a}{\gamma}, b, T\colon q_*\Big) + \gamma = 1, \quad \textit{i.e.} \ \inf_{u\in\mathcal{U}} \mathbb{E}\big[\max\{ax_1, \gamma X_1^{x_1,u}(\tau_0)\}\big] = x_1 \tag{4.3}$$

which means that the option premium $\inf_u \mathbb{E}\big[(ax_1 - \gamma X_1^{x_1,u}(\tau_0))^+\big]$ can be paid by the trust fee $(1-\gamma)X_1^{x_1,u}(\tau_0)$ at the call date τ_0.

4.3 PDE approach

As can be seen in §5.2, the probabilistic approach is based upon the theory of the random time changes and the martingale problems. However it is difficult to apply such theory to the control problem in the case of a general Markovian financial market. Therefore we finally survey an approximation method of the value of the option premium by classical solutions to the Dirichlet problem for the HJB equations corresponding to the stochastic exit time control problem (3.3).

[3] See Theorem 3 in Hajek [10].

We assume that the functions $r(t,p)$, $\widehat{d}(t,p)$ and $\sigma(t,p)$ on $[0,T] \times [0,\infty)^{N+1}$ are bounded and locally Lipschitz continuous, and take values in $\mathbf{R}$, $[0,\infty)^N$ and $\mathbf{R}^N \otimes \mathbf{R}^N$, respectively. And we assume that the investment fund $\mathcal{U} = \mathcal{U}(0,p)$ is defined by

$$\mathcal{U}(t,p) = \left\{ u \in \mathcal{D} \times \mathcal{P} : \begin{array}{l} u(s,\omega) \in \mathrm{B}_{N+1}(u^*(s,P(s,\omega)),R) \cap \mathbf{U} \\ a.e.\ (s,\omega) \in [t,T] \times \{\omega \in \Omega : P(t,\omega) = p\} \end{array} \right\}.$$

for each $(t,p) \in [0,T] \times \mathbf{R}^N$, a closed domain $\mathbf{U} = \overline{Q}_0 \times \overline{Q} \subset [0,1) \times \mathbf{R}^N$, the k-dimensional closed ball $\mathrm{B}_k(c,r)$ centered at c with radius r and a positive constant R, where a $\mathbf{U}$-valued continuous function $u^*(\cdot)$ on $[0,T] \times [0,\infty)^{N+1}$ satisfies the polynomial growth condition:

$$|u^*(t,p)| \le c_0(1+|p|^K), \qquad (t,p) \in [0,T] \times [0,\infty)^{N+1},$$

for certain constants c_0, $K > 0$. If necessary, we can think that $u^* = (\delta^*, q^*)$ is an optimal strategy for a consumption/portfolio optimization problem under constraint $(\delta, q) \in \mathbf{U}$ and $\mathrm{B}_{N+1}(u^*, R)$ is a confidence region of which the determination rests on actual results of investment managements.

As mentioned in Remark 4.1, we also assume

$$Q \cap \mathrm{B}_N(0,r_0) = \emptyset \qquad \text{for some } r_0 > 0. \tag{4.4}$$

And we shall define the set $\mathbb{U}[g](t,p) := \mathbf{U} \cap \mathrm{B}_{N+1}(g(t,p),R)$ for each $(t,p) \in [0,T] \times \mathbf{R}^N$ and $\mathbf{R}^{N+1}$-valued function g on $[0,T] \times \mathbf{R}^N$.

In the above setting, (3.3) become

$$V(x_1, e^p) = x_1 \widehat{V}(0,p,0,1), \qquad x_1 > 0,\ p \in \mathbf{R}^{N+1},$$

where $e^p := (e^{p_0}, \ldots, e^{p_N})$,

$$\widehat{V}(t,p,x,y) := \inf_{u \in \mathcal{U}(t,e^p)} \mathbb{E}_t^{p,x,y}\left[\frac{(a - Y(\tau_t))^+}{l_1(P_0(\tau_t))}\right], \qquad (t,p,x,y) \in [0,T] \times \mathbf{R}^{N+3},$$

$\tau_t := \inf\{s \ge t : Y(s) \le b\} \wedge T$ and the suffices of $\mathbb{E}$ indicate that we have specified the data $(P(t), X_1(t), Y(t)) = (e^p, e^x, y)$. (Needless to say, $\widehat{V}$ dose not depend on x in the case (A) by (4.1).) Therefore our aim is to approximate the value function $\widehat{V}$ by classical solutions to the Dirichlet problem for the corresponding HJB equations. When u^* is not the constant function and $\mathbf{U} \ne \{\delta_0\} \times \mathbf{R}^N$ for all $\delta_0 \in [0,1)$, the feature that differentiates our problem from the standard stochastic control problems is that the state space of controls depends on the data $(t, P(t))$. As can be seen below, however, the usual penalty method will lead us to the goal of this subsection. (In Lions [19, § III.1], he mentioned that it was possible to develop the argument on the case of control sets depending upon the data. However he did not develop it there.) From now onward, we consider for only the case (B). We can also develop the same arguments for the case (A), and we leave them to the reader.

Let us introduce an approximation $V_{n,m,k}$ of $\widehat{V}$. For $g = r$, $\widehat{d}$, σ and u^*, let us set

$$g_n(t,p) := g\left(t, \exp\left[\frac{2np}{(2n) \vee |p|}\right]\right), \qquad (t,p) \in [0,T] \times \mathbf{R}^{N+1},\ n \geq 1,$$

and we denote by $\{g_{n,m}\}_m$ a mollification of a bounded uniformly continuous extension $\widetilde{g}_n$ of g_n from $[0,T] \times \mathbf{R}^{N+1}$ to $\mathbf{R}^{N+2}$, i.e.,

$$g_{n,m}(t,p) = \int_{\mathbf{R}^{N+2}} \widetilde{g}_n(s,q)\zeta_m(t-s, p-q)\, ds\, dq, \qquad (t,p) \in \mathbf{R}^{N+2},$$

for a sequence $\{\zeta_m\}_m$ of $C^\infty(\mathbf{R}^{N+2})$ such that $\zeta_m \geq 0$, $\int_{\mathbf{R}^{N+2}} \zeta_m(x)\, dx = 1$ and $\operatorname{supp} \zeta_m \subset \mathrm{B}_{N+2}(0, m^{-1})$. We also put $\Phi(x) := x^+ \wedge (2a)$ and denote by Φ_m a mollification of Φ. Now we introduce the value functions

$$V_{n,m,k}(t,p,x,y) := \inf_{u \in \mathcal{U}_{n,m}} \left\{k\widetilde{J}_{n,m}(t,p,x,y,u) + J_{n,m}(t,p,x,y,u)\right\}, \quad (4.5)$$
$$V_{n,m}(t,p,x,y) := \inf_{u \in \mathcal{U}_{n,m}(t,p)} J_{n,m}(t,p,x,y,u),$$

for $(t,p,x,y) \in [0,T] \times \mathbf{R}^{N+3}$ and n, m, $k \geq 1$, where

$$J_{n,m}(t,p,x,y,u) := \mathbf{E}\left[\frac{\Phi_m(a - Y^{n,m}(\widehat{\tau}_t^{n,m}))}{\widehat{l}_1(P_0^{n,m}(\widehat{\tau}_t^{n,m}))} \,\middle|\, \begin{array}{l} P^{n,m}(t) = p \\ X^{n,m}(t) = x \\ Y^{n,m}(t) = y \end{array}\right],$$

$$\widetilde{J}_{n,m}(t,p,x,y,u) := \mathbf{E}\left[\int_t^{\widehat{\tau}_t^{n,m}} L_{n,m}(s, P^{n,m}(s), u(s))\, ds \,\middle|\, \begin{array}{l} P^{n,m}(t) = p \\ X^{n,m}(t) = x \\ Y^{n,m}(t) = y \end{array}\right],$$

$$L_{n,m}(t,p,u) := \left\{\left(|u - u^*_{n,m}(t,p)|^2 - R^2\right)^+\right\}^3,$$
$$\mathbf{U}_{n,m} := \mathbf{U} \cap \mathrm{B}_{N+1}(0, \|u^*_{n,m}\|_\infty + R),$$
$$\mathcal{U}_{n,m} := \{u \in \mathcal{D} \times \mathcal{P} : u(t,\omega) \in \mathbf{U}_{n,m} \ \textit{a.e.}\},$$
$$\mathcal{U}_{n,m}(t,p) := \left\{u \in \mathcal{D} \times \mathcal{P} : \begin{array}{l} u(s,\omega) \in \mathbb{U}[u^*_{n,m}](s, P^{n,m}(s,\omega)) \\ \textit{a.e.}\ (s,\omega) \in [t,T] \times \{\omega : P^{n,m}(t,\omega) = p\} \end{array}\right\},$$
$$\widehat{\tau}_t^{n,m} := \inf\left\{s \geq t : \begin{array}{l} (P^{n,m}(s), X^{n,m}(s), Y^{n,m}(s)) \\ \notin O_n := \mathit{int}\, \mathrm{B}_{N+2}(0,n) \times (b, b+e^n) \end{array}\right\} \wedge T,$$

and $\widehat{l}_1(p_0) := l_1(e^{p_0})$. Here, for each control $u(\cdot) = (\delta(\cdot), q(\cdot)) \in \mathcal{D} \times \mathcal{P}$, the processes $X^{n,m}$, $Y^{n,m}$ and $P^{n,m} = (P_0^{n,m}, \ldots, P_N^{n,m})$ obey the equations

$$
\begin{aligned}
dX^{n,m}(t) &= -\big(\delta(t) + 2^{-1}|\sigma_{n,m}(t, P^{n,m}(t))q(t)|^2\big)\,dt \\
&\quad + (\sigma_{n,m}(t, P^{n,m}(t))q(t))^\top dB(t) + m^{-1}\,d\widetilde{B}_{N+1}(t), \\
dY^{n,m}(t) &= \widehat{\beta}^Y_{n,m}(t, P^{n,m}(t), X^{n,m}(t))\,dt \\
&\quad + \widehat{\sigma}^Y(P^{n,m}(t), X^{n,m}(t))(\sigma_{n,m}(t, P^{n,m}(t))q(t))^\top dB(t) \\
&\quad + m^{-1}\,d\widetilde{B}_{N+2}(t), \\
dP_0^{n,m}(t) &= r_{n,m}(t, P^{n,m}(t))\,dt + m^{-1}\,d\widetilde{B}_0(t), \\
dP_i^{n,m}(t) &= -\big(\widehat{d}_{n,m,i}(t, P^{n,m}(t)) + 2^{-1}|\sigma_{n,m,i}(t, P^{n,m}(t))|^2\big)\,dt \\
&\quad + \sigma_{n,m,i}(t, P^{n,m}(t))^\top dB(t) + m^{-1}\,d\widetilde{B}_i(t),
\end{aligned}
$$

$1 \le i \le N$, respectively, where[4]

$$(\widehat{\beta}^Y_{n,m}(t,p,x), \widehat{\sigma}^Y(p,x)) := \widehat{l}_1(p_0)e^x(l_1'(p_0)r_{n,m}(t,p), 1)$$

and $\widetilde{B}(\cdot)^\top = (\widetilde{B}_0(\cdot), \ldots, \widetilde{B}_{N+2}(\cdot))^\top$ is a standard $(N+3)$-dimensional Brownian motion independent of $B(\cdot)$. We naturally consider the problems under any reference probability system $(\Omega, \{\mathcal{F}_s\}, \mathbf{P}, B, \widetilde{B})$. Then the HJB equation associated with (4.5) takes form

$$-\frac{\partial v}{\partial t} - \frac{1}{2m^2}\Delta v + \sup_{u \in \mathbf{U}_{n,m}} \{-\mathcal{G}^u_{n,m}(t,p,x,Dv,D^2v) - kL_{n,m}(t,p,u)\} = 0 \tag{4.6}$$

in $[0,T) \times O_n$, where Dv and D^2v are the first and second order differentials of v with respect to (p,x,y) respectively, and

$$
\begin{aligned}
\mathcal{G}^u_{n,m}(t,p,x,\alpha,S) &= \frac{1}{2}\operatorname{tr}\Sigma_{n,m}\Sigma^\top_{n,m}(t,p,x,u)S - \beta_{n,m}(t,p,x,u)^\top\alpha, \\
\Sigma_{n,m}(t,p,x,(\delta,q))^\top &= \sigma_{n,m}(t,p)(0, \mathbf{I}_N, q, \widehat{\sigma}^Y(p,x)q), \qquad (4.7)\\
\beta_{n,m}(t,p,x,(\delta,q))^\top &= \big(-r_{n,m}(t,p), \widehat{d}_{n,m,1}(t,p) + 2^{-1}|\sigma_{n,m,1}(t,p)|^2, \ldots, \\
&\quad \widehat{d}_{n,m,N}(t,p) + 2^{-1}|\sigma_{n,m,N}(t,p)|^2, \delta + 2^{-1}|\sigma_{n,m}(t,p)q|^2, -\widehat{\beta}^Y_{n,m}(t,p,x)\big)
\end{aligned}
$$

for $(t,p,x) \in [0,T] \times \mathbf{R}^{N+2}$, $u = (\delta, q) \in \mathbf{U}_{n,m}$, $\alpha \in \mathbf{R}^{N+3}$, symmetric matrix $S \in \mathbf{R}^{N+3} \otimes \mathbf{R}^{N+3}$ and the N-dimensional identity matrix $\mathbf{I}_N$.

Then, thanks to Theorem IV.4.1 and the arguments similar to Lemma IV.7.1 & 7.2 in Fleming and Soner [9], we see that

Lemma 4.2. *Under the assumptions as stated above, $V_{n,m,k} \in C^{1,2}([0,T) \times O_n) \cap C([0,T] \times \overline{O}_n)$ is a unique classical solution of the equation* (4.6) *with the boundary data*

---

[4] For the case (A), $(\widehat{\beta}^Y_{n,m}, \widehat{\sigma}^Y)$ is replaced by
$$(\widehat{\beta}^Y_{n,m}(t,p,y,\delta), \widehat{\sigma}^Y(y)) := y(-\delta + l_1'(p_0)r_{n,m}(t,p), 1).$$

$$v(t,p,x,y) = \frac{\Phi_m(a-y)}{\widehat{l}_1(p_0)} \qquad on \ \ ([0,T)\times\partial O_n)\cup(\{T\}\times\overline{O}_n). \tag{4.8}$$

Let us next define the value function

$$V_n(t,p,x,y) := \inf_{u\in\mathcal{U}(t,e^p)} \mathbb{E}_t^{p,x,y}\left[\frac{(a-Y(\tau_t^n))^+}{l_1(P_0(\tau_t^n))}\right],$$

for $n \geq 1$ and $(t,p,x,y) \in [0,T]\times \mathbf{R}^{N+3}$, where

$$\tau_t^n := \inf\{s\geq t : (\log P(s), \log X_1(s), Y(s)) \notin O_n\} \wedge T$$

and $\log p := (\log p_0, \ldots, \log p_N) \in \mathbf{R}^{N+1}$.

Then we obtain

Proposition 4.3. *Let the assumptions stated above hold. Then*

(i) *For each n, $m \geq 1$, $V_{n,m,k}$ converges to $V_{n,m}$ uniformly on $[0,T]\times\overline{O}_n$ as k tends to infinity.*

(ii) *For each $n \geq 1$, $V_{n,m}$ converges to V_n uniformly on $[0,T]\times\overline{O}_n$ as m tends to infinity.*

(iii) *V_n converges to $\widehat{V}$ uniformly on any compact subset of $[0,T]\times\mathbf{R}^{N+2}\times[b,\infty)$ as n tends to infinity.*

The proof relies on the standard theory for viscosity solutions, and the comparison principle and the stability property in particular. We will present its rough sketch only in §5.3. For the notion and general theory of viscosity solutions, we recommend reader to refer to the User's Guide by Crandall *et al.* [6].

5. Proofs

5.1 Proof of Theorem 3.2

Fix a $(x,p) \in (0,\infty)^{N+2}$. For the simplicity of the notation, we set

$$g^u(t) = g^{x,p,u}(t) := g\big(t, X_0^u(t), X_1^{x,u}(t), P^p(t)\big), \qquad t\in[0,T],\ u\in\mathcal{U}$$

for $g = f,\ f_n$. We first consider the stochastic exit time control problem

$$V(\theta : u) := \operatorname*{ess\,inf}_{\widehat{u}\in\mathcal{U}_\theta^u} \mathbb{E}\big[f^{\widehat{u}}(\tau_\theta^{\widehat{u}}) \mid \mathcal{F}_\theta\big],$$

for each $u \in \mathcal{U}$ and $\mathbb{F}$-stopping time θ taking values in $[0,T]$, where

$$\tau_\theta^{\widehat{u}} = \tau_\theta^{x,p,\widehat{u}} := \inf\{t\geq\theta : (X_0^{\widehat{u}}(t), X_1^{x,\widehat{u}}(t), P(t)) \notin O\}\wedge T,$$
$$\mathcal{U}_\theta^u := \big\{\widehat{u}\in\mathcal{U} : \widehat{u}(t,\omega) = u(t,\omega) \quad a.e.\ (t,\omega)\in\{t\leq\theta(\omega)\}\big\}.$$

Then we have the following DPP:

Lemma 5.1. *Suppose that Assumption 3.1 holds. Then the value function V satisfies*

$$V(\theta : u) = \operatorname*{ess\,inf}_{\widehat{u} \in \mathcal{U}_\theta^u} \mathbb{E}\big[V(\tau_\theta^{\widehat{u}} \wedge \rho : \widehat{u}) \mid \mathcal{F}_\theta\big] \tag{5.1}$$

for every $u \in \mathcal{U}$ *and* $\mathbb{F}$*-stopping times* θ, ρ *with* $\theta \leq \rho \leq T$ *a.s. Moreover the process* $\{V(\tau_0^u \wedge t : u),\ 0 \leq t \leq T\}$ *is a nonnegative* $(\mathbb{P}, \mathbb{F})$*-submartingale for each* $u \in \mathcal{U}$.

We postpone the proof of lemma, and first use this result to conclude the proof of theorem.

For each $u \in \mathcal{U}$, let us define

$$V_+(t : u) := \begin{cases} \lim_{s \downarrow t,\, s \in \mathbf{Q}} V(\tau_0^u \wedge s : u) & \text{for } t \in [0, T), \\ V(\tau_0^u : u) & \text{for } t = T. \end{cases}$$

Then $\{V_+(t : u),\ 0 \leq t \leq T\}$ is a right-continuous, left-limited $(\mathbb{P}, \mathbb{F})$-submartingale[5] with $V_+(\cdot : u) \geq V(\tau_0^u \wedge \cdot : u)$ *a.e.* for each $u \in \mathcal{U}$.

We first show

$$h_{up}(x, p) = V(x, p) = \inf_{u \in \mathcal{U}} V_+(0 : u). \tag{5.2}$$

Suppose $H_{up}(x, p) \neq \emptyset$. Then, for any $w \in H_{up}(x, p)$, there exists a $(\pi, u) \in \mathcal{P} \times \mathcal{U}$ such that $\mathbb{P}\{W^{0,\pi}(t) \geq \beta,\ t \in [0, T]\} = 1$ for some constant β and (3.1) is achieved. Since $W^{0,\pi}(\cdot)$ is a $(\mathbb{P}, \mathbb{F})$-supermartingale and $\tau^u_{\tau_0^u \wedge s} = \tau_0^u$ *a.s.*, (2.2) and (3.1) yield

$$\begin{aligned} V_+(0 : u) &\leq \lim_{s \downarrow 0,\, s \in \mathbf{Q}} \mathbb{E}\big[f^u(\tau_0^u) \mid \mathcal{F}_{\tau_0^u \wedge s}\big] \\ &\leq \lim_{s \downarrow 0,\, s \in \mathbf{Q}} \mathbb{E}\big[W^{w,\pi}(\tau_0^u) \mid \mathcal{F}_{\tau_0^u \wedge s}\big] \\ &\leq \lim_{s \downarrow 0,\, s \in \mathbf{Q}} W^{w,\pi}(\tau_0^u \wedge s) = w \quad \textit{a.s.} \end{aligned}$$

Hence $\inf_{u \in \mathcal{U}} V_+(0 : u) \leq h_{up}(x, p)$. We also observe that $\inf_{u \in \mathcal{U}} V_+(0 : u) < \infty = h_{up}(x, p)$ if $H_{up}(x, p) = \emptyset$.

For every $\varepsilon > 0$, there exists a $u_\varepsilon \in \mathcal{U}$ such that $V(x, p) + \varepsilon \geq \mathbb{E}\big[f^{u_\varepsilon}(\tau_0^{u_\varepsilon})\big]$. From the martingale representation theorem and the Bayes' rule,[6] we see that

$$\mathbb{E}\big[f^{u_\varepsilon}(\tau_0^{u_\varepsilon}) \mid \mathcal{F}_t\big] = \mathbb{E}\big[f^{u_\varepsilon}(\tau_0^{u_\varepsilon})\big] + W^{0,\pi^{u_\varepsilon}}(t) \quad \textit{a.s.}, \qquad 0 \leq t \leq T$$

for some $\pi^{u_\varepsilon} \in \mathcal{P}$. Since f is nonnegative, we know that $W^{0,\pi^{u_\varepsilon}}(\cdot) \geq -V(x, p) - \varepsilon$ *a.e.*, and

[5] See Proposition 1.3.14 in Karatzas and Shreve [16].

[6] See Problem 3.4.16 and Lemma 3.5.3 in Karatzas and Shreve [16].

$$W^{V(x,p)+\varepsilon,\pi^{u_\varepsilon}}(\tau_0^{u_\varepsilon}) = V(x,p) + \varepsilon + W^{0,\pi^{u_\varepsilon}}(\tau_0^{u_\varepsilon}) \geq f^{u_\varepsilon}(\tau_0^{u_\varepsilon}) \quad a.s.,$$

which means $V(x,p) + \varepsilon \geq h_{up}(x,p)$. Hence we obtain (5.2).

Next we prove

$$h_{low}(x,p) = V(x,p) = \sup_{u \in \mathcal{U}} V_+(0:u). \tag{5.3}$$

It is clear $0 \in H_{low}(x,p)$ and thus $H_{low}(x,p) \neq \emptyset$. If $w \in H_{low}(x,p)$ and $u \in \mathcal{U}$, there exists a portfolio process $\pi^u \in \mathcal{P}$ such that $W^{0,\pi^u}(\cdot)$ is a $(\mathbb{P},\mathbb{F})$-supermartingale and (3.2) is achieved. Hence, for every $w \in H_{low}(x,p)$ and $u \in \mathcal{U}$ we have $-\mathbb{E}\big[f^u(\tau_0^u)\big] \leq \mathbb{E}\big[W^{-w,\pi^u}(\tau_0^u)\big] \leq -w$. Therefore $h_{low}(x,p) \leq V(x,p)$.

On the other hands, by virtue of the Doob-Meyer decomposition theorem[7] and the last lemma, there exist a right-continuous $(\mathbb{P},\mathbb{F})$-martingale $M_u(\cdot)$ and a natural, integrable, increasing process $A_u(\cdot)$ with $M_u(0) = A_u(0) = 0$ such that

$$V_+(t:u) = V_+(0:u) + A_u(t) + M_u(t), \qquad 0 \leq t \leq T,$$

for each $u \in \mathcal{U}$. The martingale representation theorem and the Bayes' rule show that there exists a portfolio process π^u such that $M_u(\cdot) = -W^{0,\pi^u}(\cdot)$ *a.e.* Hence we obtain

$$\begin{aligned} W^{-V_+(0:u),\pi^u}(\tau_0^u) + f^u(\tau_0^u) &= -V_+(0:u) - M_u(\tau_0^u) + V_+(\tau_0^u : u) \\ &= A_u(\tau_0^u) \geq 0 \qquad a.s., \end{aligned}$$

which implies $h_{low}(x,p) \geq \sup_{u \in \mathcal{U}} V_+(0:u)$ and leads us to (5.3).

Hence the proof of Theorem 3.2 is completely accomplished. □

Lemma 5.1 is analogous to Karatzas and Shreve [17, Remark 5.6.7] which can be written as follows.

Lemma 5.2. *Let C be a nonnegative $\mathcal{F}_T$-measurable random variable, $\mathcal{N}$ be a certain class of $\mathbb{F}$-progressively measurable processes, and*

$$\widetilde{V}(\theta) := \operatorname*{ess\,sup}_{u \in \mathcal{N}} \frac{\mathbb{E}[H_u(T)C \mid \mathcal{F}_\theta]}{H_u(\theta)}$$

for each $\mathbb{F}$-stopping time θ taking values in $[0,T]$, where $\{H_u(t),\ 0 \leq t \leq T\}$ is a positive $\mathbb{F}$-adapted continuous process such that $H_u(s,\omega)$ depends on the path $\{u(t,\omega),\ 0 \leq t \leq s\}$ for each $u \in \mathcal{N}$ and a.e. $(s,\omega) \in [0,T] \times \Omega$. If $\sup_{u \in \mathcal{N}} \mathbb{E}[H_u(T)C] < \infty$ and $H_u(s)/H_u(v)$ is independent of $\{u(t),\ 0 \leq t \leq v\}$ for every $0 \leq v \leq s \leq T$ and $u \in \mathcal{N}$, then $\widetilde{V}$ is finite and satisfies

[7] See Theorem 1.4.10 in Karatzas and Shreve [16].

$$\widetilde{V}(\theta) = \operatorname*{ess\,sup}_{u \in \mathcal{N}} \frac{\mathbb{E}\big[H_u(\rho)\widetilde{V}(\rho) \mid \mathcal{F}_\theta\big]}{H_u(\theta)}$$

for all $\mathbb{F}$-stopping times θ, ρ with $\theta \le \rho \le T$ a.s. Moreover for each $u \in \mathcal{N}$ the process $\{H_u(t)\widetilde{V}(t),\, 0 \le t \le T\}$ is a $(\mathbb{P}, \mathbb{F})$-supermartingale which has a right-continuous and left-limited modification.

As compared with the previous lemma, the point to observe in Lemma 5.1 is that $f^u(\tau_\theta^u \wedge \rho)$ depends on $\{u(t),\, 0 \le t \le \theta\}$ for each $u \in \mathcal{U}$ and $\mathbb{F}$-stopping times θ, ρ with $\theta \le \rho \le T$ *a.s.* However, if we notice $\tau^u_{\tau_\theta^u \wedge \rho} = \tau_\theta^u$ *a.s.* and apply Ito's rule to f (f_n, to be more exact), we can prove Lemma 5.1 by proceeding along the analogous line with the proof of Remark 5.6.7 in Karatzas and Shreve [17], as it follows.

<u>*Proof of Lemma 5.1:*</u> Let θ, ρ be $\mathbb{F}$-stopping times with $\theta \le \rho \le T$ *a.s.* and $u \in \mathcal{U}$. We first note $\tau^{\widehat{u}}_{\tau_\theta^{\widehat{u}} \wedge \rho} = \tau_\theta^{\widehat{u}}$ *a.s.* because of $\theta \le \tau_\theta^{\widehat{u}} \wedge \rho \le \tau_\theta^{\widehat{u}}$ and $\tau^{\widehat{u}}_{\tau_\theta^{\widehat{u}}} = \tau_\theta^{\widehat{u}}$ *a.s.* Hence we see that

$$\begin{aligned}
V(\theta : u) &= \operatorname*{ess\,inf}_{\widehat{u} \in \mathcal{U}_\theta^u} \mathbb{E}\Big[\mathbb{E}\big[f^{\widehat{u}}(\tau_\theta^{\widehat{u}}) \mid \mathcal{F}_{\tau_\theta^{\widehat{u}} \wedge \rho}\big] \,\Big|\, \mathcal{F}_\theta\Big] \\
&= \operatorname*{ess\,inf}_{\widehat{u} \in \mathcal{U}_\theta^u} \mathbb{E}\Big[\mathbb{E}\big[f^{\widehat{u}}(\tau^{\widehat{u}}_{\tau_\theta^{\widehat{u}} \wedge \rho}) \mid \mathcal{F}_{\tau_\theta^{\widehat{u}} \wedge \rho}\big] \,\Big|\, \mathcal{F}_\theta\Big] \\
&\ge \operatorname*{ess\,inf}_{\widehat{u} \in \mathcal{U}_\theta^u} \mathbb{E}\Big[V(\tau_\theta^{\widehat{u}} \wedge \rho : \widehat{u}) \,\Big|\, \mathcal{F}_\theta\Big].
\end{aligned}$$

To prove the reverse inequality, we set

$$V_n(\theta : u) = \operatorname*{ess\,inf}_{\widehat{u} \in \mathcal{U}_\theta^u} \mathbb{E}\left[\int_\theta^{\tau_\theta^{\widehat{u}}} G^{\widehat{u}} f_n(t)\, dt \,\middle|\, \mathcal{F}_\theta\right] =: \operatorname*{ess\,inf}_{\widehat{u} \in \mathcal{U}_\theta^u} I_n(\theta : \widehat{u}), \quad n \ge 1,$$

where $G^{\widehat{u}} f_n(\cdot)$ is as in Assumption 3.1. Fix arbitrary $\widehat{u} \in \mathcal{U}_\theta^u$. Then it easily follows from Assumption 3.1 (ii) that the collection $\big\{f_n^{\widehat{u}}(\tau_\theta^{\widehat{u}} \wedge \rho) + I_n(\tau_\theta^{\widehat{u}} \wedge \rho : \widetilde{u}) : \widetilde{u} \in \mathcal{U}^{\widehat{u}}_{\tau_\theta^{\widehat{u}} \wedge \rho}\big\}$ of non-negative random variables is closed under pairwise minimization, that is,

$$I_n(\tau_\theta^{\widehat{u}} \wedge \rho : \widetilde{u}) = I_n(\tau_\theta^{\widehat{u}} \wedge \rho : u^1) \wedge I_n(\tau_\theta^{\widehat{u}} \wedge \rho : u^2) \qquad \text{for } u^1,\, u^2 \in \mathcal{U}^{\widehat{u}}_{\tau_\theta^{\widehat{u}} \wedge \rho},$$

where $\widetilde{u} \in \mathcal{U}^{\widehat{u}}_{\tau_\theta^{\widehat{u}} \wedge \rho}$ is defined by

$$\widetilde{u}(t, \omega) = \begin{cases} u^1(t, \omega) & \text{if } I_n(\tau_\theta^{\widehat{u}} \wedge \rho : u^1)(\omega) \le I_n(\tau_\theta^{\widehat{u}} \wedge \rho : u^2)(\omega) \\ u^2(t, \omega) & \text{if } I_n(\tau_\theta^{\widehat{u}} \wedge \rho : u^1)(\omega) > I_n(\tau_\theta^{\widehat{u}} \wedge \rho : u^2)(\omega) \end{cases}$$

for $t \in [0,T]$. Taking account of Assumption 3.1 (i), the argument similar to Appendix A of Karatzas and Shreve [17] ensures that there exists a sequence $\{u_k\}_{k=1}^{\infty} \subset \mathcal{U}^{\widehat{u}}_{\tau^{\widehat{u}}_\theta \wedge \rho}$ such that

$$I_n(\tau^{\widehat{u}}_\theta \wedge \rho : u_k) \searrow V_n(\tau^{\widehat{u}}_\theta \wedge \rho : \widehat{u}) \quad a.s. \qquad \text{as } k \to \infty.$$

Therefore the monotone convergence theorem and Fatou's lemma give

$$\begin{aligned}
& f^u_n(\theta) + \mathbb{E}\left[\int_\theta^{\tau^{\widehat{u}}_\theta \wedge \rho} G^{\widehat{u}} f_n(t)\, dt + V_n(\tau^{\widehat{u}}_\theta \wedge \rho : \widehat{u}) \,\middle|\, \mathcal{F}_\theta \right] \\
&= f^{\widehat{u}}_n(\theta) + \lim_{k\to\infty} \mathbb{E}\left[\int_\theta^{\tau^{\widehat{u}}_\theta \wedge \rho} G^{\widehat{u}} f_n(t)\, dt + I_n(\tau^{\widehat{u}}_\theta \wedge \rho : u_k) \,\middle|\, \mathcal{F}_\theta \right] \\
&= f^{\widehat{u}}_n(\theta) + \lim_{k\to\infty} \mathbb{E}\left[\int_\theta^{\tau^{u_k}_\theta} G^{u_k} f_n(t)\, dt \,\middle|\, \mathcal{F}_\theta \right] \\
&= \lim_{k\to\infty} \mathbb{E}\left[f^{u_k}_n(\tau^{u_k}_\theta) \mid \mathcal{F}_\theta \right] \\
&\geq V(\theta : u) - \|f - f_n\|_\infty,
\end{aligned}$$

where the second equality follows from $\tau^{u_k}_{\tau^{\widehat{u}}_\theta \wedge \rho} = \tau^{u_k}_\theta$ *a.s.*

On the other hand,

$$\begin{aligned}
& f^u_n(\theta) + \mathbb{E}\left[\int_\theta^{\tau^{\widehat{u}}_\theta \wedge \rho} G^{\widehat{u}} f_n(t)\, dt + V_n(\tau^{\widehat{u}}_\theta \wedge \rho : \widehat{u}) \,\middle|\, \mathcal{F}_\theta \right] \\
&= \mathbb{E}\left[\operatorname*{ess\,inf}_{\widetilde{u} \in \mathcal{U}^{\widehat{u}}_{\tau^{\widehat{u}}_\theta \wedge \rho}} \mathbb{E}\left[f^{\widetilde{u}}_n(\tau^{\widetilde{u}}_{\tau^{\widehat{u}}_\theta \wedge \rho}) \,\middle|\, \mathcal{F}_{\tau^{\widehat{u}}_\theta \wedge \rho} \right] \,\middle|\, \mathcal{F}_\theta \right] \\
&\leq \mathbb{E}\left[V(\tau^{\widehat{u}}_\theta \wedge \rho : \widehat{u}) \,\middle|\, \mathcal{F}_\theta \right] + \|f - f_n\|_\infty.
\end{aligned}$$

By combining the estimates above, taking the essential infimum over $\widehat{u} \in \mathcal{U}^u_\theta$ and letting $n \to \infty$, we have the DPP (5.1).

For any $\mathbb{F}$-stopping times η, ρ with $\eta \leq \rho$ *a.s.* and $A \in \mathcal{F}_\eta$, let us next put $\theta := \eta \mathbb{1}_A + \rho \mathbb{1}_{A^c}$, where $\mathbb{1}$ is the indicator function. Owing to $\tau^u_{\tau^u_0 \wedge \theta} = \tau^u_0$ *a.s.* and (5.1), we get

$$\begin{aligned}
& \mathbb{E}\left[\mathbb{1}_A V(\tau^u_0 \wedge \rho : u) \right] \\
&\quad = \mathbb{E}\left[\mathbb{E}\left[V(\tau^u_{\tau^u_0 \wedge \theta} \wedge \rho : u) \mid \mathcal{F}_{\tau^u_0 \wedge \theta} \right] \right] - \mathbb{E}\left[\mathbb{1}_{A^c} V(\tau^u_0 \wedge \theta : u) \right] \\
&\quad \geq \mathbb{E}\left[V(\tau^u_0 \wedge \theta : u) \right] - \mathbb{E}\left[\mathbb{1}_{A^c} V(\tau^u_0 \wedge \theta : u) \right] \\
&\quad = \mathbb{E}\left[\mathbb{1}_A V(\tau^u_0 \wedge \eta : u) \right],
\end{aligned}$$

which means that $\{V(\tau^u_0 \wedge t : u), 0 \leq t \leq T\}$ is a nonnegative $(\mathbb{P}, \mathbb{F})$-submartingale. Thus Lemma 5.1 is completely accomplished. □

5.2 Details for results in §4.2

We have already obtained the result for the case $q_* = 0$ in §4.1. Thus we assume $q_* \neq 0$ and fix a $u(\cdot) = (0, q(\cdot)) \in \mathcal{U}$. We will adapt the proof of Theorem 3 in Hajek [10] to deal with minimums of processes.

For each $t \in [0,T]$ and $s \geq 0$, let $\eta_0(t)$ be the non-decreasing process $\eta_0(t) := |\sigma q_*|^{-2} \int_0^t |\sigma q(v)|^2 \, dv$ $(\geq t)$ and $\eta_1(s)$ be the $\mathbb{F}$-stopping time $\eta_1(s) := \inf\{t \in [0,T] : \eta_0(t) > s\} \wedge T$ $(\leq s)$. We also define the stochastic process $Z(s) := X_1^{1,u}(\eta_1(s))$ for $s \in [0, \eta_0(T)]$. Then $Z(\eta_0(t)) = X_1^{1,u}(t)$ for each $t \in [0,T]$, and we note that the processes $Z(\cdot)$ and $X_1^{1,u_*}(\cdot)$ have the same probability law, since $Z(\cdot)$ and $Z(\cdot)^2 - \int_0^\bullet |\sigma q_*|^2 Z(v)^2 \, dv$ are continuous $(\mathbb{P}, \mathbb{F})$-martingales by means of the equality

$$
\begin{aligned}
Z(s)^2 - \int_0^s |\sigma q_*|^2 Z(v)^2 \, dv &= Z(s)^2 - \int_0^{\eta_1(s)} |\sigma q_*|^2 Z(\eta_0(t))^2 \, d\eta_0(t) \\
&= X_1^{1,u}(\eta_1(s))^2 - \int_0^{\eta_1(s)} |\sigma q(t)|^2 X_1^{1,u}(t)^2 \, dt
\end{aligned}
$$

and the optional sampling theorem. Therefore we have

$$
\begin{aligned}
\{X_1^{1,u_*}(T) \in A, \, \tau_0^{u_*} < T\} &\sim \Big\{Z(T) \in A, \, \min_{0 \leq t < T} Z(t) \leq b\Big\} \\
&= \{X_1^{1,u}(\eta_1(T)) \in A, \, \tau_0^u < \eta_1(T)\}
\end{aligned}
$$

for each $A \in \mathcal{B}(\mathbf{R})$, and thus

$$
\begin{aligned}
&\mathbb{E}\Big[\big(a - X_1^{1,u_*}(\tau_0^{u_*})\big)^+\Big] \\
&= (a-b)\mathbb{E}\big[\mathbb{1}_{\{\tau_0^u < \eta_1(T)\}}\big] + \mathbb{E}\Big[\big(a - X_1^{1,u}(\eta_1(T))\big)^+ \mathbb{1}_{\{\tau_0^u \geq \eta_1(T)\}}\Big] \\
&= \mathbb{E}\Big[\big(a - X_1^{1,u}(\tau_0^u \wedge \eta_1(T))\big)^+\Big] \\
&\leq \mathbb{E}\Big[\big(a - X_1^{1,u}(\tau_0^u)\big)^+\Big]
\end{aligned}
$$

which means that $V(x_1, p) = x_1 \mathbb{E}\Big[\big(a - X_1^{1,u_*}(\tau_0^{u_*})\big)^+\Big]$.

If $b = 0$, then $\tau_0^{u_*} \equiv T$ and

$$
V(x_1, p) = x_1 \mathbb{E}\left[\left(a - \exp\left\{(\sigma q_*)^\top B(T) - \frac{T}{2}|\sigma q_*|^2\right\}\right)^+\right] = x_1 \varphi(a, b, q_* : T).
$$

We next consider the case $b \in (0,1)$ and define a new probability measure $\widetilde{\mathbb{P}}$ by

$$\left.\frac{d\widetilde{\mathbb{P}}}{d\mathbb{P}}\right|_{\mathcal{F}_t} = \widetilde{Z}_t := \exp\left(\frac{1}{2}(\sigma q_*)^\top B(t) - \frac{1}{8}|\sigma q_*|^2 t\right), \qquad t \in [0,T].$$

According to Girsanov's theorem, $\widetilde{\mathbf{w}}(t) := -|\sigma q_*|^{-1}(\sigma q_*)^\top B(t) + 2^{-1}|\sigma q_*|t$ is a standard 1-dimensional Brownian motion under $\widetilde{\mathbb{P}}$. Since

$$\tau_0^{u_*} = \inf\left\{t \geq 0 : \widetilde{\mathbf{w}}(t) \geq -\frac{\log b}{|\sigma q_*|} =: \widehat{b}\right\} \wedge T = T_{\widehat{b}} \wedge T,$$

we have

$$V(x_1, p) = x_1 \widetilde{\mathbb{E}}\left[\frac{1}{\widetilde{Z}(T_{\widehat{b}} \wedge T)}\left(a - e^{-|\sigma q_*|\widetilde{\mathbf{w}}(T_{\widehat{b}} \wedge T)}\right)^+\right] = x_1 \psi(a, b, T\colon q_*).$$

Finally we identify (4.3). It is enough to show that the continuous function

$$g(\gamma) := \mathbb{E}\left[\left(a - \gamma X_1^{1,u_*}(\tau_0^{u_*})\right)^+\right] + \gamma - 1, \qquad \gamma \in [0,1]$$

is strictly increasing. Indeed, for each $0 \leq \gamma < \gamma + 3\gamma' \leq 1$,

$$\begin{aligned}
&g(\gamma + 3\gamma') - g(\gamma)\\
&= 3\gamma' \mathbb{E}\left[X_1^{1,u_*}(\tau_0^{u_*}) \mathbb{1}_{\{\gamma X_1^{1,u_*}(\tau_0^{u_*}) > a\}}\right]\\
&\quad + \mathbb{E}\left[\{(\gamma + 3\gamma')X_1^{1,u_*}(\tau_0^{u_*}) - a\} \mathbb{1}_{\{\gamma X_1^{1,u_*}(\tau_0^{u_*}) \leq a < (\gamma + 3\gamma')X_1^{1,u_*}(\tau_0^{u_*})\}}\right]\\
&\geq (\gamma + 3\gamma')\mathbb{E}\left[\left(X_1^{1,u_*}(\tau_0^{u_*}) - \Gamma_3\right) \mathbb{1}_{\{\Gamma_2 < X_1^{1,u_*}(\tau_0^{u_*}) < \Gamma_1\}}\right]\\
&\geq \gamma' \Gamma_2 \mathbb{P}\{\Gamma_2 < X_1^{1,u_*}(\tau_0^{u_*}) < \Gamma_1\}\\
&\geq \gamma' \Gamma_2 \Gamma_1^{-\frac{1}{2}} e^{-\frac{1}{8}|\sigma q_*|^2 T} \widetilde{\mathbb{P}}\{\Gamma_2 < e^{-|\sigma q_*|\widetilde{\mathbf{w}}(T)} < \Gamma_1,\ e^{-|\sigma q_*|\widetilde{\mathbf{w}}^*(T)} > b\}\\
&> 0,
\end{aligned}$$

where $\Gamma_j = a/(\gamma + j\gamma')$, $j = 1, 2, 3$. □

5.3 Proof of Proposition 4.3

Let $\mathcal{S}_j$ be the set of all symmetric $j \times j$ matrixes, and denote

$$F_{n,m}(t, p, x, \alpha, S) := -\frac{1}{2m^2} \operatorname{tr} \mathbf{I}_{N+3} S + \sup_{u \in \mathbb{U}[u^*_{n,m}](t,p)} \left\{-\mathcal{G}^u_{n,m}(t, p, x, \alpha, S)\right\}$$

for $(t, p, x, \alpha, S) \in [0,T] \times \mathbf{R}^{N+2} \times \mathbf{R}^{N+3} \times \mathcal{S}_{N+3}$. To prove the proposition, we will need the following lemma.

Lemma 5.3. *Let the assumptions stated in §4.3 hold, and $n,\ m \geq 1$. If v is a viscosity subsolution (resp. supersolution) of the equation*

$$-\frac{\partial v}{\partial t} + F_{n,m}(t,p,x,Dv,D^2v) = 0 \qquad in\ [0,T)\times O_n, \tag{5.4}$$

with the relaxed boundary condition

$$\min\left\{-\frac{\partial v}{\partial t} + F_{n,m}(t,p,x,Dv,D^2v),\ v - \frac{\Phi_m(a-y)}{\widehat{l}_1(p_0)}\right\} \leq 0$$

$$\left(resp.\ \max\left\{-\frac{\partial v}{\partial t} + F_{n,m}(t,p,x,Dv,D^2v),\ v - \frac{\Phi_m(a-y)}{\widehat{l}_1(p_0)}\right\} \geq 0\right)$$

on $([0,T)\times\partial O_n)\cup(\{T\}\times\overline{O}_n)$, then v satisfies the boundary condition (4.8).

The previous lemma can be proved along the lines of Proposition 1.1 in Barles and Burdeau [3] and Proposition 4.1 in Barles and Rouy [4]. Therefore we omit giving its proof here.

Fix any $n,\ m \geq 1$. We first note that the sequence $\{V_{n,m,k}\}_k$ is increasing and $V_{n,m,k} \leq V_{n,m}$, since $\mathbb{U}[u^*_{n,m}](t,p) \subset \mathbf{U}_{n,m}$ for every $(t,p) \in [0,T]\times \mathbf{R}^{N+1}$. Let us set

$$\underline{V}_{n,m}(z) := \lim_{j\to\infty} \inf\{V_{n,m,k}(z') : k \geq j,\ z' \in [0,T]\times\overline{O}_n,\ |z-z'| \leq j^{-1}\}, \tag{5.5}$$

$$V^*_{n,m}(z) := \lim_{j\to\infty} \sup\{V_{n,m}(z') : z' \in [0,T]\times\overline{O}_n,\ |z-z'| \leq j^{-1}\} \tag{5.6}$$

for $z \in [0,T]\times\overline{O}_n$. Then, for each point of $[0,T]\times\mathbf{R}^{N+2}\times\mathbf{R}^{N+3}\times\mathcal{S}_{N+3}$,

$$\lim_{k\to\infty} \sup_{u\in\mathbf{U}_{n,m}} \{-\mathcal{G}^u_{n,m}(t,p,x,\alpha,S) - kL_{n,m}(t,p,u)\}$$
$$= \sup_{u\in\mathbb{U}[u^*_{n,m}](t,p)} \{-\mathcal{G}^u_{n,m}(t,p,x,\alpha,S)\}.$$

Hence by Dini's theorem this monotone convergence is uniform on any compact subset of $[0,T]\times\mathbf{R}^{N+2}\times\mathbf{R}^{N+3}\times\mathcal{S}_{N+3}$. By means of the stability property[8] and the last lemma, therefore, we know that $\underline{V}_{n,m}$ is a viscosity supersolution of the equation (5.4) with the boundary data (4.8). Also, from Lemma IV.3.2 of Yong and Zhou [23] and Lemma 5.1 & 5.3 it easily follows that $V^*_{n,m}$ is a viscosity subsolution of the equation (5.4) with the boundary data (4.8). Hence the comparison principle[9] shows that $e^{-t}V^*_{n,m} \leq e^{-t}\underline{V}_{n,m}$

[8] See Remark 6.2 & 6.3 of Crandall *et al.* [6].
[9] See Theorem 3.3 of Crandall *et al.* [6].

on $[0,T] \times \overline{O}_n$ which means $V_{n,m,k} \to V_{n,m}$ as $k \to \infty$ for each point of $[0,T] \times \overline{O}_n$. Thus we can use Dini's theorem in order to get the first assertion (i).

As in (5.5) and (5.6), let us next define

$$\overline{V}_n(z) := \lim_{j\to\infty} \sup\{V_{n,m}(z') : m \geq j,\ z' \in [0,T] \times \overline{O}_n,\ |z - z'| \leq j^{-1}\},$$
$$\underline{V}_n(z) := \lim_{j\to\infty} \inf\{V_{n,m}(z') : m \geq j,\ z' \in [0,T] \times \overline{O}_n,\ |z - z'| \leq j^{-1}\}$$

for $z \in [0,T] \times \overline{O}_n$, and denote by V_n^* the upper semicontinuous envelope of V_n, and we put $V_{n*} := -(-V_n)^*$. We also set $F_n(\cdot) := \sup\{-\mathcal{G}_n^u(\cdot) : u \in \mathbb{U}[u_n^*](t,p)\}$, where $\mathcal{G}_n^u$ is given by replacing $r_{n,m}$, $\widehat{d}_{n,m}$, $\sigma_{n,m}$ with r_n, $\widehat{d}_n$, σ_n, respectively, in (4.7).

Since $g_n(t,p) = g(t,e^p)$ on $[0,T] \times \mathrm{B}_{N+1}(0,n)$ and $\|g_{n,m} - g_n\|_\infty \to 0$ as $m \to \infty$ for $g = r$, d, σ and u^*, by the arguments similar to the above,[10] we observe that V_n^* and $\overline{V}_n$ (resp. V_{n*} and $\underline{V}_n$) are viscosity subsolutions (resp. supersolutions) of the equation (5.4) replaced $F_{n,m}(\cdot)$ by $F_n(\cdot)$, and satisfy the boundary condition (4.8) replaced Φ_m by Φ. Therefore the comparison principle gives the second assertion (ii).

Fix any $n \geq 2$, $(t,p,x,y) \in [0,T] \times \overline{O}_n$ $(y \neq b)$ and $u \in \mathcal{U}(t,e^p)$. Then the standard estimates[11] for moments yield

$$\mathbb{E}_t^p\Big[\sup_{t\leq s\leq T} |P(s)|^{2\gamma}\Big] \leq c_1\big(1 + |e^p|^{2\gamma}\big)$$

for every $\gamma \geq 1$ and some positive constant c_1 which depends on γ, T, $\|r\|_\infty$, $\|d\|_\infty$ and $\|\sigma\|_\infty$. Because $u(t) - u^*(t,P(t)) \in B_{N+1}(0,R)$ *a.e.* and u^* satisfies the polynomial growth condition, we have

$$\begin{aligned}
&\mathbb{P}_t^{p,x,y}\{\tau_t > \tau_t^{2n}\}\\
&\leq \mathbb{P}_t^{p,x,y}\Big\{\sup_{t\leq s<\tau_t} (|\log P(s) - p|^2 + |\log X_1(s) - x|^2) \geq n^2\Big\}\\
&\quad + \mathbb{P}_t^{p,x,y}\Big\{\sup_{t\leq s<\tau_t} |\log Y(s) - \log y| \geq \log\frac{b + e^{2n}}{b + e^n}\Big\}\\
&\leq n^{-2\gamma}\,\mathbb{E}_t^{p,x,y}\Big[\sup_{t\leq s\leq T} (|\log P(s) - p|^2 + |\log X_1(s) - x|^2)^\gamma\Big]\\
&\quad + (n-1)^{-2\gamma}\,\mathbb{E}_t^{p,x,y}\Big[\sup_{t\leq s\leq T}\Big|\log\frac{Y(s)}{y}\Big|^{2\gamma}\Big]
\end{aligned}$$

---

[10] Taking in consideration of the non-degenerate condition (4.4) and the regularity of the volatility matrix σ, we should notice that Lemma 5.3 still holds, even though $F_{n,m}$ and Φ_m are changed into F_n and Φ respectively.

[11] See Corollary 2.5.10 of Krylov [18] or Lemma 3.2.5 & 3.2.6 of Nagai [20].

$$\leq c_2\left(1 + |e^p|^{4\gamma K}\right)(n-1)^{-2\gamma}$$

and

$$\left|\mathbb{E}_t^{p,x,y}\left[\frac{(a - Y(\tau_t))^+}{l_1(P_0(\tau_t))} - \frac{(a - Y(\tau_t^{2n}))^+}{l_1(P_0(\tau_t^{2n}))}\right]\right|$$
$$\leq a\,\mathbb{E}_t^{p,x,y}\left[\left(2 + \frac{1}{P_0(\tau_t)} + \frac{1}{P_0(\tau_t^{2n})}\right)\mathbb{1}_{\{\tau_t > \tau_t^{2n}\}}\right]$$
$$\leq 2ac_2\left(1 + e^{-p_0 + T\|r\|_\infty}\right)\left(1 + |e^p|^{4\gamma K}\right)(n-1)^{-2\gamma}$$

for certain positive constant c_2 depending upon c_0, γ, T, K, R, $\|r\|_\infty$, $\|d\|_\infty$ and $\|\sigma\|_\infty$. Thus we obtain the third assertion (iii), and hence the proof is complete. □

References

[1] Adachi, T.: On value of American version of Asian option, generalization of passport option and consumption/investment problems. Doctoral dissertation, Department of Computer and Mathematical Sciences, Tohoku University 2001

[2] Ahn, H., Penaud, A., Wilmott, P.: Various passport options and their valuation. Preprint, OCIAM Oxford University (1999)

[3] Barles, G., Burdeau, J.: The Dirichlet problem for semilinear second-order degenerate elliptic stochastic exit time control problems. Comm. in PDEs **20**, 129-178 (1995)

[4] Barles, G., Rouy, E.: A strong comparison result for the Bellman equation arising stochastic exit time control problems and its applications. Comm. in PDEs **23**, 1995-2033 (1998)

[5] Borkar, V.S.: Optimal Control of Diffusion Processes. Longman Sci. and Tech., Harlow, UK 1989

[6] Crandall, M.G., Ishii, H., Lions, P.-L.: User's guide to viscosity solutions of second order partial differential equations. Bull. Amer. Math. Soc. (N.S.) **27**, 1-67 (1992)

[7] Delbaen, F., Yor, M.: Passport options. Preprint, ETH. (1999)

[8] Duffie, D.: Dynamic Asset Pricing Theory. 3rd ed. Princeton Univ. Press 2001

[9] Fleming, W.H., Soner, H.M.: Controlled Markov Processes and Viscosity Solutions. Springer-Verlag, NY 1993

[10] Hajek, B.: Mean stochastic comparison of diffusions. Z. Wahrscheinlichkeitstheorie verw. Gebiete **68**, 315-329 (1985)

[11] Henderson, V.: Price comparison results and super-replication: An application to passport options. Appl. Stoch. models in Business and Industry **16**, 297-310 (2000)

[12] Henderson, V., Hobson, D.: Local times, coupling and the passport option. Finance & Stochastics **4**, 69-80 (1999)

[13] Hyer, T., Lipton-Lifschitz, A., Pugachevsky, D.: Passport to success. Risk **10**, 127-131 (1997)

[14] Ishii, H.: A boundary value problem of the Dirichlet type for Hamilton-Jacobi equations. Ann. Scuola Norm. Sup. Pisa Cl. Sci. **16**, 105-135 (1989)

[15] Karatzas, I.: Lectures on the Mathematics of Finance. Providence, RI 1997
[16] Karatzas, I., Shreve, S.E.: Brownian Motion and Stochastic Calculus. 2nd ed. Springer-Verlag, NY 1991
[17] Karatzas, I., Shreve, S.E.: Methods of Mathematical Finance. Springer-Verlag, NY 1998
[18] Krylov, N.V.: Controlled Diffusion Processes. Springer-Verlag, NY 1980
[19] Lions, P.-L.: Optimal control of diffusion processes and Hamilton-Jacobi-Bellman equations. Part 1: The dynamic programming principle and application. Comm. in PDEs **8**, 1101-1174 (1983)
[20] Nagai, H.: Stochastic Differential Equations. In Japanese. Kyoritu-Shuppan 1999
[21] Nagayama, I.: Pricing of passport option. J. Math. Sci. Univ. Tokyo **5**, 747-785 (1999)
[22] Shreve, S.E., Večeř, J.: Options on traded account: Vacation calls, vacation puts and passport options. Finance & Stochastics **4**, 255-274 (2000)
[23] Yong, J., Zhou, X.Y.: Stochastic Controls: Hamiltonian Systems and HJB Equations. Springer-Verlag, NY 1999

Adv. Math. Econ. 9, 25–32 (2006)

Advances in
MATHEMATICAL
ECONOMICS

The distribution of continuous time rank processes

Takahiko Fujita[1] **and Ryozo Miura**[2]

[1] Graduate School of Commerce and Management, Hitotsubashi University, Naka 2-1, Kunitachi, Tokyo, 186-8601, Japan
(e-mail: fujita@math.hit-u.ac.jp)

[2] Graduate School of International Corporate Strategy, Hitotsubashi University, 2-1-2 Hitotsubashi, Chiyodaku, Tokyo, 101-8439, Japan
(e-mail: rmiura@ics.hit-u.ac.jp)

Received: October 6, 2003
Revised: December 2, 2005

JEL classification: G13

Mathematics Subject Classification (2000): 60J65, 91B28

Abstract. In this paper, we will give exact calculations of probability disrtributions of continuous rank processes in Brownian case, Brownian motion with drift case, Pinned Brownian motion case. These calculations are based on the results of the joint distributions of Brownian motion and its soujourn time. Also we give new exotic options using rank statistics and calculate the price of rank options.

Key words: rank statistics, rank process, Brownian motion, Brownian motion with drift, Brownian bridge, Black Scholes model

1. Introduction

The rank statistics is an important non-parametric statistics as the order statistics is. One of the author, Miura, considered options on order statsistics ([10]), that is called α-percentile options, and investigated some researches in the finance theory. Akahori ([1]), Dassios ([3]), Embrechet, Rogers and Yor ([4]), Fujita ([7]), Yor ([12]) calculated the price of α-percentile option.

In this paper we define the rank statistics $R_{t,T}$ of a stochastic process X_t by $(\frac{1}{T})\int_0^T 1_{X_s<X_t}\,ds$, while the order statistics is defined by the number $A = m_X(T,\alpha)$ that satisfies $\frac{1}{T}\int_0^T 1_{(-\infty,A]}(X_s)\,ds = \alpha$ for $\alpha \in [0,1]$, where A is called α-percentile. The rank statistics counts the rank of X_t in $\{X_s\}_{s\in[0,T]}$. Recently rank statistics is applied to mathematical finance theory via cross sectional analysis of stock markets ([5]) and becomes more important.

We give an explicit formula for the probability distribution of a rank statistics (rank process) $R_{t,T}$ in the case where X_t is Brownian motion, Brownian motion with a constant drift, and Brownian Bridge. Using rank process, we make new derivative products like α-percentile options. For example, we can consider a new option which payoff is $\max(S_t - K, S_T - K, 0)\, 1_{R(t,T) \geqq D}$, which is a cliquet option, $\max(S_t - K, S_T - K, 0)$, penalized in the case when value S_t of the underlying asset on an interim time t is in low rank. However, we consider the simplest rank option only in the present paper, and will discuss such general options in the forthcoming paper.

We would like to give great thanks to an anonymous referee who pointed out useful remarks about our paper.

2. Facts

2.1 Brownian case

Let W_t be a standard Brownian motion.

Then

$$\begin{aligned} R_{t,T} &= \frac{1}{T}\int_0^T 1_{(W_s<W_t)}\, ds \\ &= \frac{1}{T}\int_0^t 1_{(W_t-W_s>0)}\, ds + \frac{1}{T}\int_t^T 1_{(W_s-W_t<0)}\, ds \\ &= \frac{1}{T}\int_0^t 1_{(\hat{W}_s>0)}\, ds + \frac{1}{T}\int_0^{T-t} 1_{(\tilde{W}_s<0)}\, ds \\ &= \frac{t}{T}A_1 + \frac{T-t}{T}A_2 \end{aligned}$$

where $\hat{W}_s := W_t - W_{t-s}$, $\tilde{W}_s := W_{t+s} - W_t$ (two independent Brownian motions), A_1, A_2 are two independent Arcsin random variables i.e., the density function of A_i, $f_{A_i}(x) = \frac{1_{(0,1)}(x)}{\pi\sqrt{x(1-x)}}$.

Then we can observe that in Brownian case, $R_{t,T}$ is the two indepedent weighted sum of Arcsin random variables.

2.2 Brownian motion with drift case

First we review the following results of the joint distribution of $\left(W_t, \int_0^t 1_{(-\infty,0]}(W_s)\, ds\right)$. Putting $f(t,x) = E\left[1_{[a,+\infty)}(x + W_t) \cdot e^{-\beta\int_0^t 1_{(-\infty,0]}(x+W_s)\, ds}\right]$ (for $a > 0$, $\beta > 0$), the Feynman-Kac Theorem gives that $\hat{f}(0) = \frac{e^{-\sqrt{2\xi}\, a}}{\sqrt{\xi}\,(\sqrt{\xi}+\sqrt{\xi+\beta})}$. Then the Laplace inversion gives the following:

$$P\Big(W_t \in da, \int_0^t 1_{(-\infty,0]}(W_s)\,ds \in du\Big)$$
$$= \begin{cases} \Big(\displaystyle\int_u^t \frac{a}{2\pi\sqrt{s^3(t-s)^3}} e^{\frac{-a^2}{2(t-s)}}\,ds\Big)\,da\,du & \cdots \text{if } a > 0 \\ \Big(\displaystyle\int_0^u \frac{-a}{2\pi\sqrt{s^3(t-s)^3}} e^{\frac{-a^2}{2s}}\,ds\Big)da\,du & \cdots \text{if } a < 0 \end{cases}$$

$$P\Big(W_t \in da, \int_0^t 1_{(0,\infty)}(W_s)\,ds \in du\Big)$$
$$= \begin{cases} \Big(\displaystyle\int_0^u \frac{a}{2\pi\sqrt{s^3(t-s)^3}} e^{\frac{-a^2}{2s}}\,ds\Big)da\,du & \cdots \text{if } a > 0 \\ \Big(\displaystyle\int_u^t \frac{-a}{2\pi\sqrt{s^3(t-s)^3}} e^{\frac{-a^2}{2(t-s)}}\,ds\Big)da\,du & \cdots \text{if } a < 0 \end{cases}$$

This result is obtained in ([6, 8]) to price some α-percentile options and Edokko Options which are exotic barrier options to make price manipulation more difficult.

We denote the joint density function of $\big(W_t, \int_0^t 1_{(-\infty,0]}(W_s)\,ds\big)$ by $f_t^-(a,u)$ and the joint density function of $\big(W_t, \int_0^t 1_{(0,\infty)}(W_s)\,ds\big)$ by $f_t^+(a,u)$.

Remark 2.1. This formula gives the distribution of $\int_0^t 1_{(-\infty,0]}(X_s^{T,y})\,ds$ for Pinned Brownian motion $X_s^{T,y} := W_s + \frac{s}{T}(y - W_T)$ or Brownian bidge $X_s^{T,0} = W_s - \frac{s}{T}W_T$ for $0 < u < T$,

$$P\Big(\int_0^T 1_{(-\infty,0]}(X_s^{T,y})\,ds \in du\Big) = P\Big(\int_0^T 1_{(-\infty,0]}(W_s)\,ds \in du \,\Big|\, W_T = y\Big)$$
$$= \frac{\displaystyle\int_u^T \frac{y e^{\frac{-y^2}{2(T-s)}}}{2\pi\sqrt{s^3(T-s)^3}}\,ds}{\frac{e^{\frac{-y^2}{2T}}}{\sqrt{2\pi T}}}\,du,$$

$$P\Big(\int_0^T 1_{(-\infty,0]}(X_s^{T,0})\,ds \in du\Big)$$
$$= P\Big(\int_0^T 1_{(-\infty,0]}(W_s)\,ds \in du \,\Big|\, W_T = 0\Big)$$
$$= \lim_{y\downarrow 0} \frac{\displaystyle\int_u^T \frac{y e^{\frac{-y^2}{2(T-s)}}}{2\pi\sqrt{s^3(T-s)^3}}\,ds}{\frac{e^{\frac{-y^2}{2T}}}{\sqrt{2\pi T}}}\,du$$
$$= \lim_{y\downarrow 0} \sqrt{T/(2\pi)}\, e^{y^2/(2T)} \int_{y^2/2(T-u)}^{\infty} \frac{y e^{-v}}{\sqrt{(T - y^2/2v)^3 (y^2/2v)^3}} (y^2)/(2v^2)\,dv$$

$$= (1/T)(1/\sqrt{\pi}) \int_0^\infty \frac{e^{-v}}{\sqrt{v}}\, dv$$
$$= 1/T.$$

Then we can recover the famous results for the uniform law of the occupation time of Brownian bridge. ([11])

Remark 2.2. Chesney, Jeanblanc-Picque and Yor ([2]) got the same results by another approach. Also Karatzas and Shreve ([9] p. 423, Prop. 3.9) obtained the similar results of this Theorem.

We denote the rank process of Brownian motion with drift μ, $X_t^\mu = W_t + \mu t$ by $R_{t,T}^\mu$. Then $R_{t,T}^\mu = 1/T \int_0^T 1_{(X_s^\mu < X_t^\mu)}\, ds$.

Cameron Martin relationship gives that

$$E(h(R_{t,T}^\mu)) = E\big(e^{\mu W_T - \mu^2 T/2} h(R_{t,T})\big)$$
$$= \iint_{-\infty<x<\infty,\, 0<y<1} e^{\mu x - \mu^2 T/2} h(y) f_{(W_T, R_{t,T})}(x,y)\, dy$$

where $R_{t,T} = R_{t,T}^0$. Then it is enough to know the joint distribution of $(W_T, R_{t,T})$ to obtain the distribution of $R_{t,T}^\mu$.

We already know the two independent joint distribution of $\big(\hat{W}_t, \int_0^t 1_{(\hat{W}_s>0)}\, ds\big)$ and $\big(\tilde{W}_{T-t}, \int_0^{T-t} 1_{(\tilde{W}_s<0)}\, ds\big)$.

$$f_{(\hat{W}_t, \int_0^t 1_{(\hat{W}_s>0)}\, ds)}(a,u) = f_t^+(a,u)$$
$$f_{(\tilde{W}_{T-t}, \int_0^{T-t} 1_{(\tilde{W}_s<0)}\, ds)}(a,u) = f_{T-t}^-(a,u)$$

where we recall that $\hat{W}_s = W_t - W_{t-s}$, $\tilde{W}_s = W_{s+t} - W_t$.

Putting $f_{(W_T,R_{t,T})}(x,y)$ as the joint density function of $(W_T, R_{t,T})$, we consider the joint moment generating function of $(W_T, R_{t,T})$ as $M_{(W_T,R_{t,T})}(\alpha,\beta) = E\big(e^{\alpha W_T + \beta R_{t,T}}\big)$.

$$M_{(W_T,R_{t,T})}(\alpha,\beta)$$
$$= E\big(e^{\alpha(\hat{W}_t + \tilde{W}_{T-t}) + \beta(\frac{1}{T}\int_0^t 1_{\hat{W}_s<0}\, ds + \frac{1}{T}\int_0^{T-t} 1_{\tilde{W}_s>0}\, ds)}\big)$$
$$= E\big(e^{\alpha \hat{W}_t + \frac{\beta}{T}\int_0^t 1_{\hat{W}_s>0}\, ds}\big) E\big(e^{\alpha \tilde{W}_{T-t} + \frac{\beta}{T}\int_0^{T-t} 1_{\tilde{W}_s<0}\, ds}\big)$$
$$= \iint_{-\infty<x_1<\infty,\, 0<y_1<t} e^{\alpha x_1 + \frac{\beta}{T} y_1} f_t^+(x_1,y_1)\, dx_1\, dy_1$$
$$\iint_{-\infty<x_2<\infty,\, 0<y_2<T-t} e^{\alpha x_2 + \frac{\beta}{T} y_2} f_{T-t}^-(x_2,y_2)\, dx_2\, dy_2$$

First we consider the case $0 < t < T/2$,

$$
\begin{aligned}
&M_{(W_T,R_{t,T})}(\alpha,\beta) \\
&= \iint_{-\infty<x<\infty,\,0<y<t} e^{\alpha x+\frac{\beta}{T}y}\,dx\,dy \\
&\quad \iint_{-\infty<x_1<\infty,\,0<y_1<y} f_t^+(x_1,y_1)f_{T-t}^-(x-x_1,y-y_1)\,dx_1\,dy_1 \\
&\quad + \iint_{-\infty<x<\infty,\,t<y<T-t} e^{\alpha x+\frac{\beta}{T}y}\,dx\,dy \\
&\quad \iint_{-\infty<x_1<\infty,\,0<y_1<t} f_t^+(x_1,y_1)f_{T-t}^-(x-x_1,y-y_1)\,dx_1\,dy_1 \\
&\quad + \iint_{-\infty<x<\infty,\,T-t<y<T} e^{\alpha x+\frac{\beta}{T}y}\,dx\,dy \\
&\quad \iint_{-\infty<x_1<\infty,\,y-(T-t)<y_1<t} f_t^+(x_1,y_1)f_{T-t}^-(x-x_1,y-y_1)\,dx_1\,dy_1.
\end{aligned}
$$

Next we consider the case: $T/2 < t < T$,

$$
\begin{aligned}
&M_{(W_T,R_{t,T})}(\alpha,\beta) \\
&= \iint_{-\infty<x<\infty,\,0<y<T-t} e^{\alpha x+\frac{\beta}{T}y}\,dx\,dy \\
&\quad \iint_{-\infty<x_2<\infty,\,0<y_2<y} f_t^+(x-x_2,y-y_2)f_{T-t}^-(x_2,y_2)\,dx_2\,dy_2 \\
&\quad + \iint_{-\infty<x<\infty,\,T-t<y<t} e^{\alpha x+\frac{\beta}{T}y}\,dx\,dy \\
&\quad \iint_{-\infty<x_2<\infty,\,0<y_2<T-t} f_t^+(x-x_2,y-y_2)f_{T-t}^-(x_2,y_2)\,dx_2\,dy_2 \\
&\quad + \iint_{-\infty<x<\infty,\,t<y<T} e^{\alpha x+\frac{\beta}{T}y}\,dx\,dy \\
&\quad \iint_{-\infty<x_1<\infty,\,y-t<y_2<T-t} f_t^+(x-x_2,y-y_2)f_{T-t}^-(x_2,y_2)\,dx_2\,dy_2.
\end{aligned}
$$

Then we get the following theorem.

Theorem 2.1. *If* $0 < t < T/2$,

$$
f_{(W_T,R_{t,T})}(x,y) = T\iint_A f_t^+(x_1,y_1)f_{T-t}^-(x-x_1,Ty-y_1)\,dx_1\,dy_1
$$

$$A = \begin{cases} \{(x_1,y_1) \mid -\infty < x_1 < \infty,\ 0 < y_1 < Ty\} \\ \qquad\qquad \textit{if } -\infty < x < \infty,\ 0 < y < \frac{t}{T} \\ \{(x_1,y_1) \mid -\infty < x_1 < \infty,\ 0 < y_1 < t\} \\ \qquad\qquad \textit{if } -\infty < x < \infty,\ \frac{t}{T} < y < \frac{T-t}{T} \\ \{(x_1,y_1) \mid -\infty < x_1 < \infty,\ Ty-(T-t) < y_1 < t\} \\ \qquad\qquad \textit{if } -\infty < x < \infty,\ \frac{T-t}{T} < y < 1. \end{cases}$$

If $T/2 < t < T$,

$$f_{(W_T,R_{t,T})}(x,y) = T\iint_B f_t^+(x-x_2, Ty-y_2) f_{T-t}^-(x_2,y_2)\, dx_2\, dy_2$$

$$B = \begin{cases} \{(x_2,y_2) \mid -\infty < x_2 < \infty,\ 0 < y_2 < Ty\} \\ \qquad\qquad \textit{if } -\infty < x < \infty,\ 0 < y < \frac{T-t}{T} \\ \{(x_2,y_2) \mid -\infty < x_2 < \infty,\ 0 < y_2 < T-t\} \\ \qquad\qquad \textit{if } -\infty < x < \infty,\ \frac{T-t}{T} < y < \frac{t}{T} \\ \{(x_2,y_2) \mid -\infty < x_2 < \infty,\ Ty-t < y_2 < T-t\} \\ \qquad\qquad \textit{if } -\infty < x < \infty,\ \frac{t}{T} < y < 1. \end{cases}$$

This formula gives the exact form of the joint distribution of $(W_T, R_{t,T})$ and the distribution $R_{t,T}^{\mu}$: recalling Cameron Martin relationship,

Theorem 2.2. $f_{R_{t,T}^{\mu}}(x) = \int_{-\infty}^{\infty} e^{\mu y - \mu^2 T/2} f_{(W_T,R_{t,T})}(y,x)\, dy.$

2.3 Pinned Brownian motion case

We denote the rank process of a pinned Brownian motion $X_s^{T,y} = W_s + \frac{s}{T}(y - W_T)$ by $\tilde{R}_t^{T,y}$.

Then

$$\begin{aligned} \tilde{R}_t^{T,y} &= \frac{1}{T}\int_0^T 1_{(X_s^{T,y} < X_t^{T,y})}\, ds \\ &= \frac{1}{T}\int_0^T 1_{(W_s < W_t)}\, ds \quad \text{on} \quad W_T = y. \end{aligned}$$

Then

$$\begin{aligned} E\big(h(\tilde{R}_t^{T,y})\big) &= E\big(h(R_{t,T}) \mid W_T = y\big) \\ &= \int_0^1 h(x) \frac{f_{(W_T,R_{t,T})}(y,x)}{f_{W_T}(y)}\, dx. \end{aligned}$$

The density function of $\tilde{R}_t^{T,y}$, $f_{\tilde{R}_t^{T,y}}(x)$ is

$$f_{\tilde{R}_t^{T,y}}(x) = \frac{\sqrt{2\pi T}\, 1_{(0,1)}(y) f_{(W_T,R_{t,T})}(y,x)}{e^{-y^2/(2T)}}.$$

3. Pricing of rank option

We define an exotic option with a payoff $(R^S_{t,T} - K)^+$ and call it Rank option and calculate the price in the Black Scholes Model. Other type of options using rank statics and their properties will be discussed in our coming article. In the Black Scholes Model, we consider that

$$dS_t = rS_t\,dt + \sigma S_t\,dW_t, \quad S_0 = S, \quad (S_t = Se^{\sigma W_t + (r-\sigma^2/2)t})$$
$$R^S_{t,T} = \frac{1}{T}\int_0^T 1_{(S_s<S_t)}\,ds.$$

Then

the price of Rank option
$$\begin{aligned}
&= e^{-rT}E((R^S_{t,T} - K)^+) \\
&= e^{-rT}E\left(\left(1/T\int_0^T 1_{Se^{\sigma W_s+(r-\sigma^2/2)s} < Se^{\sigma W_t+(r-\sigma^2/2)t}}\,ds - K\right)^+\right) \\
&= e^{-rT}E((R^{r/\sigma-\sigma/2}_{t,T} - K)^+) \\
&= \int_0^\infty (x-K)^+ f_{R^{r/\sigma-\sigma/2}_{t,T}}(x)\,dx
\end{aligned}$$

We note that the distribution of $R^{r/\sigma-\sigma/2}_{t,T}$ is already obtained in the previous section.

References

[1] Akahori, J.: Some formulae for a new type of path-dependent option. Ann. Appl. Probab. **5**, 383-388 (1995)

[2] Chesney, M., Jeanblanc-Picque, M., Yor, M.: Brownian excursions and Parisian barrier options. Adv. Appl. Prob. **29**, 165-184 (1997)

[3] Dassios, A.: The distribution of the quantile of a Brownian motion with drift and the pricing related path-dependent options. Ann. Appl. Probab. **5**, 389-398 (1995)

[4] Embrechts, P., Rogers, L.C.G., Yor, M.: A proof of Dassios's representation of the α-quantile of Brownian motion with drift. Ann. Appl. Probab. **5**, 757-767 (1995)

[5] Fernholz, E.R.: Stochastic Portfolio Theory, Applications of Mathematics. Stochastic Modelling and Applied Probability **48**, Springer 2000

[6] Fujita, T.: On the price of the α-percentile options. Hitotsubashi University Faculty of Commerce Working Paper Series No.24 (1997)

[7] Fujita, T.: A note on the joint distribution of α, β-percentiles and its application to the option pricing. Asia-Pacific Financial Markets **7**, 339-344 (2000)

[8] Fujita, T., Miura, R.: Edokko options: A new framework of barrier options. Asia-Pacific Financial Markets **9**, 141-151 (2002)

[9] Karatzas, I., Shreve, S.E.: Brownian Motion and Stochastic Calculus. Springer 1991
[10] Miura, R.: A note on look-back option based on order statistics. Hitotsubashi Journal of Commerce and Management **27**, 15-28 (1992).
[11] Revuz, D., Yor, M.: Continuous Martingales and Brownian Motion, Third Ed. Springer 1999
[12] Yor, M.: The distribution of Brownian quantiles. J. Appl. Prob. **2**, 405-416 (1995)

Adv. Math. Econ. 9, 33–48 (2006)

Advances in
MATHEMATICAL
ECONOMICS

Asymptotic expansion for a filtering problem and a short term rate model

Hirotaka Fushiya

Graduate School of Mathematical Sciences, The University of Tokyo, Komaba 3-8-1, Meguro-ku, Tokyo 153-8914, Japan
(e-mail: fushiya@mail4.alpha-net.ne.jp)

Received: January 11, 2005
Revised: December 1, 2005

JEL classification: C67, G12

Mathematics Subject Classification (2000): 60G35, 93E10

Abstract. We study the filtering problem in which a system process $X_t(\varepsilon)$ and a observing process $Y_t(\varepsilon)$ depend on the parameter ε, and $X_t(\varepsilon)$ converges to a deterministic function $X_t(0)$ as $\varepsilon \downarrow 0$. We give an asymptotic expansion formula in L^p for the conditional expectation of a function of $X_t(\varepsilon)$ under the σ-field generated by the process $Y_s(\varepsilon), 0 \leq s \leq t$.

Key words: filtering, nonlinear, asymptotic expansion

1. Introduction

The Filtering problem has been studied by many authors (c.f. [5] and its references). It is sometimes used for pricing in models of finance (e.g. [6]), and the asymptotic approach can also be used (e.g. [9, 10]). In the present paper, we consider an asymptotic approach to the filtering problem, which may be useful for pricing in financial models. [3] considered a similar problem.

Now let us state our result. Let $(\Omega, \mathcal{F}, \{\mathcal{F}_t\}_{t\in\mathbf{T}}, \mathbf{P})$ be a filtered probability space, $\{(W_t^1, W_t^2)\}_{t\in\mathbf{T}}$ be an $l + l'$-dimensional $\mathcal{F}_t$-Brownian motion, $\mathbf{T} = [0, T], T > 0$, and $b\colon \mathbf{T}\times\mathbf{R}^d \to \mathbf{R}^d$ and $\sigma_1 : \mathbf{T}\times\mathbf{R}^d \to \mathbf{R}^d\otimes\mathbf{R}^l$ be continuous functions. For each $\varepsilon \in [0, \infty)$, we consider the following stochastic differential equation

$$X_t(\varepsilon) = x_0 + \int_0^t b(s, X_s(\varepsilon))\, ds + \varepsilon \int_0^t \sigma_1(s, X_s(\varepsilon))\, dW_s^1, \qquad t \in \mathbf{T}. \quad (1)$$

Let $F\colon [0,\infty) \times \mathbf{T} \times \mathbf{R}^d \times \mathbf{R}^{l'} \to \mathbf{R}^{l'}$ and $\sigma_2\colon \mathbf{T} \times \mathbf{R}^{l'} \to \mathbf{R}^{l'} \otimes \mathbf{R}^{l'}$ be bounded continuous functions, and consider the following stochastic differential equation

$$Y_t(\varepsilon) = \int_0^t F(\varepsilon, s, X_s(\varepsilon), Y_s(\varepsilon))\, ds + \int_0^t \sigma_2(s, Y_s(\varepsilon))\, dW_s^2. \tag{2}$$

We think that $X_t(\varepsilon)$ is a system process and $Y_t(\varepsilon)$ is an observation process. Let $\mathcal{G}_t(\varepsilon) = \sigma(Y_s(\varepsilon);\, 0 \le s \le t)$, $t \in \mathbf{T}$, $\varepsilon \ge 0$. Our aim is to obtain an approximate expression of $\mathbf{E}[g(X_t(\varepsilon)) \mid \mathcal{G}_t(\varepsilon)]$ as $\varepsilon \downarrow 0$ for an arbitrary bounded smooth function $g(x)$.

We assume the followings.

(A.1) Stochastic Differential Equation (1) has a unique strong solutions for any $\varepsilon \in [0,1]$, and $\sup_{\varepsilon \in [0,1]} \sup_{t \in T} \mathbf{E}\left[|X_t(\varepsilon)|^p\right] < \infty$ holds for any $p \in [1,\infty)$.

(A.2) There exists a constant $K > 0$ such that

$$\|F(\varepsilon,t,x,y) - F(\varepsilon,t,x,z)\| + \|\sigma_2(t,y) - \sigma_2(t,z)\| \le K\|y-z\|$$

for every $(\varepsilon,t,x,y,z) \in [0,\infty) \times \mathbf{T} \times \mathbf{R}^d \times \mathbf{R}^{l'} \times \mathbf{R}^{l'}$.

(A.3) There is an $\eta > 0$ such that $b(t,x)$ and $\sigma_1(t,x)$ are smooth on the closed set $D_\eta = \{(t,x) \in \mathbf{T} \times \mathbf{R}^d;\ \|x - X_t(0)\| \le \eta\}$ and F is smooth on $[0,1] \times D_\eta \times \mathbf{R}^{l'}$.

(A.4) $\sigma_2(t,x)^{-1}$ exists and is bounded in (t,x).

Let $\{\widetilde{Y}_t\}_{t \in \mathbf{T}}$ be the solution of the following stochastic differential equation

$$\widetilde{Y}_t = \int_0^t \sigma_2(s, \widetilde{Y}_s)\, dW_s^2.$$

Our main theorem is the following.

Theorem 1. *Let $g\colon \mathbf{R}^d \to \mathbf{R}$ be a smooth function such that there exists a constant $N > 0$ and K satisfying*

$$|g(x)| \le K(1 + |x|^N), \qquad x \in \mathbf{R}^d$$

Then for any $t \in \mathbf{T}$, there exist measurable functionals $h^{(k)}\colon C(\mathbf{T}; \mathbf{R}^{d'}) \to \mathbf{R}$, $k = 0,1,2,\ldots$ such that

$$\lim_{\varepsilon \to 0} \mathbf{E}\left[\left|\frac{1}{\varepsilon^n}\left\{\mathbf{E}[g(X_t(\varepsilon)) \mid \mathcal{G}_t(\varepsilon)] - \sum_{k=0}^n \varepsilon^k h^{(k)}(Y_\cdot(\varepsilon))\right\}\right|^p\right] = 0,$$

for any $p \in (1,\infty)$ and $n \in \mathbf{N}$. Also $h^{(k)}(y_\cdot)$, $k = 0,1,2,\ldots$, are uniquely determined $\mathbf{P} \circ \widetilde{Y}^{-1}$-a.s. $y_\cdot$.

We apply our theorem to a certain model of 0-coupon bond price and show the calculation of functionals $h^{(k)}$ in this model in Section 4.

2. Proof of theorem

First we show the following.

Proposition 2. *Let* $G\colon \mathbf{T}\times\Omega \to \mathbf{R}^{l'}$ *be* $F(\varepsilon,t,X_t(\varepsilon),Y_t(\varepsilon))$*-adapted and satisfy* $|G_t| \le K$ *for some constant* K. *Then there exists constant* $\widetilde{C}_q > 0$ *such that*

$$\mathbf{E}\left[\sup_{t\in\mathbf{T}}\exp\left\{q\int_0^t G_s\,dW_s^2\right\}\right] \le 4\exp\left\{\frac{1}{2}q^2K^2T\right\}$$

for any $q \in \mathbf{R}$.

Proof. Using Doob's maximal inequality we have

$$\begin{aligned}
&\mathbf{E}\left[\sup_{t\in\mathbf{T}}\exp\left\{q\int_0^t G_s dW_s^2\right\}\right]\\
&\le \exp\left\{\frac{1}{4}q^2K^2T\right\}\mathbf{E}\left[\sup_{t\in\mathbf{T}}\left\{\exp\left\{\int_0^t \frac{q}{2}G_s\,dW_s^2 - \frac{1}{2}\int_0^t\left|\frac{q}{2}G_s\right|^2 ds\right\}\right\}^2\right]\\
&\le 4\exp\left\{\frac{1}{4}q^2K^2T\right\}\\
&\quad\times\mathbf{E}\left[\exp\left\{\int_0^T qG_s\,dW_s^2 - \frac{1}{2}\int_0^T |qG_s|^2\,ds\right\}\exp\left\{\frac{1}{4}\int_0^T |qG_s|^2\,ds\right\}\right]\\
&\le 4\exp\left\{\frac{1}{2}q^2K^2T\right\}.
\end{aligned}$$

□

Let $G(\varepsilon,t,x,y) = \sigma_2(t,y)^{-1}F(\varepsilon,t,x,y)$. Then $G(\varepsilon,t,x,y)$ is bounded. Let

$$\begin{aligned}
\alpha(\varepsilon,t,x.(\varepsilon),y.) = \exp\Bigg\{&\int_0^t G(\varepsilon,s,x_s,y_s)\sigma_2(s,y_s)^{-1}\,dy_s\\
&-\frac{1}{2}\int_0^t \|G(\varepsilon,s,x_s,y_s)\|^2\,ds\Bigg\}.
\end{aligned}$$

Then we have

$$\begin{aligned}
\alpha(\varepsilon,t,X.(\varepsilon),Y.(\varepsilon)) = \exp\Bigg\{&\int_0^t G(\varepsilon,s,X_s(\varepsilon),Y_s(\varepsilon))\,dW_s^2\\
&+\frac{1}{2}\int_0^t \|G(\varepsilon,s,X_s(\varepsilon),Y_s(\varepsilon))\|^2\,ds\Bigg\}.
\end{aligned}$$

Let $\mathbf{Q}(\varepsilon)$ be a probability measure defined by $d\mathbf{Q}(\varepsilon) = \alpha(\varepsilon,t,X.(\varepsilon),Y.(\varepsilon))^{-1}$ $d\mathbf{P}$. Let $\widetilde{W}_t(\varepsilon) = W_t^2 + \int_0^t G(\varepsilon,s,X_s(\varepsilon),Y_s(\varepsilon))\,ds$. Then, $\{(W_t^1,\widetilde{W}_t(\varepsilon))\}_{t\in\mathbf{T}}$ is a $\mathcal{F}_t$-Wiener process under $\mathbf{Q}(\varepsilon)$.

Also we have

$$Y_t(\varepsilon) = \int_0^t \sigma_2(s, Y_s(\varepsilon))\, d\widetilde{W}_s(\varepsilon), \qquad t \in \mathbf{T}.$$

Then, $\{X_t(\varepsilon)\}_{t\in\mathbf{T}}$ and $\{Y_t(\varepsilon)\}_{t\in\mathbf{T}}$ are independent under $\mathbf{Q}(\varepsilon)$. So we have

$$\begin{aligned}
\mathbf{E}[g(X_t(\varepsilon)) \mid \mathcal{G}_t(\varepsilon)] &= \frac{\mathbf{E}^{\mathbf{Q}(\varepsilon)}\big[g(X_t(\varepsilon))\alpha(\varepsilon, t, X_\cdot(\varepsilon), Y_\cdot(\varepsilon)) \mid \mathcal{G}_t(\varepsilon)\big]}{\mathbf{E}^{\mathbf{Q}(\varepsilon)}\big[\alpha(\varepsilon, t, X_\cdot(\varepsilon), Y_\cdot(\varepsilon)) \mid \mathcal{G}_t(\varepsilon)\big]} \\
&= \frac{\mathbf{E}^{\mathbf{Q}(\varepsilon)}\big[g(X_t(\varepsilon))\alpha(\varepsilon, t, X_\cdot(\varepsilon), y_\cdot)\big]\big|_{y_\cdot = Y_\cdot(\varepsilon)}}{\mathbf{E}^{\mathbf{Q}(\varepsilon)}\big[\alpha(\varepsilon, t, X_\cdot(\varepsilon), y_\cdot)\big]\big|_{y_\cdot = Y_\cdot(\varepsilon)}}.
\end{aligned}$$

Let

$$\begin{aligned}
G^{(0)}(t, y_t) &= G(0, t, X_t(0), y_t), \\
\alpha^{(0)}(t, y_\cdot) &= \exp\bigg\{\int_0^t G^{(0)}(s, y_s)\, dy_s - \frac{1}{2}\int_0^t \|G^{(0)}(s, y_s)\|^2\, ds\bigg\}, \\
\widetilde{G}(\varepsilon, t, x_\cdot, y_\cdot) &= \int_0^t G(\varepsilon, s, x_s, y_s)\, dy_s - \frac{1}{2}\int_0^t \|G(\varepsilon, s, x_s, y_s)\|^2\, ds \\
&\quad - \int_0^t G^{(0)}(s, y_s)\, dy_s + \frac{1}{2}\int_0^t \|G^{(0)}(s, y_s)\|^2\, ds.
\end{aligned}$$

Then we have

$$\begin{aligned}
\alpha(\varepsilon, t, X_\cdot(\varepsilon), y_\cdot(\varepsilon)) &= \alpha^{(0)}(t, y_\cdot(\varepsilon)) \exp \widetilde{G}(\varepsilon, t, X_\cdot(\varepsilon), y_\cdot(\varepsilon)), \\
\mathbf{E}[g(X_t(\varepsilon)) \mid \mathcal{G}_t(\varepsilon)] &= \frac{\mathbf{E}^{\mathbf{Q}(\varepsilon)}\big[g(X_t(\varepsilon)) \exp \widetilde{G}(\varepsilon, t, X_\cdot(\varepsilon), y_\cdot)\big]\big|_{y_\cdot = Y_\cdot(\varepsilon)}}{\mathbf{E}^{\mathbf{Q}(\varepsilon)}\big[\exp \widetilde{G}(\varepsilon, t, X_\cdot(\varepsilon), y_\cdot)\big]\big|_{y_\cdot = Y_\cdot(\varepsilon)}}.
\end{aligned}$$

The distribution of $\{(X_t(\varepsilon), Y_t(\varepsilon))\}_{t\in\mathbf{T}}$ under $\mathbf{Q}(\varepsilon)$ is equal to the distribution of $\{(X_t(\varepsilon), \widetilde{Y}_t)\}_{t\in\mathbf{T}}$ under $\mathbf{P}$. So we have

$$\mathbf{E}^{\mathbf{Q}(\varepsilon)}[|f(X_\cdot(\varepsilon), Y_\cdot(\varepsilon))|] = \mathbf{E}[|f(X_\cdot(\varepsilon), \widetilde{Y}_\cdot)|]$$

for an arbitrary functional $f\colon C(\mathbf{T}; \mathbf{R}^d) \times C(\mathbf{T}; \mathbf{R}^{l'}) \to \mathbf{R}$.

We will prove the following Proposition in Section 3.

Proposition 3. *For any polynomial order smooth function* $g(x)$ *and* $t \in \mathbf{T}$, *there exist measurable functionals* $h_1^{(k)}\colon C(\mathbf{T}; \mathbf{R}^{l'}) \to \mathbf{R}$, $k = 0, 1, 2, \ldots$, *such that*

$$\lim_{\varepsilon\to 0}\mathbf{E}\Bigg[\Bigg|\frac{1}{\varepsilon^n}\Bigg\{\mathbf{E}[g(X_t(\varepsilon))\exp\widetilde{G}(\varepsilon,t,X_\cdot(\varepsilon),y_\cdot)]\big|_{y_\cdot=\widetilde{Y}_\cdot} - \sum_{k=0}^{n}\varepsilon^k h_1^{(k)}(\widetilde{Y}_\cdot)\Bigg\}\Bigg|^p\Bigg]=0,$$

for any $p\in(1,\infty)$ *and* $n\in\mathbf{N}$. *Moreover, we have* $h_1^{(0)}(y_\cdot)=g(X_t(0))$.

We have the following by Proposition 3

Proposition 4. *For any* $t\in\mathbf{T}$, *there exist measurable functionals* $h_2^{(k)}$: $C(\mathbf{T};\mathbf{R}^{l'})\to\mathbf{R}$, $k=0,1,2,\ldots$, *such that*

$$\lim_{\varepsilon\to 0}\mathbf{E}\Bigg[\Bigg|\frac{1}{\varepsilon^n}\Bigg\{\frac{1}{\mathbf{E}\big[\exp\widetilde{G}(\varepsilon,t,X_\cdot(\varepsilon),y_\cdot)\big]\big|_{y_\cdot=\widetilde{Y}_\cdot}} - \sum_{k=0}^{n}\varepsilon^k h_2^{(k)}(\widetilde{Y}_\cdot)\Bigg\}\Bigg|^p\Bigg]=0,$$

for any $p\in(1,\infty)$ *and* $n\in\mathbf{N}$.

Proof. We have $\dfrac{1}{1-x}-(1+x+\cdots+x^n)=\dfrac{x^{n+1}}{1-x}$ for any $x\neq 1$, and $\{\mathbf{E}[\exp\{\widetilde{G}(\varepsilon,t,X_\cdot(\varepsilon),y_\cdot)\}]\}^{-1}\le\mathbf{E}[\exp\{-\widetilde{G}(\varepsilon,t,X_\cdot(\varepsilon),y_\cdot)\}]$ by Jensen's inequality.

So we have

$$\begin{aligned}
&\Bigg\{\frac{1}{\varepsilon^{np}}\mathbf{E}\Bigg[\Bigg|\frac{1}{\mathbf{E}\big[\exp\{\widetilde{G}(\varepsilon,t,X_\cdot(\varepsilon),y_\cdot)\}\big]\big|_{y_\cdot=\widetilde{Y}_\cdot}} - \sum_{k=0}^{n}\Big(\mathbf{E}\big[1-\exp\{\widetilde{G}(\varepsilon,t,X_\cdot(\varepsilon),y_\cdot)\}\big]\big|_{y_\cdot=\widetilde{Y}_\cdot}\Big)^k\Bigg|^p\Bigg]\Bigg\}^2\\
&=\Bigg\{\frac{1}{\varepsilon^{np}}\mathbf{E}\Bigg[\Bigg|\frac{\Big(\mathbf{E}\big[1-\exp\{\widetilde{G}(\varepsilon,t,X_\cdot(\varepsilon),y_\cdot)\}\big]\big|_{y_\cdot=\widetilde{Y}_\cdot}\Big)^{n+1}}{\mathbf{E}\big[\exp\{\widetilde{G}(\varepsilon,t,X_\cdot(\varepsilon),y_\cdot)\}\big]\big|_{y_\cdot=\widetilde{Y}_\cdot}}\Bigg|^p\Bigg]\Bigg\}^2\\
&\le\mathbf{E}\big[\exp\{-2p\widetilde{G}(\varepsilon,t,X_\cdot(\varepsilon),\widetilde{Y}_\cdot)\}\big]\\
&\quad\times\frac{1}{\varepsilon^{2np}}\mathbf{E}\Big[\Big|\mathbf{E}\big[1-\exp\{\widetilde{G}(\varepsilon,t,X_\cdot(\varepsilon),y_\cdot)\}\big]\big|_{y_\cdot=\widetilde{Y}_\cdot}\Big|^{2(n+1)p}\Big].
\end{aligned}$$

Using Proposition 2 and Proposition 3 with $n=1$ and $g(x)\equiv 1$, we have

$$\lim_{\varepsilon\to 0}\frac{1}{\varepsilon^{np}}\mathbf{E}\Bigg[\Bigg|\frac{1}{\mathbf{E}\big[\exp\{\widetilde{G}(\varepsilon,t,X_\cdot(\varepsilon),y_\cdot)\}\big]\big|_{y_\cdot=\widetilde{Y}_\cdot}} - \sum_{k=0}^{n}\Big(\mathbf{E}\big[1-\exp\{\widetilde{G}(\varepsilon,t,X_\cdot(\varepsilon),y_\cdot)\}\big]\big|_{y_\cdot=\widetilde{Y}_\cdot}\Big)^k\Bigg|^p\Bigg]=0.$$

Therefore we have our assertion. This completes the proof. □

Now we prove Theorem 1. Let $h^{(k)}(y.) = \sum_{j=0}^{k} h_1^{(j)}(y.)h_2^{(k-j)}(y.)$, where h_1, h_2 are as in Propositions 3 and 4. Then we have

$$\lim_{\varepsilon \to 0} \mathbf{E}\left[\left|\frac{1}{\varepsilon^n}\left\{\mathbf{E}[g(X_t(\varepsilon)) \mid \mathcal{G}_t(\varepsilon)] - \sum_{k=0}^{n} \varepsilon^k h^{(k)}(Y.(\varepsilon))\right\}\right|^p\right] = 0,$$

for any $p \in (1, \infty)$ and $n \in \mathbf{N}$.

At last we show the uniqueness of $h^{(k)}$. Suppose that $\widetilde{h}^{(k)}$, $k = 0, 1, 2, \ldots$, also satisfy

$$\lim_{\varepsilon \to 0} \mathbf{E}\left[\left|\frac{1}{\varepsilon^n}\left\{\mathbf{E}[g(X_t(\varepsilon)) \mid \mathcal{G}_t(\varepsilon)] - \sum_{k=0}^{n} \varepsilon^k \widetilde{h}^{(k)}(Y.(\varepsilon))\right\}\right|^p\right] = 0,$$

for any $p \in (1, \infty)$ and $n \in \mathbf{N}$. Since

$$\begin{aligned}
&\mathbf{E}\left[\left|\frac{1}{\varepsilon^n}\sum_{k=0}^{n}\{h^{(k)}(Y.(\varepsilon)) - \widetilde{h}^{(k)}(Y.(\varepsilon))\}\right|^p\right] \\
&= \mathbf{E}^{\mathbf{Q}(\varepsilon)}\left[\left|\frac{1}{\varepsilon^n}\sum_{k=0}^{n}\{h^{(k)}(Y.(\varepsilon)) - \widetilde{h}^{(k)}(Y.(\varepsilon))\}\alpha(\varepsilon, t, X.(\varepsilon), Y.(\varepsilon))\right|^p\right] \\
&= \mathbf{E}\left[\left|\frac{1}{\varepsilon^n}\sum_{k=0}^{n}\{h^{(k)}(\widetilde{Y}.) - \widetilde{h}^{(k)}(\widetilde{Y}.)\}\alpha(\varepsilon, t, X.(\varepsilon), \widetilde{Y}.)\right|^p\right],
\end{aligned}$$

we have by Proposition 2,

$$\lim_{\varepsilon \to 0} \mathbf{E}\left[\left|\frac{1}{\varepsilon^n}\sum_{k=0}^{n}\{h^{(k)}(\widetilde{Y}.) - \widetilde{h}^{(k)}(\widetilde{Y}.)\}\right|^p\right] = 0,$$

for any $p \in (1, \infty)$ and $n \in \mathbf{N}$. So we have

$$\mathbf{E}\left[|h^{(k)}(\widetilde{Y}.) - \widetilde{h}^{(k)}(\widetilde{Y}.)|^p\right] = 0, \qquad p \in (1, \infty),\ k = 0, 1, 2, \ldots.$$

So we have our assertion. This completes the proof. □

3. Proof of Proposition 3

In this section we show the proof of Proposition 3.

Let $\widetilde{b}$: $\mathbf{T} \times \mathbf{R}^d \to \mathbf{R}^d$ and $\widetilde{\sigma}_1 : \mathbf{T} \times \mathbf{R}^d \to \mathbf{R}^d \otimes \mathbf{R}^l$, be bounded smooth functions such that their all derivatives of any order are bounded and

$$\widetilde{\sigma}_1(t,x) = \sigma_1(t,x), \quad \widetilde{b}(t,x) = b(t,x), \qquad (t,x) \in D_\eta.$$

We define $\{\widetilde{X}_t(\varepsilon)\}_{t\in\mathbf{T}}$ to be a solution of the stochastic differential equation

$$\widetilde{X}_t(\varepsilon) = x_0 + \int_0^t \widetilde{b}(s, \widetilde{X}_s(\varepsilon))\, ds + \varepsilon \int_0^t \widetilde{\sigma}_1(s, \widetilde{X}_s(\varepsilon))\, dW_s^1. \tag{3}$$

Proposition 5. *There exists constants $C > 0$ and $\gamma > 0$ such that*

$$\mathbf{P}\Big(\sup_{t\in\mathbf{T}} \|X_t(\varepsilon) - \widetilde{X}_t(\varepsilon)\| \neq 0\Big) \le Ce^{-\gamma/\varepsilon^2}, \qquad 0 < \varepsilon \le 1.$$

Proof. Let $Z_t(\varepsilon) = \widetilde{X}_t(\varepsilon) - X_t(0)$. Then $Z_t(\varepsilon)$ satisfies

$$\begin{aligned} Z_t(\varepsilon) = &\int_0^t \{\widetilde{b}(s, Z_s(\varepsilon) + X_s(0)) - \widetilde{b}(s, X_s(0))\}\, ds \\ &+ \varepsilon \int_0^t \widetilde{\sigma}_1(s, Z_s(\varepsilon) + X_s(0))\, dW_s^1. \end{aligned}$$

Let $K' = \sup_{t\in\mathbf{T},\, x\in\mathbf{R}^d} \|\widetilde{b}(t,x)\|$, then we have

$$\|Z_t(\varepsilon)\| \le K' \int_0^t \|Z_s(\varepsilon)\|\, ds + \varepsilon \Big\| \int_0^t \widetilde{\sigma}_1(s, Z_s(\varepsilon) + X_s(0))\, dW_s^1 \Big\|, \qquad \varepsilon \in (0,1],\ t \in \mathbf{T}.$$

Let $M_t = \int_0^t \widetilde{\sigma}_1(s, Z_s(\varepsilon) + X_t(0))\, dW_s^1$. Then for each $i = 1, 2, \ldots, l$, there is an 1-dimensional Brownian Motion $B(t)$ such that $M_t^i = B(\langle M^i \rangle_t)$. Note that

$$\langle M^i \rangle_t = \int_0^t \|\widetilde{\sigma}_1^i(s, Z_s(\varepsilon) + X_s(0))\|^2\, ds \le k^2 T,$$

where $k = \sup_{t\in\mathbf{T},\, x\in\mathbf{R}^d} \|\widetilde{\sigma}_1(t,x)\|$. So there are absolute constants A and A', such that

$$\mathbf{P}\Big(\sup_{t\in\mathbf{T}} |M_t^i| > \eta'/\varepsilon\Big) \le \mathbf{P}\Big(\sup_{0\le t\le k^2T} |B_t| > \eta'/\varepsilon\Big) \le Ae^{-A'\eta'^2 k^2 T/\varepsilon^2}$$

for any $\varepsilon \in (0,1]$, $\eta' > 0$. If $\sup_{t\in\mathbf{T}} \|M_t\| \le l\eta'/\varepsilon$, then $\|Z_t(\varepsilon)\| \le K' \int_0^t \|Z_s(\varepsilon)\|\, ds + l\eta'$. So we have

$$\mathbf{P}\left(\sup_{t\in\mathbf{T}}\|Z_t(\varepsilon)\| > l\eta' e^{K'T}\right) \le Ale^{-A'\eta'^2 k^2 T/\varepsilon^2}$$

from Gronwall's inequality. Letting $\eta' = \eta(le^{K'T})^{-1}$, we have by the pathwise uniqueness of the stochastic differential equation,

$$\mathbf{P}\left(\sup_{t\in\mathbf{T}}\|X_t(\varepsilon) - \widetilde{X}_t(\varepsilon)\| \neq 0\right) \le \mathbf{P}\left(\sup_{t\in\mathbf{T}}\|\widetilde{X}_t(\varepsilon) - X_t(0)\| > \eta\right)$$
$$\le Ce^{-C'\eta^2/\varepsilon^2}. \tag{4}$$

This completes the proof. □

The following is due to [8], Theorem 4.6.4, p. 172.

Proposition 6. *$\{\widetilde{X}_t(\varepsilon)\}_{t\in\mathbf{T}}$ is smooth in ε in $\mathbf{L}^p$-sence, for any $p \in (1,\infty)$. Moreover, there exists L^p bounded continuous process $\{\widetilde{X}_t^{(k)}\}_{t\in\mathbf{T}} = \left\{\frac{\partial^k}{\partial\varepsilon^k}\widetilde{X}_t(\varepsilon)\Big|_{\varepsilon=0}\right\}$, $k\in\mathbf{N}$, such that*

$$\lim_{\varepsilon\to 0}\mathbf{E}\left[\sup_{t\in\mathbf{T}}\left\|\frac{1}{\varepsilon^n}\left\{\widetilde{X}_t(\varepsilon) - \widetilde{X}_t(0) - \sum_{k=1}^{n}\varepsilon^k\widetilde{X}_t^{(k)}\right\}\right\|^p\right] = 0,$$
$$p\in(1,\infty),\ n\in\mathbf{N}.$$

$G(\varepsilon,t,x,y)$ has a Taylor expansion with respect to ε. So there exist smooth functions $G^{(k)}\colon \mathbf{T}\times\mathbf{R}^{d(k+1)}\times\mathbf{R}^{l'}\to\mathbf{R}$ which are polynomials in x and satisfy

$$\lim_{\varepsilon\to 0}\frac{1}{\varepsilon^{np}}\mathbf{E}\left[\sup_{t\in\mathbf{T}}\left\|G(\varepsilon,t,\widetilde{X}_t(\varepsilon),\widetilde{Y}_t)\right.\right.$$
$$\left.\left.-\sum_{k=0}^{n}\varepsilon^k G^{(k)}\left(t,\widetilde{X}_t(0),\widetilde{X}_t^{(1)},\widetilde{X}_t^{(2)},\ldots,\widetilde{X}_t^{(k)},\widetilde{Y}_t\right)\right\|^p\right] = 0$$

for any $n\in\mathbf{N}$ and $p\in(1,\infty)$.

Let us denote $G^{(k)}(t,y) = G^{(k)}\left(t,\widetilde{X}_t(0),\widetilde{X}_t^{(1)},\widetilde{X}_t^{(2)},\ldots,\widetilde{X}_t^{(k)},y\right)$.

Proposition 7. *For any $t\in\mathbf{T}$, $p>1$ and $n\in\mathbf{N}$,*

$$\lim_{\varepsilon\to 0}\frac{1}{\varepsilon^{np}}\mathbf{E}\left[\sup_{t\in\mathbf{T}}\left|\exp\widetilde{G}(\varepsilon,t,\widetilde{X}.(\varepsilon),\widetilde{Y}.) - \sum_{k'=0}^{n}\frac{1}{k'!}\left\{\int_0^t\sum_{k=1}^{n}\varepsilon^k G^{(k)}(s,\widetilde{Y}_s)\,d\widetilde{Y}_s\right.\right.\right.$$
$$\left.\left.\left.-\frac{1}{2}\int_0^t\left\{\left\|\sum_{k=0}^{n}\varepsilon^k G^{(k)}(s,\widetilde{Y}_s)\right\|^2 - \|G^{(0)}(s,\widetilde{Y}_s)\|^2\right\}ds\right\}^{k'}\right|^p\right] = 0.$$

Proof. We have

$$\lim_{\varepsilon\to 0}\frac{1}{\varepsilon^{k'np}}\mathbf{E}\left[\sup_{t\in\mathbf{T}}\left|\{\widetilde{G}(\varepsilon,t,\widetilde{X}_{\cdot}(\varepsilon),\widetilde{Y}_{\cdot})\}^{k'}-\left\{\int_0^t\sum_{k=1}^{n}\varepsilon^k G^{(k)}(s,\widetilde{Y}_s)\,d\widetilde{Y}_s\right.\right.\right.$$

$$\left.\left.\left.-\frac{1}{2}\int_0^t\left(\left\|G^{(0)}(s,\widetilde{Y}_s)+\sum_{k=1}^{n}\varepsilon^k G^{(k)}(s,\widetilde{Y}_s)\right\|^2-\|G^{(0)}(s,\widetilde{Y}_s)\|^2\right)ds\right\}^{k'}\right|^p\right]=0$$

for any $n,\ k'\in\mathbf{N}$ and $p\in(1,\infty)$. On the other hand,

$$e^x=\sum_{k=0}^{n}\frac{x^k}{k!}+\int_0^x\left\{\int_0^{y_1}\left\{\int_0^{y_2}\cdots\left\{\int_0^{y_n}e^{y_{n+1}}\,dy_{n+1}\right\}\cdots dy_3\right\}dy_2\right\}dy_1.$$

So we have

$$\left|e^x-\sum_{k=0}^{n}\frac{x^k}{k!}\right|\le\frac{|x|^{n+1}}{(n+1)!}e^{|x|}.$$

Therefore,

$$\left|\exp\{\widetilde{G}(\varepsilon,t,\widetilde{Y}_{\cdot})\}-\sum_{k'=0}^{n}\frac{\{\widetilde{G}(\varepsilon,t,\widetilde{Y}_{\cdot})\}^{k'}}{k'!}\right|^p$$
$$\le\left\{\frac{|\widetilde{G}(\varepsilon,t,\widetilde{Y}_{\cdot})|^{n+1}}{(n+1)!}\exp|\widetilde{G}(\varepsilon,t,\widetilde{Y}_{\cdot})|\right\}^p.$$

We see that,

$$\lim_{\varepsilon\to 0}\frac{1}{\varepsilon^{nq}}\mathbf{E}\left[\sup_{t\in\mathbf{T}}|\widetilde{G}(\varepsilon,t,\widetilde{Y}_{\cdot})|^{(n+1)q}\right]=0,$$

for any $q\in(1,\infty)$ and there exists constants C_q for any $q\in(1,\infty)$ such that

$$\begin{aligned}&\mathbf{E}\left[\sup_{t\in\mathbf{T}}\left\{\exp|\widetilde{G}(\varepsilon,t,\widetilde{Y}_{\cdot})|\right\}^q\right]\\&\le\mathbf{E}\left[\sup_{t\in\mathbf{T}}\exp\{q\widetilde{G}(\varepsilon,t,\widetilde{Y}_{\cdot})\}\right]+\mathbf{E}\left[\sup_{t\in\mathbf{T}}\exp\{-q\widetilde{G}(\varepsilon,t,\widetilde{Y}_{\cdot})\}\right]\\&\le C_q\end{aligned}$$

by Proposition 2. Therefore,

$$\lim_{\varepsilon\to 0}\frac{1}{\varepsilon^{np}}\mathbf{E}\left[\sup_{t\in\mathbf{T}}\left|\exp\{\widetilde{G}(\varepsilon,t,\widetilde{Y}_{\cdot})\}-\sum_{k'=0}^{n}\frac{\{\widetilde{G}(\varepsilon,t,\widetilde{Y}_{\cdot})\}^{k'}}{k'!}\right|^p\right]=0$$

for any $p\in(1,\infty)$. So,

$$\lim_{\varepsilon\to 0}\frac{1}{\varepsilon^{np}}\mathbf{E}\Bigg[\sup_{t\in\mathbf{T}}\Bigg|\exp\widetilde{G}(\varepsilon,t,\widetilde{X}.(\varepsilon),\widetilde{Y}.)-\sum_{k'=0}^{n}\frac{1}{k'!}\Bigg\{\int_0^t\sum_{k=1}^{n}\varepsilon^k G^{(k)}(s,\widetilde{Y}_s)\,d\widetilde{Y}_s$$
$$-\frac{1}{2}\int_0^t\Bigg(\Bigg\|\sum_{k=0}^{n}\varepsilon^k G^{(k)}(s,\widetilde{Y}_s)\Bigg\|^2-\|G^{(0)}(s,\widetilde{Y}_s)\|^2\Bigg)ds\Bigg\}^{k'}\Bigg|^p\Bigg]$$
$$\le\lim_{\varepsilon\to 0}\frac{1}{\varepsilon^{np}}\mathbf{E}\Bigg[\sup_{t\in\mathbf{T}}\Bigg|\exp\{\widetilde{G}(\varepsilon,t,y.)\}-\sum_{k'=0}^{n}\frac{\{\widetilde{G}(\varepsilon,t,\widetilde{Y}.)\}^{k'}}{k'!}\Bigg|^p\Bigg]$$
$$+\lim_{\varepsilon\to 0}\frac{1}{\varepsilon^{np}}\mathbf{E}\Bigg[\sup_{t\in\mathbf{T}}\Bigg|\sum_{k'=0}^{n}\frac{1}{k'!}\Bigg\{\{\widetilde{G}(\varepsilon,t,\widetilde{Y}.)\}^{k'}-\Bigg\{\int_0^t\sum_{k=1}^{n}\varepsilon^k G^{(k)}(s,\widetilde{Y}_s)\,dW_s^2$$
$$+\frac{1}{2}\int_0^t\Bigg(\Bigg\|\sum_{k=0}^{n}\varepsilon^k G^{(k)}(s,\widetilde{Y}_s)\Bigg\|^2-\|G^{(0)}(s,\widetilde{Y}_s)\|^2\Bigg)ds\Bigg\}^{k'}\Bigg\}\Bigg|^p\Bigg]=0$$

for any $p\in(1,\infty)$. So we have our assertion. This completes the proof. □

Now let us prove Proposition 3. Let $\widetilde{g}\colon\mathbf{R}^d\to\mathbf{R}$ be bounded smooth function with compact support such that

$$\widetilde{g}(x)=g(x),\quad x\in\Big\{x\in\mathbf{R};\ \|x\|\le\sup_{t\in\mathbf{T}}\|X_t(0)\|+\eta\Big\}.$$

Then, there exist smooth functions $\widetilde{g}^{(k)}\colon\mathbf{R}^d\times\mathbf{R}^{dk}\to\mathbf{R}$, $k=0,1,2,\ldots$ for which $\widetilde{g}^{(k)}(\cdot,x)$, $k=0,1,2,\ldots$, are polynomials in x and

$$\lim_{\varepsilon\to 0}\frac{1}{\varepsilon^{np}}\mathbf{E}\Bigg[\sup_{t\in\mathbf{T}}\Bigg\|\widetilde{g}(\widetilde{X}_t(\varepsilon))-\sum_{k=0}^{n}\varepsilon^k\widetilde{g}^{(k)}\big(\widetilde{X}_t(0),\widetilde{X}_t^{(1)},\widetilde{X}_t^{(2)},\ldots,\widetilde{X}_t^{(k)}\big)\Bigg\|^p\Bigg]=0,\tag{5}$$

for any $n\ge 1$ and $p\in[1,\infty)$, because $\widetilde{X}_t(\varepsilon)$ has an asymptotic expansion by Proposition 6 and $\widetilde{g}$ is smooth. We know that there also exist functionals $\widetilde{G}^{(k)}(t,\{\widetilde{X}^{(j)}_{\cdot}\}_{j=0}^k,y.)$ such that

$$\lim_{\varepsilon\to 0}\frac{1}{\varepsilon^{np}}\mathbf{E}\Bigg[\sup_{t\in\mathbf{T}}\Bigg|\exp\widetilde{G}(\varepsilon,t,\widetilde{X}.(\varepsilon),\widetilde{Y}.)-\sum_{k=0}^{n}\varepsilon^k\widetilde{G}^{(k)}\big(t,\{\widetilde{X}^{(j)}_{\cdot}\}_{j=0}^k,\widetilde{Y}.\big)\Bigg|^p\Bigg]=0,\tag{6}$$

by Proposition 7. Here $\widetilde{X}^{(0)}_{\cdot}=\widetilde{X}_{\cdot}(0)$. There exists a constant C_q for any $q\in[1,\infty)$ such that

$$\mathbf{E}\big[|g(X_t(\varepsilon))|^q\big]+\mathbf{E}\big[|\widetilde{g}(\widetilde{X}_t(\varepsilon))|^q\big]\le C_q,\qquad\varepsilon\in(0,1],$$

by the assumption for g and Assumption (A.1). So we have

$$\frac{1}{\varepsilon^{np}}\mathbf{E}\Big[\big|g(X_t(\varepsilon))\exp\widetilde{G}(\varepsilon,t,X.(\varepsilon),\widetilde{Y}.)-\widetilde{g}(\widetilde{X}_t(\varepsilon))\exp\widetilde{G}(\varepsilon,t,\widetilde{X}.(\varepsilon),\widetilde{Y}.)\big|^p\Big]$$
$$\leq \frac{1}{\varepsilon^{np}}\mathbf{E}\Big[\Big|1_{\{\sup_{t\in\mathbf{T}}|X_t(\varepsilon)-\widetilde{X}_t(\varepsilon)|\neq 0\}}\big\{\big|g(X_t(\varepsilon))\exp\widetilde{G}(\varepsilon,t,X.(\varepsilon),\widetilde{Y}.)\big|$$
$$+\big|\widetilde{g}(\widetilde{X}_t(\varepsilon))\exp\widetilde{G}(\varepsilon,t,\widetilde{X}.(\varepsilon),\widetilde{Y}.)\big|\big\}\Big|^p\Big]$$
$$\leq \frac{2^{p+2}(C_{4p})^{\frac{1}{4}}}{\varepsilon^{np}}\Big\{\mathbf{P}\Big(\sup_{t\in\mathbf{T}}|X_t(\varepsilon)-\widetilde{X}_t(\varepsilon)|\neq 0\Big)\Big\}^{\frac{1}{2}}$$
$$\times\Big\{\mathbf{E}\Big[\big|\exp\widetilde{G}(\varepsilon,t,X.(\varepsilon),\widetilde{Y}.)\big|^{4p}+\big|\exp\widetilde{G}(\varepsilon,t,\widetilde{X}.(\varepsilon),\widetilde{Y}.)\big|^{4p}\Big]\Big\}^{\frac{1}{4}}.$$

Since $\mathbf{E}\big[\big|\exp\widetilde{G}(\varepsilon,t,X.(\varepsilon),\widetilde{Y}.)\big|^p\big]$ and $\mathbf{E}\big[\big|\exp\widetilde{G}(\varepsilon,t,\widetilde{X}.(\varepsilon),\widetilde{Y}.)\big|^p\big]$ are bounded in ε by Proposition 2, we have

$$\lim_{\varepsilon\to 0}\frac{1}{\varepsilon^{np}}\mathbf{E}\Big[\Big|g(X_t(\varepsilon))\exp\widetilde{G}(\varepsilon,t,X.(\varepsilon),\widetilde{Y}.)$$
$$-\widetilde{g}(\widetilde{X}_t(\varepsilon))\exp\widetilde{G}(\varepsilon,t,\widetilde{X}.(\varepsilon),\widetilde{Y}.)\Big|^p\Big]=0 \quad (7)$$

for any $n\geq 1$ by Proposition 5. Let

$$h_1^{(k)}(y.)=\mathbf{E}\left[\sum_{j=0}^{k}\widetilde{g}^{(j)}(\widetilde{X}_t(0),\widetilde{X}_t^{(1)},\ldots,\widetilde{X}_t^{(k)})\widetilde{G}^{(k-j)}(t,\{\widetilde{X}^{(l)}_{.}\}_{l=0}^{k-j},y.)\right].$$

Then we have

$$\varlimsup_{\varepsilon\to 0}\Big\{\mathbf{E}\Big[\Big|\frac{1}{\varepsilon^n}\Big\{\mathbf{E}[g(X_t(\varepsilon))\exp\widetilde{G}(\varepsilon,t,X.(\varepsilon),y.)]\big|_{y.=\widetilde{Y}.}-\sum_{k=0}^{n}\varepsilon^k h_1^{(k)}(\widetilde{Y}.)\Big\}\Big|^p\Big]\Big\}^{\frac{1}{p}}$$
$$\leq\varlimsup_{\varepsilon\to 0}\frac{1}{\varepsilon^n}\Big\{\mathbf{E}\Big[\Big|\widetilde{g}(\widetilde{X}_t(\varepsilon))\exp\widetilde{G}(\varepsilon,t,\widetilde{X}.(\varepsilon),\widetilde{Y}.)$$
$$-\sum_{k=0}^{n}\varepsilon^k\Big\{\sum_{j=0}^{k}\widetilde{g}^{(j)}(\widetilde{X}_t(0),\widetilde{X}_t^{(1)},\ldots,\widetilde{X}_t^{(k)})\widetilde{G}^{(k-j)}(t,\{X^{(j)}\}_{j=1}^{k},\widetilde{Y}.)\Big\}\Big|^p\Big]\Big\}^{\frac{1}{p}}$$
$$+\varlimsup_{\varepsilon\to 0}\frac{1}{\varepsilon^n}\Big\{\mathbf{E}\big[\big|g(X_t(\varepsilon))\exp\widetilde{G}(\varepsilon,t,X.(\varepsilon),\widetilde{Y}.)$$
$$-\widetilde{g}(\widetilde{X}_t(\varepsilon))\exp\widetilde{G}(\varepsilon,t,\widetilde{X}.(\varepsilon),\widetilde{Y}.)\}\big|^p\big]\Big\}^{\frac{1}{p}}=0$$

by (5), (6) and (7). Note that $h_1^{(0)}(y.)=\widetilde{g}^{(0)}(\widetilde{X}_t(0))\widetilde{G}^{(0)}(t,X^{(0)}_{.},y.)=\widetilde{g}(\widetilde{X}_t(0))=g(X_t(0))$. This completes the proof of Proposition 3. □

4. Example

In this section, we show the calculation of $h^{(0)}(y.)$, $h^{(1)}(y.)$ and $h^{(2)}(y.)$ in a certain financial model.

Let $(\Omega, \mathcal{F}, \{\mathcal{F}_t\}_{t\in\mathbf{T}}, \mathbf{P})$ be a probability space, and $\mathbf{T} = [0,T]$, and a, b, σ_1, ε, x_0 are constants such that $a, \sigma_1, x_0 \in (0,\infty)$, $b \in [0,\infty)$, and $\varepsilon \in [0,1]$. Let $\{(W_t^1, W_t^2)_{t\in\mathbf{T}}\}$ be a 2-dim $\mathcal{F}_t$-Brownian Motion, and $\{X_t(\varepsilon)\}_{t\in\mathbf{T}}$ be a solution to the following stochastic differential equation.

$$X_t(\varepsilon) = x_0 + \int_0^t (-aX_s(\varepsilon) + b)\, ds + \varepsilon \int_0^t \sigma_1 \sqrt{|X_t(\varepsilon)|}\, dW_s^1.$$

We have $X_t(\varepsilon) \geq 0$ *a.s.* We regard $X_t(\varepsilon)$ as the spot rate process and $\mathbf{P}$ is a risk neutral measure. Then the price of a 0-coupon bond with maturity T, is given by $\mathbf{E}\left[\exp\left(-\int_t^T X_s(\varepsilon)\, ds\right) \,\Big|\, \mathcal{F}_t\right]$. Let A and B be the solution to the following differential equations,

$$\begin{aligned} B'(\varepsilon,t) &= -aB(\varepsilon,t) - \frac{1}{2}\varepsilon^2\sigma_1^2\{B(\varepsilon,t)\}^2 + 1, & B(\varepsilon,0) &= 0,\\ A'(\varepsilon,t) &= -bB(\varepsilon,t), & A(\varepsilon,0) &= 0. \end{aligned}$$

Then we have

$$\mathbf{E}\left[\exp\left(-\int_t^T X_s(\varepsilon)\, ds\right) \,\Big|\, \mathcal{F}_t\right] = \exp\{A(\varepsilon, T-t) - B(\varepsilon, T-t)X_t(\varepsilon)\}.$$

(See Duffie [1], 5-H The Feynman-Kac Solution.) Since $B(\varepsilon,t) \geq 0$, $A(\varepsilon,t) \leq 0$, we have $\exp\{A(\varepsilon,T-t) - B(\varepsilon,T-t)x\} \leq 1,\ x \geq 0$. Let $F(\varepsilon,t,x) = \exp\{A(\varepsilon,T-t) - B(\varepsilon,T-t)x\} \wedge 1$. Then F is a bounded continuous function and $F(\varepsilon,t,X_t(\varepsilon)) = \mathbf{E}\left[\exp\left(-\int_t^T X_s(\varepsilon)\, ds\right) \,\Big|\, \mathcal{F}_t\right]$, $x \geq 0$.

We assume that we can only observe the process $\{Y_t(\varepsilon)\}_{t\in\mathbf{T}}$ given by

$$Y_t(\varepsilon) = \int_0^t F(\varepsilon, s, X_s(\varepsilon))\, ds + \sigma_2 W_t^2.$$

Let $\mathcal{G}_t(\varepsilon) = \sigma(Y_s(\varepsilon);\ 0 \leq s \leq t)$,

$$\begin{aligned} \widetilde{G}(\varepsilon,t,x.,y.) = &\int_0^t \sigma_2^{-1} F(\varepsilon,s,x_s)\, dy_s - \frac{1}{2}\int_0^t \sigma_2^{-2}\|F(\varepsilon,s,x_s)\|^2\, ds\\ &- \int_0^t \sigma_2^{-1} F(0,s,y_s)\, dy_s + \frac{1}{2}\int_0^t \sigma_2^{-2}\|F(0,s,y_s)\|^2\, ds. \end{aligned}$$

Now we give an asymptotic expansion of $\mathbf{E}[F(\varepsilon,t,X_t(\varepsilon)) \mid \mathcal{G}_t(\varepsilon)]$. We have

$$\begin{aligned}&\mathbf{E}[F(\varepsilon,t,X_t(\varepsilon)) \mid \mathcal{G}_t(\varepsilon)]\\&\quad= \frac{\mathbf{E}^{\mathbf{Q}(\varepsilon)}\left[F(\varepsilon,t,X_t(\varepsilon))\exp\{\widetilde{G}(\varepsilon,t,X_\cdot(\varepsilon),y_\cdot)\}\right]\big|_{y_\cdot=Y_\cdot(\varepsilon)}}{\mathbf{E}^{\mathbf{Q}(\varepsilon)}\left[\exp\{\widetilde{G}(\varepsilon,t,X_\cdot(\varepsilon),y_\cdot)\}\right]\big|_{y_\cdot=Y_\cdot(\varepsilon)}}.\end{aligned}$$

Let η be a constant satisfying $\eta < \frac{1}{2}x_0\exp(-aT)$, and let

$$D_\eta = \left\{(t,x)\in\mathbf{T}\times\mathbf{R};\ x_0\exp(-aT)-\eta \le x \le x_0 + \frac{b}{a}+\eta\right\}.$$

Then $-ax+b$ and $\sqrt{|x|}$ are smooth and bounded on the closed set D_η, and $F(\varepsilon,t,x)$ is, too. So there exists $\{\widetilde{X}_t(\varepsilon)\}_{t\in\mathbf{T}}$ that has an asymptotic expansion

$$\lim_{\varepsilon\to 0}\mathbf{E}\left[\left|\frac{1}{\varepsilon^n}\left\{\widetilde{X}_t(\varepsilon)-\widetilde{X}_t(0)-\sum_{k=1}^{n}\varepsilon^k\widetilde{X}_t^{(k)}\right\}\right|^p\right]=0.$$

Now we show the calculation of $h^{(0)}(y_\cdot)$, $h^{(1)}(y_\cdot)$ and $h^{(2)}(y_\cdot)$. Since $\widetilde{X}_t^{(k)} = \frac{\partial}{\partial\varepsilon}\widetilde{X}_t(\varepsilon)\Big|_{\varepsilon=0}$, we have

$$\begin{aligned}\widetilde{X}_t(0) &= \frac{b}{a}+x_0e^{-at},\\ \widetilde{X}_t^{(1)} &= e^{-at}\int_0^t e^{as}\sigma_1\sqrt{|\widetilde{X}_s(0)|}\,dW_s^1,\end{aligned}$$

and

$$\widetilde{X}_t^{(2)} = e^{-at}\int_0^t e^{as}\sqrt{\frac{\sigma_1}{|\widetilde{X}_s(0)|}}\,\widetilde{X}_s^{(1)}\,dW_s^1.$$

Let $\widetilde{F}(\varepsilon,t,x)\colon \mathbf{T}\times\mathbf{R}\to\mathbf{R}$ be a bounded smooth function that is equal to $F(\varepsilon,t,x)$ on the closed set D_η. Then we have

$$\begin{aligned}\lim_{\varepsilon\to 0}\mathbf{E}\Bigg[\Bigg|&\frac{\mathbf{E}\left[F(\varepsilon,t,X_t(\varepsilon))\exp\{\widetilde{G}(\varepsilon,t,X.(\varepsilon),y.)\}\right]}{\mathbf{E}\left[\exp\{\widetilde{G}(\varepsilon,t,X.(\varepsilon),y.)\}\right]}\Bigg|_{y.=\sigma_2W^2.}\\&-\frac{\mathbf{E}\left[\widetilde{F}(t,\widetilde{X}_t(\varepsilon))\exp\{\widetilde{G}(\varepsilon,t,\widetilde{X}.(\varepsilon),y.)\}\right]}{\mathbf{E}\left[\exp\{\widetilde{G}(\varepsilon,t,\widetilde{X}.(\varepsilon),y.)\}\right]}\Bigg|_{y.=\sigma_2W^2.}\Bigg|^p\Bigg]=0.\end{aligned}$$

There exist $F_k\colon \mathbf{T}\times\mathbf{R}^k\to\mathbf{R}$ such that

$$\lim_{\varepsilon\to 0}\mathbf{E}\left[\sup_{t\in\mathbf{T}}\left|\frac{1}{\varepsilon^n}\left\{\widetilde{F}(\varepsilon,t,\widetilde{X}_t(\varepsilon))-\sum_{k=0}^{n}\varepsilon^k F_k\big(t,\widetilde{X}_t^{(1)},\dots,\widetilde{X}_t^{(k)}\big)\right\}\right|^p\right]=0$$

for any $p>1$ and $n\in\mathbf{N}$. There exist $A_0(t)$, $A_2(t)$, $B_0(t)$ and $B_2(t)$ such that

$$\lim_{\varepsilon\to 0}\sup_{t\in\mathbf{T}}\left|\frac{1}{\varepsilon^2}\{A(\varepsilon,t)-A_0(t)-\varepsilon^2A_2(t)\}\right|=0$$

$$\lim_{\varepsilon\to 0}\sup_{t\in\mathbf{T}}\left|\frac{1}{\varepsilon^2}\{B(\varepsilon,t)-B_0(t)-\varepsilon^2B_2(t)\}\right|=0$$

for any $p>1$ and $n\in\mathbf{N}$.

$$A_0(t)=-\frac{b}{a^2}e^{-at}-\frac{b}{a}t+\frac{b}{a^2},$$

$$A_2(t)=\frac{b\sigma_1^2}{4a^2}\{e^{-2at}-4ate^{-at}-4e^{-at}+2at\}+\frac{3b\sigma_1^2}{4a^4},$$

$$B_0(t)=-\frac{1}{a}(e^{-at}-1),$$

and

$$B_2(t)=\frac{\sigma_1^2}{2a^3}(e^{-2at}-2ate^{-at}+1).$$

Using these, we have

$$F_0(t)=\exp\{A_0(T-t)+B_0(T-t)\widetilde{X}_t(0)\},$$

$$F_1\big(t,\widetilde{X}_t^{(1)}\big)=-F_0(t)B_0(T-t)\widetilde{X}_t^{(1)},$$

and

$$F_2\big(t,\widetilde{X}_t^{(1)},\widetilde{X}_t^{(2)}\big)=F_0(t)\Big\{A_2(T-t)-B_2(T-t)\widetilde{X}_t(0)-B_0(T-t)\widetilde{X}_t^{(2)}+\frac{1}{2}B_0(T-t)^2\big(\widetilde{X}_t^{(1)}\big)^2\Big\}.$$

Furthermore, there exist functionals $\widetilde{G}^{(k)}\colon \mathbf{T}\times(\mathbf{C}(\mathbf{T};\mathbf{R}))^k\times\mathbf{C}(\mathbf{T};\mathbf{R})\to\mathbf{R}$ such that

$$\lim_{\varepsilon\to 0}\mathbf{E}\left[\sup_{t\in\mathbf{T}}\left|\frac{1}{\varepsilon^n}\left\{\exp\widetilde{G}(\varepsilon,t,\widetilde{X}_\cdot,\sigma_2W_\cdot^2)-1-\sum_{k=1}^{n}\varepsilon^k\widetilde{G}^{(k)}\big(t,\{\widetilde{X}_\cdot^{(j)}\}_{j=1}^k,\sigma_2W_\cdot^2\big)\right\}\right|^p\right]=0$$

for any $t\geq 0$, $p\in(1,\infty)$ and $n\in\mathbf{N}$. We have

$$\widetilde{G}^{(1)}(t,\widetilde{X}^{(1)}_{\cdot},y_{\cdot}) = \int_0^t \sigma_2^{-1}F_1(s)\,dy_s - \int_0^t \sigma_2^{-2}F_0(s)F_1(s)\,ds,$$

where we mean $\int_0^t F_1(s)\,dy_s = F_1(t)y_t - \int_0^t y_s\,dF_1(s)$. Therefore, for each $t \geq 0$ there exist functionals $h^{(k)}\colon \mathbf{C}(\mathbf{T};\mathbf{R}) \to \mathbf{R}$ such that

$$\lim_{\varepsilon\to 0}\mathbf{E}\left[\left|\frac{1}{\varepsilon^n}\left\{\frac{\mathbf{E}[\widetilde{F}(t,\widetilde{X}_t(\varepsilon))\widetilde{G}(\varepsilon,t,\widetilde{X}_{\cdot}(\varepsilon),y_{\cdot})]}{\mathbf{E}[\widetilde{G}(\varepsilon,t,\widetilde{X}_{\cdot}(\varepsilon),y_{\cdot})]}\right|_{y_{\cdot}=\sigma_2 W^2_{\cdot}} - \sum_{k=0}^{n}\varepsilon^k h^{(k)}(\sigma_2 W^2_{\cdot})\right\}\right|^p\right] = 0$$

for any $p \in (1,\infty)$ and $n \in \mathbf{N}$. We have

$$h^{(0)}(y_{\cdot}) = F_0(t),$$
$$h^{(1)}(y_{\cdot}) = \mathbf{E}[F_1(t,\widetilde{X}^{(1)}_t)] = 0,$$

and

$$\begin{aligned}
&h^{(2)}(y_{\cdot})\\
&= \mathbf{E}\Big[F_2(t,\widetilde{X}^{(1)}_t,\widetilde{X}^{(2)}_t) + F_1(t,\widetilde{X}^{(1)}_t)\widetilde{G}^{(1)}(t,\widetilde{X}^{(1)}_{\cdot},y_{\cdot})\\
&\quad - \frac{1}{2}\big(\widetilde{G}^{(1)}(t,\widetilde{X}^{(1)}_{\cdot},y_{\cdot})\big)^2\Big]\\
&= F_0(t)\{A_2(T-t) - B_2(T-t)\}\widetilde{X}_t(0) + \frac{1}{2}(B_0(T-t))^2 e^{-2at}\int_0^t v(s)\,ds\\
&\quad + \sigma_2^{-1}\{F_0(t)B_0(T-t)e^{-at}\}y_t\int_0^t v(s)\,ds\\
&\quad - \sigma_2^{-1}F_0(t)B_0(T-t)e^{-at}\int_0^t F_0(s)B_0(T-s)e^{-as}y_s v(s)\,ds\\
&\quad - \sigma_2^{-1}F_0(t)B_0(T-t)e^{-at}\\
&\qquad \times \int_0^t \{\{F_0(s)B_0(T-s)e^{-as}\}'y_s - F_0(s)e^{-as}\}\int_0^s v(u)\,du\,ds\\
&\quad - \frac{1}{2}\sigma_2^{-2}F_0(t)\int_0^t \Big\{-F_0(t)B_0(T-t)e^{-at}y_t + F_0(u)B_0(T-u)e^{-au}y_u\\
&\quad + \int_0^t 1_{\{u\leq s\leq t\}}\{F_0(s)B_0(T-s)e^{-as}\}'y_s\,ds\\
&\quad - \int_0^t 1_{\{u\leq s\leq t\}}\sigma_2^{-1}F_0(s)e^{-as}\,ds\Big\}^2 v(u)\,du,
\end{aligned}$$

where $v(t) = \sigma_1^2 e^{2at} \widetilde{X}_t(0)$.

References

[1] Duffie, D., Dynamic Asset Pricing Theory, 3rd edition. Princeton University Press 2001

[2] Fujisaki, M., Kallianpur, G., Kunita, H.: Stochastic differential equations for the non linear filtering problem. Osaka J. Math. **9**, 19-40 (1972)

[3] Hisanaga, T.: The filtering problem for affine term structure model of the bond. in Japanese. Master Thesis, University of Tokyo 1996

[4] Kallianpur, G., Striebel, C.: Estimation of stochastic processes, arbitrary system process with additive white noise observation errors. Ann. Math. Statist. **39**, 785-801 (1968)

[5] Kallianpur, G.: Stochastic filtering: A part of stochastic nonlinear analysis. Proceedings of the Nobert Wiener Centenary Congress, 371-385 (1994)

[6] Kallianpur, G., Xiong, J.: Asset pricing with stochastic volatility. Appl. Math. Optim. **43**, 23-44 (2001)

[7] Kunita, H.: Asymptotic behavior of the nonlinear filtering errors of Markov processes. J. Multivariate Analysis **1**, 365-393 (1971)

[8] Kunita, H.: Stochastic Flows and Stochastic Differential Equations. Cambridge University press 1990

[9] Kunitomo, N., Takahashi, A.: The asymptotic expansion approach to the valuation of interest rate contingent claims. Mathematical Finance **11**, 117-151 (2001)

[10] Kunitomo, N., Takahashi, A.: On validity of the asymptotic expansion approach in contingent claim analysis. Ann. Appl. Probab. **13**, 914-952 (2003)

[11] Lamberton, D., Lapeyre, B.: Introduction to Stochastic Calculus Applied to Finance. Chapman & Hall, London 1996

Adv. Math. Econ. 9, 49–71 (2006)

Advances in
MATHEMATICAL
ECONOMICS

Law invariant risk measures have the Fatou property*

Elyès Jouini[1], **Walter Schachermayer**[2†], **and Nizar Touzi**[3]

[1] Université Paris Dauphine and CEREMADE, Place du Maréchal de Lattre de Tassigny, F-75775 Paris Cedex 16, France
(e-mail: jouini@ceremade.dauphine.fr)

[2] Vienna University of Technology, Wiedner Hauptstrasse 8-10/105, A-1040 Wien, Austria and Université Paris Dauphine, Place du Maréchal de Lattre de Tassigny, F-75775 Paris Cedex 16, France
(e-mail: wschach@fam.tuwien.ac.at)

[3] CREST, Laboratoire de Finance et Assurance, 15 Bd Gabriel Péri, F-92245 Malakoff Cedex, France and Imperial College London, Tanaka Business School.
(e-mail: touzi@ensae.fr; n.touzi@ic.ac.uk)

Received: May 9, 2005
Revised: January 6, 2006

JEL classification: C65, G19

Mathematics Subject Classification (2000): 46E30, 60B05

Abstract. S. Kusuoka [K 01, Theorem 4] gave an interesting dual characterization of *law invariant* coherent risk measures, satisfying the Fatou property. The latter property was introduced by F. Delbaen [D 02]. In the present note we extend Kusuoka's characterization in two directions, the first one being rather standard, while the second one is somewhat surprising. Firstly we generalize — similarly as M. Fritelli and E. Rossaza Gianin [FG 05] — from the notion of coherent risk measures to the more general notion of convex risk measures as introduced by H. Föllmer and A. Schied [FS 04]. Secondly — and more importantly — we show that the hypothesis of Fatou property may actually be dropped as it is automatically implied by the hypothesis of law invariance.

We also introduce the notion of the Lebesgue property of a convex risk measure, where the inequality in the definition of the Fatou property is replaced by an equality, and give some dual characterizations of this property.

Key words: law-invariance, cash-invariance, Fatou and Lebesgue properties

* We thank S. Kusuoka, P. Orihuela and A. Schied for their advise and help in preparing this paper.

† Financial support from the Austrian Science Fund (FWF) under the grant P15889 and from Vienna Science and Technology Fund (WWTF) under Grant MA13 is gratefully acknowledged.

1. Introduction

This paper is a twin to [JST 05] and we shall use similar notation. In particular we rather use the language of "monetary utility functions" which — up to the sign — is identical to the notion of convex risk measures [FS 04]. We do so in order to point out more directly how the present theory is embedded into the framework of classical utility theory.

Throughout the paper we work on a standard probability space $(\Omega, \mathcal{F}, \mathbf{P})$, i.e., we suppose that $(\Omega, \mathcal{F}, \mathbf{P})$ does not have atoms and that $\mathbb{L}^2(\Omega, \mathcal{F}, \mathbf{P})$ is separable.

A *monetary utility function* is a concave non-decreasing map $U\colon \mathbb{L}^\infty(\Omega, \mathcal{F}, \mathbf{P}) \to [-\infty, \infty[$ with $\mathrm{dom}(U) = \{X \mid U(X) \in \mathbb{R}\} \neq \emptyset$, and

$$U(X + c) = U(X) + c, \quad \text{for} \quad X \in \mathbb{L}^\infty,\ c \in \mathbb{R}.$$

Note that a monetary utility function is Lipschitz with respect to $\|\,.\,\|_\infty$, and that $\mathrm{dom}(U) = \mathbb{L}^\infty$. By adding a constant to U if necessary, we may and shall always assume that $U(0) = 0$.

Defining $\rho(X) = -U(X)$ the above definition of a monetary utility function yields the definition of a convex risk measure [FS 04]. Convex risk measures are in turn a generalization of the concept of *coherent risk measures* [ADEH 97], which are particularly relevant in applications, and where one imposes the additional requirement of positive homogeneity $\rho(\lambda X) = \lambda\rho(X)$, for $X \in \mathbb{L}^\infty$ and $\lambda \geq 0$. A characterization of coherent (resp. convex) risk measures $\rho\colon \mathbb{L}^\infty(\Omega, \mathcal{F}, \mathbf{P}) \to \mathbb{R}$ in terms of their Fenchel transform, defined on $\mathbb{L}^1(\Omega, \mathcal{F}, \mathbf{P})$, was obtained in [D 02] under the condition that ρ satisfies the Fatou property, i.e.,

$$\rho(X) \leq \liminf_{n\to\infty} \rho(X_n) \ \text{ whenever } \ \sup_n \|X_n\|_\infty < \infty \ \text{ and } \ X_n \xrightarrow{\mathbf{P}} X, \quad (1)$$

where $\xrightarrow{\mathbf{P}}$ denotes convergence in probability. In the present context, this condition is equivalent to the upper semi-continuity condition with respect to the $\sigma(\mathbb{L}^\infty, \mathbb{L}^1)$-topology.

For fixed $X \in \mathbb{L}^1(\Omega, \mathcal{F}, \mathbf{P})$, we introduce the function

$$U_\alpha(X) := \alpha^{-1} \int_0^\alpha q_X(\beta)\, d\beta, \qquad \alpha \in \,]0, 1[, \quad (2)$$

$U_0(X) = \operatorname{ess\,inf}(X)$, and $U_1(X) = \mathbf{E}[X]$, where q_X denotes the quantile function of the random variable X, i.e. the generalized inverse of its cumulative distribution function (see (3) below). For every $\alpha \in [0, 1]$, U_α is a positively homogeneous monetary utility function, which is in addition *law invariant*. The corresponding coherent risk measure $\rho_\alpha = -U_\alpha$ is the so-called *average value at risk* at level α, sometimes denoted by $\mathrm{AV@R}_\alpha$ (see [FS 04]). The family $\{U_\alpha,\ 0 \leq \alpha \leq 1\}$ plays an important role as any *law invariant* monetary utility function U may be represented in terms of the utility functions U_α, $\alpha \in [0,1]$. This result was obtained by [K 01] in the context of coherent risk measures, and later extended by [FG 05] to the context of convex risk measures, see also [FS 04], Theorem 4.54 and 4.57 as well as Corollary 4.72. The precise statement of this result is the following.

Theorem 1.1. *Suppose that* $(\Omega, \mathcal{F}, \mathbf{P})$ *is a standard probability space. For a function* $U\colon \mathbb{L}^\infty(\Omega, \mathcal{F}, \mathbf{P}) \to \mathbb{R}$ *the following are equivalent:*
(a) U *is a law invariant monetary utility function satisfying the Fatou property.*
(b) There is a convex function $v\colon \mathcal{P}([0,1]) \to [0,\infty]$ *such that*

$$U(X) = \inf_{m \in \mathcal{P}([0,1])} \left\{ \int_0^1 U_\alpha(X)\, dm(\alpha) + v(m) \right\} \quad \textit{for every } X \in \mathbb{L}^\infty.$$

Here, $\mathcal{P}([0,1])$ denotes the set of all Borel probability measures on the compact space $[0,1]$. The crucial observation of Kusuoka [K 01] is that, for law invariant monetary utility functions, condition (b) is equivalent to
(c) *There is a law invariant, lower semi-continuous, convex function* $V\colon \mathbb{L}^1(\Omega, \mathcal{F}, \mathbf{P}) \to [0,\infty]$ *such that* $\mathrm{dom}(V) \subseteq \mathcal{P}(\Omega, \mathcal{F}, \mathbf{P})$ *and*

$$U(X) = \inf_{Y \in \mathbb{L}^1} \{\mathbf{E}[XY] + V(Y)\} \quad \textit{for every} \quad X \in \mathbb{L}^\infty,$$

where $\mathcal{P}(\Omega, \mathcal{F}, \mathbf{P})$ denotes the set of $\mathbf{P}$-absolutely continuous probability measures on $(\Omega, \mathcal{F}, \mathbf{P})$, which we identify with a subset of $\mathbb{L}^1(\Omega, \mathcal{F}, \mathbf{P})$. For completeness, we report a proof of the equivalence between conditions (b) and (c) in Section 3.

The equivalence of (a) and (c) is due to F. Delbaen in the framework of (not necessarily *law invariant*) coherent risk measures [D 02], and was extended to convex risk measures in [FS 04].

The first main contribution of this paper is to drop the Fatou property in condition (a) of the above Theorem 1.1 by proving that it is automatically satisfied by law-invariant monetary utility functions. In fact, we prove more generally that the Fatou property is implied by the concavity, the $\mathbb{L}^\infty$-u.s.c. and the law-invariance properties. This result is stated in Section 2 and proved in Section 4. The reader only interested in this result may directly proceed to these sections.

We next introduce the following natural notion.

Definition 1.2. *A utility function* $U\colon \mathbb{L}^\infty \to \mathbb{R} \cup \{-\infty\}$ *satisfies the* Lebesgue property *if for every uniformly bounded sequence* $(X_n)_{n=1}^\infty$ *tending a.s. to* X *we have*

$$U(X) = \lim_{n \to \infty} U(X_n).$$

Clearly the Lebesgue property is a stronger condition than the Fatou property defined in (1), as the inequality has been replaced by an equality. In fact, this property was — under different names — already investigated in the previous literature, as was kindly pointed out to us by A. Schied.

The second contribution of this paper is a characterization of the Lebesgue property for a monetary utility function U in terms of the corresponding Fenchel transform V introduced in condition (c) of Theorem 1.1. If in addition U is law-invariant, this implies a characterization in terms of the function v introduced in the above Theorem 1.1 (b). These results are stated in Section 2 and proved in Section 5.

2. AV@R representation of law-invariant monetary utilities

2.1 Definitions

Let $(\Omega, \mathcal{F}, \mathbf{P})$ be an atomless probability space, and assume that $\mathbb{L}^2(\Omega, \mathcal{F}, \mathbf{P})$ is separable. The assumption of $\mathcal{F}$ being free of atoms is crucial (otherwise one is led to combinatorial problems which are irrelevant from the economic point of view). On the other hand, the separability assumption is convenient for the arguments below, but does not reduce the generality: indeed in all the arguments below we shall only encounter (at most) countably many random variables $(X_n)_{n=1}^{\infty}$; hence we may assume w.l.g. that the σ-algebra $\mathcal{F}$ is generated by countably many random variables, i.e., that $\mathbb{L}^2(\Omega, \mathcal{F}, \mathbf{P})$ is separable.

We denote by $\mathcal{P}(\Omega, \mathcal{F}, \mathbf{P})$ the set of $\mathbf{P}$-absolutely continuous probability measures on $(\Omega, \mathcal{F}, \mathbf{P})$, which we identify with a subset of $\mathbb{L}^1(\Omega, \mathcal{F}, \mathbf{P})$. We also denote by $\mathcal{P}([0,1])$ (resp. $\mathcal{P}(]0,1])$) the set of all Borel probability measures on the compact space $[0,1]$ (resp. on the locally compact space $]0,1]$).

A *measure preserving transformation* of $(\Omega, \mathcal{F}, \mathbf{P})$ is a bi-measurable bijection $\tau \colon \Omega \to \Omega$ leaving $\mathbf{P}$ invariant, i.e., $\tau(\mathbf{P}) = \mathbf{P}$. For $1 \leq p \leq \infty$, the transformation τ induces an isometric isomorphism, still denoted by τ, on $\mathbb{L}^p(\Omega, \mathcal{F}, \mathbf{P})$, mapping X to $X \circ \tau$.

A map $f \colon \mathbb{L}^\infty \to \mathbb{R}$ is called *law invariant*, if $f(X)$ depends only on the law of X for every $X \in \mathbb{L}^\infty$. The function f is called *transformation invariant* if $f \circ \tau = f$ for every measure preserving transformation τ, where we abuse notations by writing $f \circ \tau(X) := f(X \circ \tau)$.

We shall verify in Lemma A.4 that these notions of law invariance and transformation invariance may be used in a synonymous way in the present context of monetary utility function, as a consequence of the concavity and the $\|.\|_\infty$-continuity property of monetary utility functions.

An important example of law invariant and transformation invariant function is the so-called quantile function defined by

$$q_X(\alpha) := \inf\{x \in \mathbb{R} \mid \mathbf{P}[X \leq x] \geq \alpha\}, \qquad X \in \mathbb{L}^\infty,\ \alpha \in [0,1]. \tag{3}$$

The functions U_α, $0 \leq \alpha \leq 1$, introduced in (2) provide the simplest example of law invariant monetary utility functions, which correspond to the so-called average value at risk.

2.2 Strong and weak upper semi-continuity of law invariant maps

We now have assembled all the concepts that are needed to formulate our first main result.

Theorem 2.1. *Suppose that $(\Omega, \mathcal{F}, \mathbf{P})$ is a standard probability space. For a function $U\colon \mathbb{L}^\infty(\Omega, \mathcal{F}, \mathbf{P}) \to \mathbb{R}$ the following are equivalent:*
(i) U is a law invariant monetary utility function.
(ii) There is a law invariant, lower semi-continuous, convex function $V\colon \mathbb{L}^1(\Omega, \mathcal{F}, \mathbf{P}) \to [0,\infty]$ such that $\mathrm{dom}(V) \subseteq \mathcal{P}(\Omega, \mathcal{F}, \mathbf{P})$ and

$$U(X) = \inf_{Y \in \mathbb{L}^1} \{\mathbf{E}[XY] + V(Y)\} \quad \text{for} \quad X \in \mathbb{L}^\infty.$$

(iii) There is a convex function $v\colon \mathcal{P}([0,1]) \to [0,\infty]$ such that

$$U(X) = \inf_{m \in \mathcal{P}([0,1])} \left\{ \int_0^1 U_\alpha(X)\, dm(\alpha) + v(m) \right\} \quad \text{for} \quad X \in \mathbb{L}^\infty.$$

If any of these conditions is satisfied, then U satisfies the Fatou property.

This result shows that law invariant monetary utility functions admit a representation in terms of the corresponding Fenchel transform without any further assumption. In particular the AV@R representation of such utility functions holds without any further condition. Our novel contribution is that the Fatou property is automatically implied by the law invariance and the strong upper semi-continuity; recall that monetary utility functions are $\mathbb{L}^\infty$-Lipschitz continuous. We state this fact in a slightly more general framework:

Theorem 2.2. *Suppose that $(\Omega, \mathcal{F}, \mathbf{P})$ is a standard probability space. Let $U\colon \mathbb{L}^\infty \to \mathbb{R} \cup \{-\infty\}$ be a concave function, which is law invariant and u.s.c. with respect to the topology induced by $\|\,.\,\|_\infty$. Then U is u.s.c. with respect to the $\sigma(\mathbb{L}^\infty, \mathbb{L}^1)$-topology.*

We prove this result, which we consider as the main contribution of this paper, in section 4. The reader only interested in Theorem 2.2 may directly proceed to this section.

Finally we observe that Theorem 2.1 implies in particular that in Theorem 7 of [K 01] the assumption of the Fatou property may also be dropped. For the sake of completeness we formulate this result.

A monetary utility function $U\colon \mathbb{L}^\infty \to \mathbb{R}$ is called *comonotone* if $U(X_1 + X_2) = U(X_1) + U(X_2)$, for comonotone $X_1, X_2 \in \mathbb{L}^\infty$ (compare [JST 05]). Note that this implies in particular that U is positively homogeneous, i.e., $U(\lambda X) = \lambda U(X)$, for $\lambda \geq 0$, so that $\rho(X) := -U(X)$ is a coherent risk measure.

Theorem 2.3. *Suppose that $(\Omega, \mathcal{F}, \mathbf{P})$ is a standard probability space. For a function $U\colon \mathbb{L}^\infty(\Omega, \mathcal{F}, \mathbf{P}) \to \mathbb{R}$ the following are equivalent:*
(i) U is a comonotone, law invariant, monetary utility function.
(ii) There is a probability measure m on $[0,1]$ such that

$$U(X) = \int_0^1 U_\alpha(X)\, dm(\alpha), \qquad X \in \mathbb{L}^\infty.$$

In fact, this latter result is known, and may be found in [FS 04], Theorem 4.87, as was kindly pointed out to us by A. Schied.

2.3 Dual characterization of the Lebesgue property

Under the additional assumption of U satisfying the Lebesgue property of Definition 1.2, we have the following variant of Theorem 2.1.

Theorem 2.4. *For a function $U\colon \mathbb{L}^\infty(\Omega, \mathcal{F}, \mathbf{P}) \to \mathbb{R}$ the following are equivalent:*
(i) U is a law invariant monetary utility function satisfying the Lebesgue property.
(ii) There is a law invariant, lower semi-continuous, convex function $V\colon \mathbb{L}^1(\Omega, \mathcal{F}, \mathbf{P}) \to [0, \infty]$ such that $\mathrm{dom}(V) \subseteq \mathcal{P}(\Omega, \mathcal{F}, \mathbf{P})$,

$$U(X) = \inf_{Y \in \mathbb{L}^1} \{\mathbf{E}[XY] + V(Y)\}, \qquad X \in \mathbb{L}^\infty, \tag{4}$$

and $\{V \leq c\}$ is uniformly integrable, for each $c > 0$.
(iii) There is a convex function $v\colon \mathcal{P}(]0,1]) \to [0, \infty]$ such that

$$U(X) = \inf_{m \in \mathcal{P}(]0,1])} \left\{ \int_0^1 U_\alpha(X)\, dm(\alpha) + v(m) \right\}, \qquad X \in \mathbb{L}^\infty, \tag{5}$$

and such that, for $c > 0$, $\{v \leq c\}$ is relatively compact in the Prokhorov topology on $\mathcal{P}(]0,1])$, i.e., for $c > 0$ and $\varepsilon > 0$ there exists $\alpha > 0$ such that $m(]0, \alpha]) < \varepsilon$, whenever $v(m) \leq c$.

To relate Theorem 2.4 to Theorem 2.1 it is instructive to consider a very easy example, namely $U_0(X) = \operatorname{ess\,inf}(X)$, which is a *law invariant* monetary utility function. It is straight-forward to verify that U_0 fails the Lebesgue property. In this case the functions V (resp. v) appearing in (ii) and (iii) of Theorem 2.1 simply are identically zero on $\mathcal{P}(\Omega, \mathcal{F}, \mathbf{P})$ (resp. on $\mathcal{P}(]0,1])$), so that they do not satisfy the uniform integrability (resp. relative compactness) requirements in (ii) and (iii) of Theorem 2.1.

We also stress the difference of $\mathcal{P}([0,1])$ versus $\mathcal{P}(]0,1])$ in Theorem 2.1 and 2.4 respectively. The above formulation of Theorem 2.1 using $\mathcal{P}([0,1])$ was stated by S. Kusuoka and seems more natural (although it would be possible to also formulate Theorem 2.1 using $\mathcal{P}(]0,1])$ instead of $\mathcal{P}([0,1])$. For the formulation of Theorem 2.3, however, it is indispensable to pass to $\mathcal{P}([0,1])$). Think again of $U^0(X) = \operatorname{ess\,inf}(X)$. In this case, the measure m appearing in Theorem 2.3 (ii) equals the Dirac-measure δ_0.

3. Reduction of the probability space by law invariance

In this section we shall show the equivalence of (ii) and (iii) in Theorem 2.1. We shall see that a rather straight-forward application of the formula of integration by parts translates (ii) into (iii) and vice versa. To do so rigourously, it will be convenient to develop some functional analytic machinery.

As in [JST 05] we denote by $\mathcal{D}_{\searrow}$ the set of non-increasing, right continuous, $\mathbb{R}_+$-valued functions f on $]0,1]$ such that $f(1) = 0$ and

$$\|f\|_1 = \int_0^1 f(x)\,dx = 1.$$

We define the map $T\colon \mathcal{D}_{\searrow} \to \mathcal{M}(]0,1])$ by $T(f) = m$ where the measure m on the locally compact space $]0,1]$ is defined by

$$dm(x) = -x\,df(x), \qquad x \in\,]0,1]. \tag{6}$$

To verify that (6) well-defines a probability measure on $]0,1]$ suppose first that f is differentiable and bounded on $]0,1]$. We then may apply the classical formula of integration by parts to obtain

$$\begin{aligned}\|m\|_1 = m(]0,1]) &= \int_0^1 dm(x)\\ &= -\int_0^1 x f'(x)\,dx\\ &= -\Big[x f(x)\Big]_0^1 + \int_0^1 f(x)\,dx = \|f\|_1 = 1.\end{aligned} \tag{7}$$

This isometric identity also remains valid for arbitrary $f \in \mathcal{D}_{\searrow}$: indeed, by considering $f \wedge c$, for $c > 0$ renormalizing and letting $c \to \infty$, one reduces to the case of bounded f; for general bounded $f \in \mathcal{D}_{\searrow}$ it suffices to interpret the above partial integration formula in a generalized sense, using Stieltjes integration.

In fact, the map $T\colon \mathcal{D}_{\searrow} \to \mathcal{M}(]0,1])$ defines a bijection between $\mathcal{D}_{\searrow}$ and the set $\mathcal{P}(]0,1])$ of probability measures on the locally compact space $]0,1]$. Indeed, one may interpret (6) just as well as a definition of the function f (right-continuous and satisfying $f(1) = 0$) for given $m \in \mathcal{P}(]0,1])$.

We still observe that T maps, for $\alpha \in]0,1]$, the functions $g_\alpha = \alpha^{-1}\mathbf{1}_{]0,\alpha[} \in \mathcal{D}_{\searrow}$ to the Dirac measure δ_α on $]0,1]$; this property could just as well have been used to define the map T (extending subsequently the definition by linearity and continuity).

Proof of Theorem 2.1 (ii) ⇔ (iii).
Step 1: Given a convex function $v\colon \mathcal{P}(]0,1]) \to [0,\infty]$ as in (iii) we define the function $V\colon \mathbb{L}^1(\Omega,\mathcal{F},\mathbf{P}) \to [0,\infty]$ by

$$V(Y) = v(T(-q_{-Y})),\ Y \in \mathcal{P}(\Omega,\mathcal{F},\mathbf{P}) \text{ and } V(Y) = +\infty \text{ otherwise}, \quad (8)$$

where T is defined in (6). This is a convex *law invariant* function on $\mathbb{L}^1$.

Conversely, given a *law invariant* convex function $V\colon \mathbb{L}^1(\Omega,\mathcal{F},\mathbf{P}) \to [0,\infty]$ we may well-define $\mathcal{V}\colon \mathcal{D}_{\searrow} \to [0,\infty]$ by

$$\mathcal{V}(-q_{-Y}) := V(Y), \quad (9)$$

where $-q_{-Y}$ runs through $\mathcal{D}_{\searrow}$ when Y ranges through $\mathcal{P}(\Omega,\mathcal{F},\mathbf{P})$. We then define $v\colon \mathcal{P}(]0,1]) \to [0,\infty]$ by

$$v(m) = \mathcal{V}(T^{-1}(m)), \qquad m \in \mathcal{P}(]0,1]). \quad (10)$$

This establishes a bijective correspondence between the functions V and v as appearing in items (ii) and (iii) of Theorem 2.4. We have to show that two such functions V and v define the same function $U\colon \mathbb{L}^\infty \to \mathbb{R}$ via (4) and (5) respectively.

So fix v and V satisfying (10). Write U^V for the function defined by (4) and U^v for the function defined by (5).

First note that

$$\begin{aligned} U^V(X) &= \inf_{Y\in\mathbb{L}^1}\left\{\int_0^1 q_X(\alpha)(-q_{-Y}(\alpha))\,d\alpha - V(Y)\right\} \\ &= \inf_{f\in\mathcal{D}_{\searrow}}\left\{\int_0^1 q_X(\alpha)f(\alpha)\,d\alpha - \mathcal{V}(f)\right\}. \end{aligned} \quad (11)$$

Indeed, looking at the right hand side of (4), the term $V(Y)$ is invariant, when Y runs through all elements of $\mathbb{L}^1(\Omega,\mathcal{F},\mathbf{P})$ with fixed quantile function

$-q_{-Y}(\,.\,) \in \mathcal{D}_{\searrow}$. On the other hand the term $\mathbf{E}[XY]$ becomes minimal, for fixed X and law of Y, if X and Y are anti-comonotonic (compare [JST 05]), in which case

$$\mathbf{E}[XY] = \int_0^1 q_X(\alpha)(-q_{-Y}(\alpha))\,d\alpha,$$

which readily shows (11). Suppose now that $f(\alpha) = -q_{-Y}(\alpha)$ is bounded and differentiable on $]0,1]$ to again apply integration by parts. Let $F(\alpha) = \int_0^\alpha q_X(\beta)\,d\beta$ so that $U_\alpha(X) = \alpha^{-1}F(\alpha)$, for $\alpha \in]0,1]$. We then have

$$\begin{aligned}\int_0^1 q_X(\alpha)f(\alpha)\,d\alpha &= \Big[F(\alpha)f(\alpha)\Big]_0^1 - \int_0^1 F(\alpha)f'(\alpha)\,d\alpha \\ &= -\int_0^1 U_\alpha(X)\alpha f'(\alpha)\,d\alpha \\ &= \int_0^1 U_\alpha(X)\,dm(\alpha). \qquad (12)\end{aligned}$$

Note that the latter integral is just the term appearing in (5). Similarly as in (7) one verifies that (12) in fact holds true for arbitrary $f \in \mathcal{D}_{\searrow}$, which readily shows that the functions U^V and U^v defined by (4) and (5) respectively coincide.

We still have to verify that the function V in Theorem 2.1 (ii) may be assumed to be lower semi-continuous with respect to $\|\,.\,\|_1$. In fact, this is a triviality: we may always pass from a law invariant, convex function $\widetilde{V}\colon \mathbb{L}^1 \to [0,\infty]$ to its lower semi-continuous envelope V, i.e., the largest lower semi-continuous function dominated by V. It now suffices to note that the passage from $\widetilde{V}$ to V does not affect the conjugate function U defined in (1), in other words $U^V(X) = U^{\widetilde{V}}(X)$.

<u>*Step 2:*</u> We now show that we may choose the function v in (iii) to be defined on $\mathcal{P}([0,1])$. Given a convex, lower semi-continuous, *law invariant* function $V\colon \mathbb{L}^1 \to [0,\infty]$ as in (ii), define the corresponding function $v\colon \mathcal{P}(]0,1]) \to [0,\infty]$ as in the above step 1. We define the lower semi-continuous envelope $\overline{v}$ of v on $\mathcal{P}([0,1])$ by

$$\overline{v}(m) := \inf\Big\{ \lim_{n\to\infty} v(m_n) \;\Big|\; (m_n)_{n=1}^\infty \in \mathcal{P}(]0,1]) \text{ and } \lim_{n\to\infty} m_n = m \Big\},$$

where the limit is taken with respect to the weak topology on $\mathcal{P}([0,1])$, i.e., the one generated by the continuous functions on $[0,1]$. Noting that, for $X \in \mathbb{L}^\infty(\Omega,\mathcal{F},\mathbf{P})$, the function $\alpha \mapsto U_\alpha(X)$ is continuous on $[0,1]$, we get

$$\begin{aligned}&\inf_{m\in\mathcal{P}(]0,1])}\Big\{\int_0^1 U^\alpha(X)\,dm(\alpha) + v(m)\Big\} \qquad (13)\\ &= \inf_{m\in\mathcal{P}([0,1])}\Big\{\int_0^1 U^\alpha(X)\,dm(\alpha) + \overline{v}(m)\Big\}.\end{aligned}$$

Hence we have found a (lower semi-continuous, convex) function $\overline{v}$, defined on $\mathcal{P}([0,1])$, such that the above infima coincide. We note in passing that, if v satisfies the Prokhorov condition of (iii) of Theorem 2.4, then $\overline{v}(m) = \infty$, whenever $m(\{0\}) > 0$.

Conversely starting with a function $v\colon \mathcal{P}([0,1]) \to [0,\infty]$, which we assume w.l.g. convex and l.s.c. by passing to this envelope, we may associate a convex, l.s.c., *law invariant* function $V\colon \mathbb{L}^1(\Omega,\mathcal{F},\mathbf{P}) \to [0,\infty]$ as in the above step 1. Note that the definition of V only uses the restriction of v to $\mathcal{P}(]0,1])$. By (13) and the arguments in step 1, we conclude again that

$$\inf_{m\in\mathcal{P}([0,1])}\left\{\int_0^1 U^\alpha(X)dm(\alpha) + v(m)\right\}$$
$$= \inf_{Y\in\mathbb{L}^1}\{\mathbf{E}[XY] + V(Y)\}.$$

This finishes the proof of Theorem 2.1. □

We observe that, in the above proof of Theorem 2.1 (ii) ⇔ (iii), we have in fact translated statement (iii) of Theorem 2.1 into the subsequent equivalent form:

(iii′) *There is a convex function* $\mathcal{V}\colon \mathcal{D}_\searrow \to [0,\infty]$ *such that*

$$U(X) = \inf_{f\in\mathcal{D}_\searrow}\left\{\int_0^1 q_X(\alpha)f(\alpha)\,d\alpha - \mathcal{V}(f)\right\}. \tag{14}$$

Indeed, the translation of the *law invariant* function V on $\mathbb{L}^1$ into the function $\mathcal{V}$ on $\mathcal{D}_\searrow$ was done in (9) above and in (11) it was shown that the function $U(X)$ in (14) indeed equals the function $U^V(X)$.

We also remark that the above proof also shows that in item (ii) above one may equivalently drop the word "convex" and/or the word "lower semi-continuous".

We have imposed in item (ii) the condition of lower semi-continuity of the function V in order to make sure that the terms "*law invariant*" and "*transformation invariant*" are equivalent (see Lemma A.4 below).

4. The Fatou property for law invariant utility functions

In this section we shall prove Theorem 2.2 which will follow from the subsequent result whose proof will be reported at the end of this section.

Proposition 4.1. *Let* C *be a convex,* σ^**-closed, law invariant subset of* $\mathbb{L}^\infty(\Omega,\mathcal{F},\mathbf{P})^*$. *Then* $C\cap\mathbb{L}^1(\Omega,\mathcal{F},\mathbf{P})$ *is* σ^**-dense in* C.

Hence for a law invariant convex σ^*-lower semi-continuous function $V\colon \mathbb{L}^\infty(\Omega,\mathcal{F},\mathbf{P})^* \to [0,\infty]$, V equals the σ^*-lower semi-continuous extension of the restriction of V to $\mathbb{L}^1(\Omega,\mathcal{F},\mathbf{P})$, i.e.

$$V(\mu) = \inf\Big\{\lim_{\alpha\in I} V(f_\alpha) \;\Big|\; (f_\alpha)_{\alpha\in I} \in \mathbb{L}^1,\ \sigma^*\text{-}\lim_{\alpha\in I} f_\alpha = \mu\Big\}, \qquad \mu \in (\mathbb{L}^\infty)^*.$$

Some explanation seems in order. On $(\mathbb{L}^\infty)^*$ we consider the $\sigma^* = \sigma((\mathbb{L}^\infty)^*,\mathbb{L}^\infty)$ topology and identify $\mathbb{L}^1(\Omega,\mathcal{F},\mathbf{P})$ with a subspace of $\mathbb{L}^\infty(\Omega,\mathcal{F},\mathbf{P})^*$. A measure preserving transformation $\tau\colon (\Omega,\mathcal{F},\mathbf{P}) \to (\Omega,\mathcal{F},\mathbf{P})$ defines an isometry, denoted again by τ, on $\mathbb{L}^p(\Omega,\mathcal{F},\mathbf{P})$, for $1 \le p \le \infty$, via

$$\begin{aligned} \tau\colon \mathbb{L}^p &\to \mathbb{L}^p \\ f &\mapsto f\circ\tau. \end{aligned} \tag{15}$$

The transpose of $\tau\colon \mathbb{L}^\infty \to \mathbb{L}^\infty$, denoted by τ^*, defines an isometry on $(\mathbb{L}^\infty)^*$ via

$$\begin{aligned} \tau^*: \quad (\mathbb{L}^\infty)^* &\to (\mathbb{L}^\infty)^* \\ \langle \tau^*(\mu), f\rangle &= \langle \mu, \tau(f)\rangle, \qquad \mu \in (\mathbb{L}^\infty)^*,\ f \in \mathbb{L}^\infty. \end{aligned} \tag{16}$$

A function V on $(\mathbb{L}^\infty)^*$ is called *transformation invariant* if $V = V\circ\tau^*$ for every measure preserving transformation $\tau\colon (\Omega,\mathcal{F},\mathbf{P}) \to (\Omega,\mathcal{F},\mathbf{P})$. A similar definition applies to subsets of $(\mathbb{L}^\infty)^*$.

A σ^*-closed convex subset C of $(\mathbb{L}^\infty)^*$ is called *law invariant* if, for $X_1,\ X_2 \in \mathbb{L}^\infty$ with $\mathrm{law}(X_1) = \mathrm{law}(X_2)$ we have

$$\{\langle \mu, X_1\rangle \mid \mu \in C\} = \{\langle \mu, X_2\rangle \mid \mu \in C\}.$$

A convex σ^*-lower semi-continuous function $V\colon (\mathbb{L}^\infty)^* \to \mathbb{R}\cup\{+\infty\}$ is called *law invariant* if, for each $c \in \mathbb{R}$, the level set $\{V \le c\}$ is *law invariant.*

In Lemma A.5 below we justify that in our setting we may use the notions of *law invariance* and *transformation invariance* synonymously.

Admitting the above Proposition 4.1 the proof of Theorem 2.2 is straightforward.

Proof of Theorem 2.2. Given a concave, u.s.c. (w.r. to $\|\cdot\|_\infty$) function $U\colon \mathbb{L}^\infty(\Omega,\mathcal{F},\mathbf{P}) \to \mathbb{R}\cup\{-\infty\}$ we may define the conjugate

$$V\colon \mathbb{L}^\infty(\Omega,\mathcal{F},\mathbf{P})^* \to \mathbb{R}\cup\{+\infty\} \tag{17}$$

$$V(\mu) = \sup_{X\in\mathbb{L}^\infty} \{U(X) - \langle \mu, X\rangle\}, \qquad \mu \in (\mathbb{L}^\infty)^*. \tag{18}$$

We know from the general theory [R 97] and [ET 74] that V is convex and l.s.c. with respect to $\sigma((\mathbb{L}^\infty)^*,\mathbb{L}^\infty)$ and

$$U(X) = \inf_{\mu \in (\mathbb{L}^\infty)^*} \{V(\mu) + \langle \mu, X \rangle\}, \qquad X \in \mathbb{L}^\infty.$$

If U is *transformation invariant* then V is so too. Admitting the above Proposition 4.1 we conclude that V equals the σ^*-lower semi-continuous extension of its restriction to $\mathbb{L}^1$, so that

$$U(X) = \inf_{Y \in \mathbb{L}^1} \{V(Y) + \mathbf{E}[YX]\}, \qquad X \in \mathbb{L}^\infty.$$

Hence U is σ^* upper semi-continuous as it is the infimum of a family of σ^* continuous functions. □

To prepare the proof of Proposition 4.1 we need some auxiliary results.

Lemma 4.2. *For $p \in [1, \infty]$, Let D be a convex, $\| \cdot \|_p$-closed, law invariant subset of $\mathbb{L}^p(\Omega, \mathcal{F}, \mathbf{P})$, and let $X \in D$. Then, for any sub-sigma-algebra $\mathcal{G}$ of $\mathcal{F}$, we have $\mathbf{E}[X \mid \mathcal{G}] \in D$.*

We provide two somewhat alternative arguments for the cases $p = \infty$ and $p < \infty$.

Proof of Lemma 4.2 ($p = \infty$).
Step 1: We first suppose that $\mathcal{G}$ is trivial so that $\mathbf{E}[X \mid \mathcal{G}] = \mathbf{E}[X]$.

Given $X \in \mathbb{L}^\infty$ and $\varepsilon > 0$, we may find natural numbers $M \leq N$ and a partition $A_1, \ldots, A_N$ of Ω into $\mathcal{F}$-measurable sets of probability N^{-1}, such that

(i) $\operatorname{osc}\{X \mid A_i\} < \varepsilon$, for $i = M+1, \ldots, N$,
(ii) $M/N < \varepsilon$.

Here $\operatorname{osc}\{X \mid A_i\}$ denotes the essential oscillation of X on A_i, i.e. the difference of the essential sup and the essential inf of X onl A_i.

For $1 \leq i < j \leq N$ fix a measure-preserving map $\tau_{i,j} \colon A_i \to A_j$ and let $\tau_{j,i} = \tau_{i,j}^{-1}$. For $\tau_{i,i}$ we choose the identity on A_i.

For a permutation $\pi \colon \{1, \ldots, N\} \to \{1, \ldots, N\}$ we denote by $\tau^\pi : \Omega \to \Omega$ the measure preserving transformation defined via $\tau^\pi|_{A_i} = \tau_{i,\pi(i)}$.

Denoting by Π_N the set of permutations of $\{1, \ldots, N\}$, the element

$$\overline{X} := \frac{1}{N!} \sum_{\pi \in \Pi_N} X \circ \tau^\pi$$

is in D, as D is convex and *transformation invariant* (Lemma A.4). An elementary estimate yields

$$\|\overline{X} - \mathbf{E}[X]\|_\infty \leq \varepsilon + \frac{M}{N} \operatorname{osc}(X).$$

As D is $\|\,.\,\|_\infty$-closed we infer that $\mathbf{E}[X]$ is in D too.

Step 2: Now suppose that $\mathcal{G}$ is finite, hence generated by a partition $\{B_1, \ldots, B_n\}$ of Ω with $\mathbf{P}[B_j] > 0$.

In this case it suffices to apply step 1 on each atom B_j to obtain the conclusion of the lemma.

Step 3: For a general sub-sigma-algebra $\mathcal{G}$ of $\mathcal{F}$ and given $X \in \mathbb{L}^\infty$, we may find, for $\varepsilon > 0$, a finite sub-sigma-algebra $\mathcal{H}$ of $\mathcal{G}$ such that

$$\left\| \mathbf{E}[X \mid \mathcal{G}] - \mathbf{E}[X \mid \mathcal{H}] \right\|_\infty < \varepsilon.$$

Hence the general case follows from step 2. □

Proof of Lemma 4.2 ($p \in [1, \infty[$). Assume to the contrary that $\mathbf{E}[X \mid \mathcal{G}]$ does not lie in the $\|\,.\,\|_p$-closed convex hull of the set D. Then, it follows from the Hahn-Banach separation Theorem that

$$\mathbf{E}\{Z\mathbf{E}[X \mid \mathcal{G}]\} > \sup_{Y \in D} \mathbf{E}[ZY] \quad \text{for some} \quad Z \in \mathbb{L}^q(\Omega, \mathcal{F}, \mathbf{P}), \tag{19}$$

where $p^{-1} + q^{-1} = 1$. Let $F_{Z|\mathcal{G}}(x) := \mathbf{P}[Z \le x \mid \mathcal{G}]$ be the $\mathcal{G}$-conditional cumulative distribution function of Z, and let $q_{Z|\mathcal{G}}(\alpha) := \inf\{x \mid F_{Z|\mathcal{G}}(x) \ge \alpha\}$ be its inverse. Let ν be a random variable on $(\Omega, \mathcal{F}, \mathbf{P})$ with uniform distribution on $(0, 1)$ conditionally on $\mathcal{G}$, and define

$$\begin{aligned} \nu_Z := {} & F_{Z|\mathcal{G}}(Z)\, \mathbf{1}_{\{\Delta F_{Z|\mathcal{G}}(Z) = 0\}} \\ & + \left(F_{Z|\mathcal{G}}(Z-) + \nu \Delta F_{Z|\mathcal{G}}(Z)\right) \mathbf{1}_{\{\Delta F_{Z|\mathcal{G}}(Z) > 0\}}, \end{aligned} \tag{20}$$

so that $Z = q_{Z|\mathcal{G}}(\nu_Z)$ a.s. Next, set $\widehat{X} := q_{X|\mathcal{G}}(\nu_Z)$, and observe that $\widehat{X}$ has the same $\mathcal{G}$-conditional distribution as X (in particular $\widehat{X} \in D$), and $\widehat{X}$ is comonotone to Z conditionally to $\mathcal{G}$, see [JN 04]. It then follows from (19) that

$$\mathbf{E}\{Z\mathbf{E}[X \mid \mathcal{G}]\} > \mathbf{E}\left[Z\widehat{X}\right] = \mathbf{E}\left\{\mathbf{E}\left[Z\widehat{X} \mid \mathcal{G}\right]\right\}. \tag{21}$$

From the $\mathcal{G}$-conditional comonotonicity of $\widehat{X}$ and Z, we have $\mathbf{E}[Z\widehat{X} \mid \mathcal{G}] \ge \mathbf{E}[Z \mid \mathcal{G}]\, \mathbf{E}[\widehat{X} \mid \mathcal{G}]$, see Proposition 4 in [JN 04]. Recalling that $\widehat{X}$ and X have the same $\mathcal{G}$-conditional distribution, this provides $\mathbf{E}\{Z\mathbf{E}[X \mid \mathcal{G}]\} > \mathbf{E}\{\mathbf{E}[Z \mid \mathcal{G}]\, \mathbf{E}[\widehat{X} \mid \mathcal{G}]\} = \mathbf{E}\{Z\mathbf{E}[X \mid \mathcal{G}]\}$, which is the required contradiction.
□

For $\mu \in \mathbb{L}^\infty(\Omega, \mathcal{F}, \mathbf{P})^*$ and a sub-σ-algebra $\mathcal{G}$ of $\mathcal{F}$, we define the conditional expectation

$$\mu \in \mathbb{L}^\infty(\Omega, \mathcal{F}, \mathbf{P})^* \longmapsto \mathbf{E}[\mu \mid \mathcal{G}] \in \mathbb{L}^\infty(\Omega, \mathcal{F}, \mathbf{P})^* \tag{22}$$

as the transpose of the $\mathcal{G}$-conditional expectation operator on $\mathbb{L}^\infty(\Omega, \mathcal{F}, \mathbf{P})$, i.e.

$$\langle \mathbf{E}[\mu | \mathcal{G}], \xi \rangle = \langle \mu, \mathbf{E}[\xi | \mathcal{G}] \rangle \quad \text{for } \mu \in \mathbb{L}^\infty(\Omega, \mathcal{F}, \mathbf{P})^* \text{ and } \xi \in \mathbb{L}^\infty(\Omega, \mathcal{F}, \mathbf{P}). \tag{23}$$

If the singular part of μ is zero, i.e. μ is absolutely continuous with respect to $\mathbf{P}$ with density $d\mu/d\mathbf{P} = Z$, then it is immediately checked that this definition coincides with the classical notion of conditional expectation in the sense that $\mathbf{E}[\mu \mid \mathcal{G}] = \mathbf{E}[Z \mid \mathcal{G}] \cdot \mathbf{P}$.

Lemma 4.3. *If C is a σ^*-closed, convex law invariant subset of $\mathbb{L}^\infty(\Omega, \mathcal{F}, \mathbf{P})^*$, $\mu \in C$, and $\mathcal{G}$ is a sub-sigma-algebra of $\mathcal{F}$, then $\mathbf{E}[\mu \mid \mathcal{G}] \in C$.*
Hence $C \cap \mathbb{L}^1$ is σ^*-dense in C.

Proof. Fix $\mu \in C$ and the sigma-algebra $\mathcal{G}$, and suppose that $\mathbf{E}[\mu \mid \mathcal{G}] \notin C$. By the Hahn-Banach theorem there is $X \in \mathbb{L}^\infty$ such that

$$a := \sup_{\nu \in C} \langle X, \nu \rangle < \langle X, \mathbf{E}[\mu \mid \mathcal{G}] \rangle =: b.$$

Let D_X denote the $\| \, . \, \|_\infty$-closed convex hull of the set $\{X \circ \tau \mid \tau$ measure preserving transformation of $\Omega\}$. As C is *law invariant* and therefore *transformation invariant* by Lemma A.5, we get

$$a = \sup_{\nu \in C, \, Z \in D_X} \langle Z, \nu \rangle.$$

By the previous Lemma 4.2 we conclude that

$$a \geq \sup_{\nu \in C} \langle \mathbf{E}[X \mid \mathcal{G}], \nu \rangle \geq \langle \mathbf{E}[X \mid \mathcal{G}], \mu \rangle.$$

Whence

$$\langle \mathbf{E}[X \mid \mathcal{G}], \mu \rangle \leq a < b = \langle X, \mathbf{E}[\mu \mid \mathcal{G}] \rangle = \langle \mathbf{E}[X \mid \mathcal{G}], \mu \rangle,$$

a contradiction proving the first assertion of the lemma.

As regards the final assertion, note that the net $\mathbf{E}[\mu \mid \mathcal{G}]$, when $\mathcal{G}$ runs through the finite sub-sigma-algebras of $\mathcal{F}$ converges to μ with respect to $\sigma((\mathbb{L}^\infty)^*, \mathbb{L}^\infty)$. □

Proof of Proposition 4.1. The first assertion is proved in Lemma 4.3, and the second one follows by applying it to the level sets $\{V \leq c\}$, for $c \in \mathbb{R}$. □

Remark 4.4. Proposition 4.1 can be re-phrased as follows: *an $\| \, . \, \|_\infty$-closed, convex, law invariant subset $C \subseteq \mathbb{L}^\infty(\Omega, \mathcal{F}, \mathbf{P})$ is $\sigma(\mathbb{L}^\infty, \mathbb{L}^1)$-closed.* Indeed, consider the polar $C^\circ = \{\mu \in (\mathbb{L}^\infty)^* \mid \langle \mu, f \rangle \leq 1 \text{ for } f \in C\}$, which is a $\sigma((\mathbb{L}^\infty)^*, \mathbb{L}^\infty)$-closed, convex, *law invariant* subset of $(\mathbb{L}^\infty)^*$. The assertion that $C^\circ \cap \mathbb{L}^1$ is $\sigma((\mathbb{L}^\infty)^*, \mathbb{L}^\infty)$-dense in C° is tantamount to the $\sigma(\mathbb{L}^\infty, \mathbb{L}^1)$-closedness of C.

5. The Lebesgue property for law invariant utility functions

In this section, we provide a proof of Theorem 2.4. We first state (without proof) an easy result from measure theory which will be used in the implication (ii) $\Longrightarrow$ (i) below.

Lemma 5.1. *Let C be a uniformly integrable subset of $\mathbb{L}^1(\Omega, \mathcal{F}, \mathbf{P})$ and $(X_n)_{n=1}^{\infty}$ a uniformly bounded sequence in $\mathbb{L}^{\infty}(\Omega, \mathcal{F}, \mathbf{P})$ tending a.s. to X. Then*

$$\lim_{n\to\infty} \inf_{Y\in C} \mathbf{E}[X_n Y] = \inf_{Y\in C} \mathbf{E}[XY].$$

Proof of Theorem 2.4.
(i) $\Rightarrow$ (ii): As the Lebesgue property implies the Fatou property we know from the general theory ([D 02] and [FS 04]) that the function

$$V(Y) = \sup_{X\in\mathbb{L}^\infty} \{U(X) - \mathbf{E}[XY]\}, \qquad Y \in \mathbb{L}^1,$$

defines the conjugate function of U, for which we then have the dual relation

$$U(X) = \inf_{Y\in\mathbb{L}^1} \{V(Y) + \mathbf{E}[XY]\}, \qquad X \in \mathbb{L}^\infty.$$

Clearly V is lower semi-continuous and V is *law invariant* iff U is so.

We have to show that $\{V \leq c\}$ is uniformly integrable, for each $c > 0$. Suppose to the contrary that for some $c > 0$ the set $\{V \leq c\}$ fails to be uniformly integrable. Then there exists $\alpha > 0$, a sequence $(Y_n)_{n=1}^{\infty}$ in $\{V \leq c\}$, and a sequence $(A_n)_{n=1}^{\infty}$ in $\mathcal{F}$, such that $\lim_{n\to\infty} \mathbf{1}_{A_n} = 0$ a.s. and

$$\mathbf{E}[\mathbf{1}_{A_n} Y_n] \geq \alpha > 0.$$

For $X_n = -\frac{2c}{\alpha} \mathbf{1}_{A_n}$ we find

$$\begin{aligned} U(X_n) &\leq V(Y_n) + \mathbf{E}[X_n Y_n] \\ &\leq c - \alpha \frac{2c}{\alpha} = -c \end{aligned} \tag{24}$$

while $U(\lim_{n\to\infty} X_n) = U(0) = 0$, a contradiction to the Lebesgue property of U.

(ii) $\Rightarrow$ (i): For given $V \colon \mathbb{L}^1 \to [0, \infty]$, we know from the general theory ([D 02] and [FS 04]) that U as defined in (4) is a monetary utility function satisfying the Fatou property, i.e., for uniformly bounded $(X_n)_{n=1}^{\infty}$ tending a.s. to X we have

$$U(X) \geq \lim_{n\to\infty} U(X_n), \tag{25}$$

where we may assume w.l.g. that the limit on the right hand side exists. Hence we only have to show the reverse inequality of (25).

So let $(X_n)_{n=1}^\infty$ be as above such that $(U(X_n))_{n=1}^\infty$ converges. As U is a monetary utility function and $(X_n)_{n=1}^\infty$ is uniformly bounded, this limit is finite.

For $\varepsilon > 0$ and $n \in \mathbb{N}$ we may use (4) to find $c_n \geq 0$ such that

$$U(X_n) \geq \inf_{V(Y) \leq c_n} \mathbf{E}[X_n Y] + c_n - \varepsilon. \tag{26}$$

Using again the fact that $(X_n)_{n=1}^\infty$ is uniformly bounded we conclude that $(c_n)_{n=1}^\infty$ is bounded, so that we may find a cluster point $c \geq 0$ and there is an infinite subset I of $\mathbb{N}$ such that for $n \in I$ we have $|c_n - c| < \varepsilon$. We then may apply the preceding Lemma 5.1 to estimate

$$\begin{aligned} U(X) &\leq \inf_{V(Y) \leq c+\varepsilon} \mathbf{E}[XY] + (c + \varepsilon) \\ &= \lim_{n \in I} \inf_{V(Y) \leq c+\varepsilon} \mathbf{E}[X_n Y] + c + \varepsilon \\ &\leq \lim_{n \in I} \inf_{V(Y) \leq c_n} \mathbf{E}[X_n Y] + c + \varepsilon \\ &\leq \lim_{n \to \infty} U(X_n) + 3\varepsilon. \end{aligned} \tag{27}$$

(ii) $\Longleftrightarrow$ (iii) In view of the first step of the proof of Theorem 2.1 (ii) $\Leftrightarrow$ (iii) in Section 3, it only remains to show that the notion of uniform integrability in (ii) corresponds to the notion of relative compactness with respect to the Prokhorov topology in (iii). To do so, note that if $m \in \mathcal{P}(]0,1])$ and $f \in \mathcal{D}_\searrow$ are related via $T(f) = m$, see (6), we have for $\alpha \in]0,1]$ (arguing once more by approximation with bounded, differentiable functions f)

$$\begin{aligned} m(]0,\alpha[) &= \int_0^\alpha dm(x) \\ &= -\int_0^\alpha x f'(x)\,dx \\ &= -\Big[x f(x)\Big]_0^\alpha + \int_0^\alpha f(x)\,dx \\ &= \int_0^\alpha (f(x) - f(\alpha))\,dx. \end{aligned} \tag{28}$$

The set $\{Y \in \mathbb{L}^1 \mid V(Y) \leq c\}$ is uniformly integrable iff the integral $\int_0^\alpha (f(x) - f(\alpha))\,dx$ tends to zero, for $\alpha \to 0$, uniformly over the set $\{f = -q_{-Y} \in \mathcal{D}_\searrow \mid V(Y) \leq c\}$. In view of (28) this is tantamount to the fact that $m(]0,\alpha[)$ tends to zero, for $\alpha \to 0$, uniformly over the set $\{m \in \mathcal{P}(]0,1]) \mid v(m) \leq c\}$. □

In the above proof of the equivalence of (i) and (ii) of Theorem 2.4 we have not used the law invariance of U and V respectively, which is irrelevant for this equivalence (while for the formulation of (iii) it is, of course, indispensable).

In fact this is part of a more general characterization of the Lebesgue property in equivalent terms as mentioned in the beginning of this section. As these results are somewhat scattered in the previous literature [D 03, FS 04, K 05] we resume them in the subsequent theorem and give proofs. In the subsequent theorem, we identify $\mathbb{L}^1(\Omega, \mathcal{F}, \mathbf{P})$ with a subspace of $\mathbb{L}^\infty(\Omega, \mathcal{F}, \mathbf{P})^*$.

Theorem 5.2. *Suppose that* $\mathbb{L}^1(\Omega, \mathcal{F}, \mathbf{P})$ *is separable, let* $U\colon \mathbb{L}^\infty(\Omega, \mathcal{F}, \mathbf{P}) \to \mathbb{R}$ *be a monetary utility function satisfying the Fatou property and let* $V\colon \mathbb{L}^\infty(\Omega, \mathcal{F}, \mathbf{P})^* \to [0, \infty]$ *be its conjugate function defined on the dual* $\mathbb{L}^\infty(\Omega, \mathcal{F}, \mathbf{P})^*$*, i.e.*

$$V(\mu) := \sup_{X \in \mathbb{L}^\infty} \{U(X) - \langle \mu, X \rangle\}, \qquad \mu \in \mathbb{L}^\infty(\Omega, \mathcal{F}, \mathbf{P})^*. \tag{29}$$

The following assertions are equivalent:
(i) U *satisfies the Lebesgue property.*
(ii) $U(x)$ *is continuous from below in the sense of [FS 04], i.e. for every sequence* $(X_n)_{n=1}^\infty \in \mathbb{L}^\infty$ *increasing monotonically to* $X \in \mathbb{L}^\infty$ *we have* $\lim_{n\to\infty} U(X_n) = U(X)$.
(iii) $\operatorname{dom}(V) = \{V < \infty\} \subseteq \mathbb{L}^1(\Omega, \mathcal{F}, \mathbf{P})$.
(iv) For each $c \in \mathbb{R}$*,* $\{V \le c\}$ *is a weakly compact subset of* $\mathbb{L}^1(\Omega, \mathcal{F}, \mathbf{P})$.
(v) For every $X \in \mathbb{L}^\infty(\Omega, \mathcal{F}, \mathbf{P})$ *the infimum in the equality*

$$U(X) = \inf_{Y \in \mathbb{L}^1} \{V(Y) + \mathbf{E}[XY]\},$$

is attained.

Remark 5.3. In the above theorem, the only requirement on the probability space is that $\mathbb{L}^1(\Omega, \mathcal{F}, \mathbf{P})$ is separable (we need this assumption for the implication (v) $\Rightarrow$ (iv)). In particular, $(\Omega, \mathcal{F}, \mathbf{P})$ need not be atomless.

Remark 5.4. The notion of continuity from below was introduced in [FS 04, Proposition 4.21], where the equivalence of (ii) and (iii) was shown. Property (v) was studied in [D 03] where, applying James' theorem, F. Delbaen showed the equivalence of (iv) and (v) in the context of coherent risk measures. After finishing the paper we were kindly informed by F. Delbaen that he has an argument to directly deduce the above implication (v) $\Rightarrow$ (iv) from James' theorem also for the case of convex risk measures without referring to a variant of this theorem such as Theorem A.1 below [D 05].

Proof of Theorem 5.2.
(i) $\Leftrightarrow$ (iv): We have shown this equivalence in the proof of Theorem 2.4 above.

(iii) $\Leftrightarrow$ (iv): the implication (iv) $\Rightarrow$ (iii) being obvious note for the converse that a subset $C \subseteq \mathbb{L}^1(\Omega, \mathcal{F}, \mathbf{P})$ is relatively weakly compact iff its $\sigma((\mathbb{L}^\infty)^*, \mathbb{L}^\infty)$-closure is contained in $\mathbb{L}^1(\Omega, \mathcal{F}, \mathbf{P})$. As the level sets $\{\mu \in (\mathbb{L}^\infty)^* \mid V(\mu) \leq c\}$ are the $\sigma((\mathbb{L}^\infty)^*, \mathbb{L}^\infty)$ closure of $\{Y \in \mathbb{L}^1 \mid V(Y) \leq c\}$ in view of the Fatou property of U, we obtain (iii) $\Rightarrow$ (iv).
(i) $\Rightarrow$ (ii): obvious.
(ii) $\Rightarrow$ (iv): This implication was shown in (i) $\Rightarrow$ (ii) of Theorem 2.4.
(iv) $\Rightarrow$ (v): For $X \in \mathbb{L}^\infty(\Omega, \mathcal{F}, \mathbf{P})$ the function

$$c \mapsto \inf_{V(Y) \leq c} \mathbf{E}[XY]$$

is decreasing, convex and bounded on $[0, \infty[$ so that the function

$$c \mapsto \inf_{V(Y) \leq c} \mathbf{E}[XY] + c$$

attains its minimum at some $\bar{c} \in [0, \infty[$. Hence

$$U(X) = \inf_{V(Y) \leq \bar{c}} \mathbf{E}[XY] + \bar{c}. \tag{30}$$

As $\{V(Y) \leq \bar{c}\}$ is a weakly compact set in $\mathbb{L}^1(\Omega, \mathcal{F}, \mathbf{P})$ the infimum in (30) is attained.
(v) $\Rightarrow$ (iv): To prove this implication first suppose that U is positively homogenous, i.e. $\rho = -U$ is a coherent risk measure. In this case $\{V < \infty\} = \{V = 0\}$.

If $\{Y \in \mathbb{L}^1 \mid V(Y) = 0\}$ fails to be weakly compact, then we deduce from James' theorem (see, e.g., [FLP 01, FHMPZ 01]) that there is some $X \in \mathbb{L}^\infty(\Omega, \mathcal{F}, \mathbf{P})$ such that X does not attain its infimum on $\{Y \in \mathbb{L}^1 \mid V(Y) = 0\}$. Hence in the equation

$$U(X) = \inf_{Y \in \mathbb{L}^1, V(Y) = 0} \mathbf{E}[XY]$$

the infimum is not attained.

Now we drop the assumption that U is positively homogenous. In this case one needs to apply a variant of James' theorem, which was shown to us by P. Orihuela — following closely the arguments of [G 87] — and which we state and prove in the appendix A.1. This theorem implies that, whenever (iv) fails, we may find $X \in \mathbb{L}^\infty(\Omega, \mathcal{F}, \mathbf{P})$ such that in

$$U(X) = \inf_{Y \in \mathbb{L}^1} \{\mathbf{E}[XY] + V(Y)\}$$

the infimum is not attained. $\square$

We still note that we may rephrase condition (iii) of Theorem 2.1 again in terms of the set $\mathcal{D}_{\searrow}$ (similarly as in (14) above for the case of Theorem 2.1):

(iii′) *There is a convex function* $\mathcal{V}\colon \mathcal{D}_{\searrow} \to [0,1]$ *such that*

$$U(X) = \inf_{f \in \mathcal{D}_{\searrow}} \left\{ \int_0^1 q_X(\alpha) f(\alpha)\, d\alpha - \mathcal{V}(f) \right\}.$$

The verification that this condition is indeed equivalent to condition (ii) and (iii) in Theorem 2.1 is similar as for (14) above.

A. Appendix

The proof of the variant of James' theorem below was communicated to us by P. Orihuela. We sincerely thank him for allowing us to include it in this paper.

Theorem A.1. *Let* $(E, \|\,.\,\|)$ *be a separable Banach space and* $V\colon E \to \mathbb{R} \cup \{\infty\}$ *a proper convex l.s.c. function such that* $\mathrm{dom}(V) = \{V < \infty\}$ *is a bounded subset of* E. *Suppose that there is* $c \in \mathbb{R}$ *such that the level set* $L_c = \{V \leq c\}$ *fails to be weakly compact.*

Then there is $x^* \in E^*$ *such that, for*

$$U(x^*) = \inf_{x \in E} \{\langle x, x^* \rangle + V(x)\} \tag{31}$$

the infimum is not attained.

To prove the theorem we recall the inequality of Simons which isolates the combinatorial part in James' theorem.

Proposition A.2 ([S 72, G 87]). *Let* B *be a set and* $(f_n)_{n=1}^{\infty}$ *a sequence of functions on* B *taking their values in a compact interval* $[a,b]$. *Denote by* C *the convex set*

$$C = \left\{ \sum_{n=1}^{\infty} c_n f_n \,\middle|\, c_n \geq 0, \sum_{n=1}^{\infty} c_n = 1 \right\},$$

and suppose that every element $f \in C$ *attains its infimum on* B. *Then*

$$\inf_{b \in B} \liminf_{n \to \infty} f_n(b) \leq \sup_{f \in C} \inf_{b \in B} f(b). \tag{32}$$

We also need an elementary estimate.

Lemma A.3. *Let* $V\colon E \to \mathbb{R} \cup \{\infty\}$ *be as in Theorem A.1; suppose that* $\operatorname{dom}(V)$ *is contained in the unit ball of E and that* $\inf_{x\in E} V(x) < 0$.

Denoting by

$$\operatorname{Epi}(V) = \{(x,t) \in E \times \mathbb{R} \mid V(x) \le t\}, \tag{33}$$

$$\textit{and} \quad \operatorname{Epi}(V,\mu) = \{(x,t) \in E \times \mathbb{R} \mid V(x) \le t \le \mu\}, \qquad \mu \in \mathbb{R}, \tag{34}$$

let $(x^*,\lambda) \in E^* \times \mathbb{R}$, $\|x^*\| \le 1$, $\lambda > 0$.

Then, for $\mu \ge 2\lambda^{-1}$, *we have*

$$\inf_{(x,t)\in\operatorname{Epi}(V)} \langle (x^*,\lambda),(x,t)\rangle = \inf_{(x,t)\in\operatorname{Epi}(V,\mu)} \langle (x^*,\lambda),(x,t)\rangle.$$

Proof. Fix $x_0 \in X$, $\|x_0\| \le 1$, such that $V(x_0) \le 0$. Then, for every $(x,t) \in \operatorname{Epi}(V)$ such that

$$\langle (x^*,\lambda),(x,t)\rangle \le \langle (x^*,\lambda),(x_0,0)\rangle,$$

we have

$$\lambda t \le \langle x^*, x_0 - x\rangle \le 2. \qquad \square$$

Proof of Theorem A.1. Assume w.l.g. that $\operatorname{dom}(V)$ is contained in the unit ball of E and that $\inf_{x\in E} V(x) = -1$. Assume that for every $x^* \in E^*$ the infimum in

$$U(x^*) := \inf_{x\in E}\{\langle x, x^*\rangle + V(x)\} \tag{35}$$

is attained and let us work towards a contradiction.

Consider the Banach space $E^{**} \times \mathbb{R}$, in which the epigraph (33) of V, is a norm-closed convex set.

Note that the optimisation problem (35) may be rewritten as

$$U(x^*) = \inf_{(x,t)\in\operatorname{Epi}(V)} \{\langle (x^*,1),(x,t)\rangle\}, \tag{36}$$

and that, for $x^* \in E^*$, the inf in (35) is attained iff the inf in (36) is attained. Hence the inf in (35) is attained for each $x^* \in E^*$ iff each (x^*,λ), where $x^* \in E^*$ and $\lambda > 0$, attains its inf on $\operatorname{Epi}(V)$.

By hypothesis there is some level $c > 0$ such that $L_c = \{V \le c\}$ is not weakly compact in E.

By the convexity of V this holds true for every $c > \inf_{x\in E} V(x) = -1$ so that we may choose $c = 0$.

Hence there is $(x^{**},0) \in (E^{**} \times \mathbb{R}) \setminus (E \times \mathbb{R})$ which is in the $\sigma(E^{**} \times \mathbb{R}, E^* \times \mathbb{R})$-closure of $\operatorname{Epi}(V)$. We may apply Hahn-Banach to separate $\operatorname{Epi}(V)$ strictly from $(x^{**},0)$, i.e. there are $(x^{***},\lambda) \in E^{***} \times \mathbb{R}$ with $\|x^{***}\| \le 1$ and $\alpha < \beta$ such that

$$\langle (x^{***},\lambda),(x^{**},0)\rangle < \alpha < \beta < \inf_{(x,t)\in \mathrm{Epi}(V)} \langle (x^{***},\lambda),(x,t)\rangle. \tag{37}$$

Clearly we must have $\lambda \geq 0$. In fact, we may assume that $\lambda > 0$. Indeed if (37) holds true for some (x^{***},λ) then it also holds true for (x^{***},λ') provided that $\lambda \leq \lambda' < \inf_{(x,t)\in \mathrm{Epi}(V)}\langle (x^{***},\lambda),(x,t)\rangle - \beta$. Indeed, the passage from λ to λ' does not affect the first inequality of (37) while the last one remains valid in view of $t \geq -1$, for $(x,t) \in \mathrm{Epi}(V)$.

Fix a dense sequence $(x_j)_{j=1}^{\infty}$ in E and use the $\sigma(E^{***},E^{**})$-densitiy of the unit ball of E^* in the unit ball of E^{***} to find a sequence $(x_n^*)_{n=1}^{\infty}$ with $\|x_n^*\| \leq 1$ such that

$$|\langle x_n^* - x^{***}, x_j\rangle| < n^{-1}, \qquad j = 1,\ldots,n,$$

and $\langle x_n^*, x^{**}\rangle < \alpha$.

By hypothesis each (x_n^*,λ) as well as any countable convex combination of this sequence attains its inf at some $(x,\mu) \in \mathrm{Epi}(V)$ for which we find $\mu \leq 2\lambda^{-1}$ by Lemma A.3. Let $\mu_0 = 2\lambda^{-1}$ and define B as the truncated epigraph (34) of V at level μ_0, i.e.

$$B = \mathrm{Epi}(V,\mu_0) = \{(x,t) \in E \times \mathbb{R} \mid V(x) \leq t \leq \mu_0\},$$

which is a bounded subset of $E \times \mathbb{R}$.

We now are in a position to apply Simons' inequality. Letting $C = \left\{\sum_{n=1}^{\infty} c_n(x_n^*,\lambda) \mid c_n \geq 0,\ \sum_{n=1}^{\infty} c_n = 1\right\}$ we have

$$a := \sup_{(x^*,\lambda)\in C}\ \inf_{(x,t)\in B} \langle (x^*,\lambda),(x,t)\rangle \leq \alpha. \tag{38}$$

Indeed, for every $(x^*,\lambda) \in C$ we have $\langle (x^*,\lambda),(x^{**},0)\rangle \leq \alpha$; noting that $(x^{**},0)$ is in the $\sigma(E^{**}\times\mathbb{R}, E^*\times\mathbb{R})$-closure of $B = \mathrm{Epi}(V,\mu_0)$ and (x^*,λ) is continuous with respect to this topology, we obtain (38).

On the other hand

$$b := \inf_{(x,t)\in B}\ \liminf_{n\to\infty} \langle (x_n^*,\lambda),(x,t)\rangle \geq \beta. \tag{39}$$

Indeed, by construction we have $\lim_{n\to\infty}\langle x_n^*, x\rangle = \langle x^{***}, x\rangle$, for every $x \in E$, so that (39) follows from (37). Hence (32) yields the desired contradiction

$$b \leq a \leq \alpha < \beta \leq b. \qquad \square$$

We finish the paper by two easy measure theoretic results.

Lemma A.4. *Let $(\Omega,\mathcal{F},\mathbf{P})$ be a standard probability space, $1 \leq p \leq \infty$, and C a norm closed subset of $\mathbb{L}^p(\Omega,\mathcal{F},\mathbf{P})$. T.f.a.e.*
(i) C is law invariant, i.e., $X_1 \in C$ and $\mathrm{law}(X_1) = \mathrm{law}(X_2)$ implies that $X_2 \in C$.
(ii) C is transformation invariant, i.e., for $X \in C$ and a bi-measurable measure preserving transformation $\tau\colon (\Omega,\mathcal{F},\mathbf{P}) \to (\Omega,\mathcal{F},\mathbf{P})$ we have $X\circ\tau \in C$.

Proof. (i) $\Rightarrow$ (ii): Note that $\mathrm{law}(X) = \mathrm{law}(X \circ \tau)$ for X and τ as in (ii).
(ii) $\Rightarrow$ (i): Let $X_1, X_2 \in \mathbb{L}^p$ with $\mathrm{law}(X_1) = \mathrm{law}(X_2)$. For $\varepsilon > 0$ let $(A_i)_{i=1}^\infty$ be a partition of $\mathbb{R}$ into countably many sets of diameter less than ε; for example, one may choose the half-open intervals $\{]\frac{k}{2^n}, \frac{k+1}{2^n}]\}_{k \in \mathbb{Z}}$, for n sufficiently large. The sets

$$B_i^1 = \{X_1 \in A_i\}, \quad B_i^2 = \{X_2 \in A_i\},$$

satisfy $\mathbf{P}[B_i^1] = \mathbf{P}[B_i^2]$, for each $i \in \mathbb{N}$. Using the hypothesis that $(\Omega, \mathcal{F}, \mathbf{P})$ is a standard probability space, we may find a bi-measurable measure preserving transformation $\tau \colon (\Omega, \mathcal{F}, \mathbf{P}) \to (\Omega, \mathcal{F}, \mathbf{P})$ mapping each B_i^1 onto B_i^2. We then have

$$\|X_2 - X_1 \circ \tau\|_\infty \leq \varepsilon.$$

Assumption (ii) and $X_1 \in C$ implies that $X_1 \circ \tau \in C$. The $\|\,.\,\|_p$-closedness of C then implies that $X_2 \in C$. □

In the next lemma we formulate an analogous result for the case of $\mathbb{L}^\infty(\Omega, \mathcal{F}, \mathbf{P})^*$.

Lemma A.5. *Let $(\Omega, \mathcal{F}, \mathbf{P})$ be a standard probability space and C a σ^*-closed, convex subset of $\mathbb{L}^\infty(\Omega, \mathcal{F}, \mathbf{P})^*$. T.f.a.e.*
(i) C is law invariant, i.e., for $X_1, X_2 \in \mathbb{L}^\infty$ with $\mathrm{law}(X_1) = \mathrm{law}(X_2)$, we have

$$\{\langle \mu, X_1 \rangle \mid \mu \in C\} = \{\langle \mu, X_2 \rangle \mid \mu \in C\}.$$

(ii) C is transformation invariant, i.e., $C = \tau^*(C)$ for each measure preserving transformation $\tau \colon (\Omega, \mathcal{F}, \mathbf{P}) \to (\Omega, \mathcal{F}, \mathbf{P})$ (see (16)).
(iii) The conjugate function Φ of C defined by

$$\Phi(X) = \sup_{\mu \in C} \langle \mu, X \rangle, \qquad X \in \mathbb{L}^\infty,$$

is law invariant.

Proof. (i) $\Leftrightarrow$ (iii): W.l.g. assume $C \neq \emptyset$. As C is σ^*-closed and convex, for $X \in \mathbb{L}^\infty$ the set $I(X) := \{\langle \mu, X \rangle \mid \mu \in C\}$ is the closed non-empty interval $[-\Phi(-X), \Phi(X)]$. Obviously C is *law invariant* iff Φ is *law invariant*.
(ii) $\Leftrightarrow$ (iii): By Lemma A.4 the function Φ is *law invariant* iff it is *transformation invariant*, i.e., $\Phi = \Phi \circ \tau$ for each bi-measurable measure preserving $\tau \colon (\Omega, \mathcal{F}, \mathbf{P}) \to (\Omega, \mathcal{F}, \mathbf{P})$. Hence the equivalence of (ii) and (iii) is obvious. □

References

[ADEH 97] Artzner, P., Delbaen, F., Eber, J.M., Heath, D.: Coherent measures of risk. Mathematical Finance **9**, 203-228 (1999)

[D 02] Delbaen, F.: Coherent risk measure of risk on general probability spaces. In: Advances in Finance and Stochastics, Essays in Honor of Dieter Sondermann (Sandmann, K., Schonbucher, P.J. eds.). pp.1-37 Springer, Berlin 2002

[D 03] Delbaen, F.: Coherent risk measures. Lecture Notes of Scuola Normale Pisa (2003)

[D 05] Delbaen, F.: Private communication referring to a forthcoming paper "Coherent risk measures" (2005)

[ET 74] Ekeland, I., Temam, R.: Analyse Convexe et Problèmes Variationnels. Dunod Gauthier-Villars 1974

[FHMPZ 01] Fabian, M., Habala, P., Montesinos, V., Pelant, J., Zizler, V.: Functional Analysis and Infinite Dimensional Geometry. Springer Verlag, New York 2001

[FLP 01] Fonf, V.P., Lindenstrauss, J., Phelps, R.R.: Infinite dimensional convexity. In: Handbook of the Geometry of Banach Spaces. Vol. I. pp.599-670 North-Holland-Amsterdam 2001

[FG 05] Frittelli, M., Rossaza Gianin, E.: Law invariant convex risk measures. Advances in Mathematical Economics **7**, 33-46 (2005)

[FS 04] Föllmer, H., Schied, A.: Stochastic Finance, Second Edition. de Gruyter 2004

[G 87] Godefroy, G.: Boundaries of a convex set and interpolation sets. Mathematische Annalen **277**, 173-184 (1987)

[JST 05] Jouini, E., Schachermayer, W., Touzi, N.: Optimal risk sharing with *law invariant* monetary utility functions. preprint (2005)

[JN 04] Jouini, E., Napp, C.: Conditional comonotonicity. Decisions in Economics and Finance **28**, 153-166

[K 05] Krätschmer, V.: Robust representation of convex risk measures by probability measures. to appear in Finance and Stochastics (2005)

[K 01] Kusuoka, S.: On law-invariant coherent risk measures. Advances in Mathematical Economics **3**, 83-95 (2001)

[Ph 93] Phelps, R.R.: Convex functions, monotone operators and differentiability. Lecture Notes in Math. **1364**, Springer 1993

[R 97] Rockafellar, R.T.: Convex Analysis. Princeton Landmarks in Mathematics, Princeton University Press 1997

[S 72] Simons, S.: A convergence theorem with boundary. Pacific Journal of Mathematics **40**, 703-708 (1972)

Adv. Math. Econ. 9, 73–97 (2006)

Advances in
MATHEMATICAL
ECONOMICS

The dawn of modern theory of games

Mikio Nakayama*

Department of Economics, Keio University, 2-15-45 Mita, Tokyo 108-8345
(e-mail: nakayama@econ.keio.ac.jp)

Received: January 16, 2006
Revised: January 24, 2006

JEL classification: B41

Mathematics Subject Classification (2000): 91A99

Abstract. The modern theory of games initiated by John von Neumann with the minimax theorem in 1928 has now grown to be an indispensable analytical framework for social sciences, and economics in particular. In this paper, we shall review the early history of game theory from von Neumann to John F. Nash, the founder of the noncooperative game theory, including Émile Borel, Hugo Steinhaus and Oskar Morgenstern, thereby pointing out a hint of why game theory has come to be widely applied in economics.

Key words: Borel, Steinhaus, Kakutani's fixed-point theorem, Morgenstern, cooperative games, stable sets, Nash, noncooperative games, Nash equilibrium

1. Introduction

The Nobel prize of 2005 in economics was awarded to Robert J. Aumann and Thomas C. Shelling. This is the second time that the prize is awarded to game theorists since 1994 when John F. Nash, John C. Harsanyi and Reinhard Selten won the prize for the first time in game theory.

Among these laureates, John F. Nash is known as the founder of *noncooperative game theory* and appears in university undergraduate text books of economics with his noncooperative equilibrium concept, the Nash equilibrium. Harsanyi and Selten developed further to deepen and widen the basis and scope of the noncooperative theory initiated by Nash, thereby making the theory widely applicable to social sciences, especially to economics. The Nobel prize in 1994 was due to this contribution.

* The author thanks Akira Yamazaki and Toru Maruyama for helpful comments and suggestions.

This time, contribution was not solely by noncooperative game theory. In fact, Aumann's one of the earliest economic contributions [1] is on the application of *cooperative game theory* to market equilibrium, which is even earlier than major economic applications of noncooperative game theory. Therefore, we might as well expect that the Nobel prize in 2005 will trigger a wide dissemination of cooperative game theory as a fruitful analytical tool in economics for the first time sixty-one years after its birth in the book, *Theory of Games and Economic Behavior* [31].

In view of these facts, it seems worth investigating how and why the mathematical theory of games was to be born. It is commonly accepted that the modern theory of games was initiated by John von Neumann's minimax theorem [28] in 1928. But, it is also well known that earlier than von Neumann a famous mathematician, Émile Borel had written a paper on two-person zero-sum games. Why is Émile Borel not considered as the initiator of game theory? Also, a mathematician, Hugo Steinhaus studied almost in the same period a special case of a two-person zero-sum game called a persuit game. These two mathematicians, though of course with excellent talent, could not reach the minimax theorem; only von Neumann could establish the fundamental theorem. But why?

In this paper, we shall review what these mathematicians were trying to accomplish as their professional works. As mentioned above, modern theory of games consists of noncooperative theory and cooperative theory. The cooperative game theory was initiated by von Neumann and an economist, Oskar Morgenstern in 1944. We will see that game theory established by von Neumann and Morgenstern, in particular, is not merely an application of mathematics to social sciences, but rather, an attempt to build a formal basis to study social sciences in the same degree of rigor as in mathematics. Also, we will realize that Nash's noncooperative game theory is not just a mathematical exercise, but a methodological innovation for social sciences, and economics in particular.

We will first review what was going on around the minimax theorem. The most dramatic event would be the debate in *Econometrica* between Maurice Fréchet and von Neumann on who first created the theory of games [9]. Fréchet asserted that Émile Borel was the initiator, but von Neumann decisively refuted this. We also review Steinhaus's two-person game and the game of fair division, whose solution was due to B. Knaster and S. Banach noted in Steinhaus [40]. This problem was later formulated as a formal game by Harold Kuhn [13].

In a closely related model to the minimax theorem, von Neumann contributed to central economic theory by the article, "Über ein Ökonomisches Gleichungssystem und ein Verallgemeinerung des Brouwerschen Fixpunktsatzes." This paper is well known also by the lemma that led to Kakutani's fixed point theorem [11].

Finally, we shall review the original work made by John F. Nash ([23, 24, 25]), emphasizing in particular his farsightedness of future developments of noncooperative games related to the now important issue of bounded rationality.

2. Minimax theorem

2.1 Minimax theorem and mixed strategies

To begin with, we shall review von Neumann's minimax theorem and Morgenstern's idea of probabilistic decisions, i.e., the idea of *mixed strategies*.

A two-person zero-sum game is represented by $\Gamma = (N, X, Y, g)$ where

- $N = \{1, 2\}$: the set of players
- $X = \{x_1, \ldots, x_{\Sigma_1}\}$: a finite set of *pure* strategies x of player 1
- $Y = \{y_1, \ldots, y_{\Sigma_2}\}$: a finite set of *pure* strategies of player 2
- $g\colon X \times Y \to R$: the payoff function of player 1
- $-g\colon X \times Y \to R$: the payoff function of player 2

Example 2.1. The so-called *Morra*, or also called *gangster baccarat*, or *Paper, Stone, Scissors*:

$$\begin{aligned} \Sigma_1 = \Sigma_2 = 3, \quad & g(1,1) = 0, && g(1,2) = 1, && g(1,3) = -1,\\ & g(2,1) = -1, && g(2,2) = 0, && g(2,3) = 1,\\ & g(3,1) = 1, && g(3,2) = -1, && g(3,3) = 0. \end{aligned}$$

$$\begin{pmatrix} 0 & 1 & -1 \\ -1 & 0 & 1 \\ 1 & -1 & 0 \end{pmatrix}$$

Definition 2.1. *A mixed strategy of player 1 is an element ξ of the set*

$$\{\xi \mid \xi_1 + \cdots + \xi_{\Sigma_1} = 1,\ \xi_1 \geq 0, \ldots, \xi_{\Sigma_1} \geq 0\}.$$

The mixed strategy of player 2 η is defined similarly.

Definition 2.2. *The payoff $h(\xi, \eta)$ to player 1 for the strategy pair (ξ, η) is given by*

$$h(\xi, \eta) = \sum_{x=1}^{\Sigma_1} \sum_{y=1}^{\Sigma_2} g(x, y) \xi_x \eta_y$$

Theorem 2.1 (Minimax Theorem). *In two-person zero sum games,*

$$\mathrm{Max}_\xi \, \mathrm{Min}_\eta \, h(\xi, \eta) = \mathrm{Min}_\eta \, \mathrm{Max}_\xi \, h(\xi, \eta).$$

Remark 2.1. The inequality

$$\mathrm{Max}_\xi \, \mathrm{Min}_\eta \, h(\xi, \eta) \leq \mathrm{Min}_\eta \, \mathrm{Max}_\xi \, h(\xi, \eta)$$

is obvious.

The minimax theorem has been proved in many ways by topological ones using fixed point theorems e.g., von Neumann [30], convex analyses using separation theorems e.g., Ville [44] or completely algebraic ones e.g., Loomis [16]. The original von Neumann's proof, however, does not use the Brouwer fixed point theorem: it is a mixture of continuity and topological considerations, leading to a form of one-dimensional Kakutani's fixed point theorem which appeared ten years or more later (see also Myerson [19]).

The minimax theorem was believed by the founder to open the new way of mathematics for economics. But Paul Samuelson noted the opposite view:

> When he claimed it meant economics had to find a completely new mathematics, I objected, saying that it sounded to me like constrained maximization theory á la Newton and Weierstrass (and, one would add today, Kuhn and Tucker). Von Neumann retorted belligerently, 'Will you bet a cigar on that?' ... After these many decades, I claim one cigar. [35]

After the World War II, proofs via the linear programming (LP) approach appeared; and hence, Samuelson's claim.

The concept of mixed strategies in its rigorous form was first defined by Émile Borel [4] as early as 1921. Oskar Morgenstern [20]also developed the idea of mixed strategies in 1928 in an informal form of the *Sherlock Holmes story* and later talked this story in the Colloquium held by K. Menger. Morgenstern writes in [21]

> ... after the meeting broke up, a mathematician named Eduard Čech came up to me and said that the questions I had raised were identical with those dealt with by John von Neumann in a paper on the Theory of Games published in 1928, the same year that I had published my book on economic forecasting.

This is the first time that Morgenstern knew the name, von Neumann, but they did not meet until 1939 in Princeton.

The paper on minimax theorem [28] is not just a paper proving a new theorem; but rather, an attempt to build a rigorous base allowing formal analyses on rational behavior of economic agents, which can also be seen by the following quote from Punzo [33]:

> The Viennese group and von Neumann were working at the implementation of a scientific programme and not just on the solution

of a logico-mathematical puzzle. They were striving to develope a syntax of formal rules for model building which would be appropriate to economics.

Just like the work *Mathematische Grundlagen der Quantenmechanik* [29] was an attempt to formalize the new physics at that time,[1] therefore, this paper and later book *Theory of Games and Economic Behavior* [31] joint with Oskar Morgenstern should be viewed as attempts to build a rigorous framework for social sciences, especially for economics.

2.2 Zermelo's theorem

We state here the so called Zermelo's theorem [46] in 1913 following the tradition of game theory. Von Neumann and Morgenstern exhibited in their book [31] the content of the following theorem as an application of the minimax theorem without referring to Zermelo. Later, this theorem is restated by Aumann [2] as Zermelo's theorem [2].

Theorem 2.2. *In chess, either white can force a win, or black can force a win, or both can force at least a draw.*

This theorem can be expressed in the following two-person zero-sum game $\Gamma = (N, X, Y, g)$:

player's strategy: Player i's strategy is a plan of moves against every conceivable contingency in the game. The number of strategies of a player in chess is finite, though very large.

The payoff function of Γ is defined by

player 1's payoff function:

$$g(x,y) = \begin{cases} 1 & \text{if player 1 wins} \\ -1 & \text{if player 1 looses} \\ 0 & \text{if draw occurs} \end{cases}$$

Let G be the matrix with (x, y)-element being $g(x, y)$.

---

[1] Leonard [15] notes that three papers to be contained in the book in 1932 already had appeared in 1927. Thus, the ideas of two-person zero-sum games and the axiomatization of quantum mechanics were undoubtedly developed simultaneously.

[2] Recently, Schwalbe and Walker [37] have reported that this theorem is not exactly the same to what Zermelo proved. One of the theorems proved by Zermelo states, in particular, that the number of steps needed to win from a winning position is not more than the number of positions in the game.

Player 1 can force a win: $\iff$ G has at least one row x with $g(x, y) = 1$ for all $y = 1, \ldots, \Sigma_2$.

- This x is a maximin strategy of player 1; and any y is a minimax strategy of player 2.

Player 2 can force a win: $\iff$ G has at least one column y with $g(x, y) = -1$ for all $x = 1, \ldots, \Sigma_1$

- This y is a minimax strategy of player 2; and any x is a maximin strategy of player 1.

Both can force a draw: $\iff$ G has at least one pair (x, y) with $g(x, y) = 0$ for all x and y.

- This x is a maximin strategy of player 1, and this y is a minimax strategy of player 2.

3. Émile Borel

3.1 Probability of winning

In this short paper [4], Émile Borel defined the concept of mixed strategies, and analyzed a two-person constant-sum game with payoffs being the probability of winning in the game. The game is assumed to satisfy the following properties:

- n: the number of codes (pure strategies) of each player.
- a: the probability of player 1 winning; and b that of player 2 winning, so that $a + b = 1$.
- $\begin{cases} a = 1/2 + \alpha_{ik}, \\ b = 1/2 + \alpha_{ki}, \end{cases}$ where $-1/2 \leq \alpha_{ik},\ \alpha_{ki} \leq 1/2$.
- $\alpha_{ik} + \alpha_{ki} = 0$.
- $\alpha_{ii} = 0$.

Borel then goes on to deal with the matrix by what is today called *the iterated elimination of weakly dominated strategies.*

Letting p and q be the mixed strategies of player 1 and 2 over the remaining n $(< m)$ strategies, respectively, the payoff to player 1, i.e., the probability of player 1 winning in the game is given by

$$\sum_{i=1}^{n} \sum_{k=1}^{n} \left(\frac{1}{2} + \alpha_{ik} \right) p_i q_k = \frac{1}{2} + \alpha,$$

where

$$\alpha = \sum_{i=1}^{n} \sum_{k=1}^{n} \alpha_{ik} p_i q_k.$$

The "best" strategy for player 1 is the one such that $\alpha = 0$ whatever the probabilities $q = (q_1, \ldots, q_n)$ may be. That this is the maximin strategy of player 1 should be clear. The solution is given for the case where $n = 3$.

The game of Morra can be expressed by the matrix $A = (a_{ik})$ such that $m = 3$; $\alpha_{12} = \alpha_{23} = \frac{1}{2}$, $\alpha_{13} = -\frac{1}{2}$, namely,

$$\begin{pmatrix} 1/2 & 1 & 0 \\ 0 & 1/2 & 1 \\ 1 & 0 & 1/2 \end{pmatrix}$$

which will be equivalent to the one given in Example 1.1 by the utility transformation

$$f(a_{ik}) = 2a_{ik} - 1, \qquad i,\, k = 1,\, 2,\, 3.$$

Borel says without proof that when $n > 7$, the existence of the minimax solution will be restricted only for particular values of α_{ik}'s, which clearly contradicts the minimax theorem to be appeared seven years later.

3.2 Émile Borel, initiator of game theory?

Émile Borel had begun to study the two-person zero-sum game in 1921, which is seven years earlier than von Neumann's minimax theorem. Borel published seven works or more dealing with the theory of games as listed below.

(1) "La théorie du jeu et les équation intégrales á noyau symétrique gauche," *Compte Rendus Académie des Science*, vol.173, 1304–1308 (1921).
(2) "Sur les jeu où intervient l'hasard et l'habileté des joueurs," *Association Française pour l'Advancement des Sciences*, 79–85 (1923).
(3) "Sur les jeu où intervient l'hasard et l'habileté des joueurs," *Theorie des Probabilités*, Paris: Librairie Scientifique, J. Hermann, 204–224 (1924).
(4) "Un théorem sur les systémes de formes linéaires á detérminants symétrique gauche," *Compte Rendus Académie des Science*, vol.183, 925–927, avec erratum, 996 (1926).
(5) "Algèbre et calcul des probalilités," *Compte Rendus Académie des Science*, vol.184, 52–53 (1927).
(6) *Traité du calcul des probalilités st ses applications, Applications des jeux de hasard*, Paris: GauthierVillars, vol.IV, Fascicule 2, 122 (1938).
(7) "Jeux où la psychologie joue un role fondamental," in (6) 71–87.

Maurice Fréchet [9] wrote in 1953 a letter to *Econometrica* claiming that Émile Borel should be the one to initiate the modern theory of games. The main reason is the above works on the theory of games published earlier than von Neumann's work. Being written in French, however, Fréchet says that they could not attract attention of scholars who use English in their research.

In these works, Fréchet saw that Borel clearly recognized the importance of 'the skill of the player' as well as chance. Fréchet also notes the fact that Borel indicated applications to practical problems such as the art of war and certain economic problems, which are more useful than those considered by Joseph Bertrand in his *Calcul des Probabilities*.

In addition, the main part of the commentary appears to be written under the belief that von Neumann already knew these earlier works of Borel. Fréchet points out that the concept of strategy and the timing of choosing strategies are given the same explanations by von Neumann as those given by Borel. It is only after reading von Neumann's rejoindar that he knew that von Neumann did not know the work of Borel[3].

Fréchet went on saying that the kind of minimax theorem is not new in the history of mathematics. To quote from Fréchet [9],

> I have it, ... that the same theorem and even more general theorems had been independently demonstrated by several authors well *before* the notes of Borel and the first paper of von Neumann.

The precedents that Fréchet meant are the separation theorem due to H. Minkowski and J. Farkas, and the system of linear inequalties of E. Stiemke from which the minimax theorem can be deduced.

Von Neumann [32], after having read the letter, denied this view firmly on the ground that Borel did not prove the fundamental minimax theorem, that he even believed this to be false for a large number of strategies, and that there is nothing that deserves publishing before the minimax theorem. As noted before, von Neumann did not know that Borel had begun to study the theory as early as 1921. He wrote in [32]:

> I developed my idea on the subject before I read his papers, whose negative conclusions on the decisive point (the "minimax theorem," ...) would have been primarily discouraging.

In view of the fact that von Neumann was only a student when Borel wrote the first paper on the theory, the above quote expresses a true feeling that a young student might have against already famous mathematician.

As for the view that the minimax theorem was *well-known*, he politely rejects this view saying that "It is common and tempting fallacy to view the later steps in a mathematical evolution as much more obvious and cogent after the fact than they were beforehand."

It is true that Borel had an interest in applying mathematics to military, economic and even to social problems. If his 1921–1938 works had attracted

---

[3] In the footnote 8 of 1928 paper [28], von Neumann wrote:

> While this paper was put into its final form, I learned of the note of E. Borel in the Comptes Rendus of Jan.10.1927....

world-wide attentions, he might have become the 'initiator' of, say, The Operations Research, that has been established after the World War II. But, what von Neumann aimed is not a mere application of mathematics to social problems. Being engaged himself in the programme of the formalist school, he undoubtedly aimed at formalizing or mathematizing economic and social sciences at that time, which led him to the minimax theorem, the groundwork for the rational behavior of economic agents.

4. Hugo Steinhaus (and B. Knaster, S. Banach)

Hugo Steinhaus completed his doctorate in 1911 under David Hilbert. He is remembered as a collaborator of S. Banach, but his interest extends to medicine, electricity, biology, geology and anthropology. At that time Lwów and Wroclaw have a number of excellent mathematicians such as W. Sierpinski, S. Banach, S. Ulam, K. Kratowski, etc. As far as game theory is concerned, however, Steinhaus worked in isolation being unaware of Borel and von Neumann's ongoing works.

4.1 Games of pursuit

The paper [39] was published in a journal editors of which were students of the university in Lwów, Poland. The original paper is not available now even in Polish, and the photostatic copy was provided by Polish mathematician Stan Ulam, who was a friend of von Neumann after immigrating to USA. The English translation is provided by Harold Kuhn.

The paper discusses three models of games: chess, naval pursuit and games of chance, among which we shall comment on the second one, the naval pursuit.

The model:

- A ship 1 is pursuing ship 2.
- $P_1 = (x_1, y_1)$: position of ship 1
- $P_2 = (x_2, y_2)$: position of ship 2
- $B(P_1, P_2)$: *mode* of pursuit, indicating the angle between the line of sight, connecting P_1 and P_2, and the direction of steering of pursuing ship.
- $C(P_1, P_2)$: *mode* of escape, representing the angle of escaping ship.
- the speed of each ship is given.

Let $t = F(B, C)$ be the duration of the chase from the beginning to the end of the manoeuvre. Then:

escaping ship 2's problem: Given B, find a *mode* of escape $C_0 = F_1(B)$ that gives the maximum value of t,

$$t_{max} = F(B, C_0).$$

pursuing ship 1's problem: Find a *mode* of pursuit B_0 that attains the minimum value of t,

$$t_{min} = F(B_0, F_1(B_0)).$$

solution: When the speed of the pursuing ship exceeds that of the escaping ship, a finite value of $t_{min} = t_0$ is obtained.

Remark 4.1.

$$\begin{aligned} t_0 = F(B_0, F_1(B_0)) &= \min_B F(B, F_1(B)) \\ &= \min_B \max_C F(B, C) \geq \max_C \min_B F(B, C) \\ &= \min_B F(B, C_0). \end{aligned}$$

Steinhaus wrote in the letter attached to [39] in 1925 that he did not know the above inequality holding in equality.

Remark 4.2. The problem is reminiscient of the *Stackelberg Oligopoly* in that the escaping ship is best replying to the pursuing ship, and knowing this the pursuing ship chooses it's best strategy. The only difference appears to be that the game is zero-sum.

4.2 Games of fair division

Steinhaus was also interested in games of fair division [40], which seek a fair scheme or rule to divide a fixed size of, say, a cake ([40] and [41]). Games of fair division constitute an intuitive and interesting class of games that provide prototype considerations on fairness and equity.

Below is a summary of an n-person *divide and choose* method given by B. Knaster ans S. Banach reported by Steinhaus [40].

- There is a cake to be divided for n persons $1, 2, \ldots, n$.
- 1 cuts from the cake an arbitrary part.
- 2 has then the right, but is not obliged, to diminish the slice cut.
- Whatever 2 does, 3 has the right, but is not obliged, to diminish still the already diminished or not diminished slice; and so on up to n.
- The last diminisher must take as his part the slice he was the last to touch.
- The remaining $n - 1$ persons then start the game with the remainder of the cake.
- After $n - 2$ persons are thus disposed of, the remaining two persons now apply the two-person divide-and-choose method.

Harold Kuhn reformulated in [13] the game of fair division in an extensive form and show the method to obtain the fair division by a linear programming.

In [10], a physicist *George Gamow* who is famous as an initiator of the Big Bang Theory, and Marvin Stern also tell a story of dividing a fixed amount of brandy to three glasses, extending the divide-and-choose method. The three actors are Gamow, Stern and von Kalman who is known with the *Kalman filter*. How can do you think they attain a fair division?

5. von Neumann's expanding economy model

In this section, we shall present a summary of von Neumann's *Expanding Economy Model* (EEM) [30] based on the concise introduction by Gerald L. Thompson in [43]. The model was one of the earliest general equilibrium models, first presented in the winter 1932 at the mathematical seminar of Princeton University. Later, in 1935, von Neumann was invited to talk in Karl Menger's mathematical seminar in Vienna.

Beside the economic importance, this paper contains an important lemma leading immediately to the famous Kakutani's fixed point theorem. Von Neumann called the lemma a generalized fix-point theorem, and mentioned about a *new* proof of the minimax theorem by way of this lemma.

5.1 The model

The Model:

- a closed economy with m processes and n goods.
- x_i is the *intensity* of operation of the ith process, normalized so that

$$x \geq 0 \quad \text{and} \quad xf = 1,$$

  where $f = (1, \ldots, 1) \in R^m$.
- $A = (a_{ij})$ is the *input* matrix, where a_{ij} is the units of good j required in the process i operating with intensity 1.
- $B = (b_{ij})$ is the *output* matrix, where b_{ij} is the units of good j produced by the process i operating with intensity 1.
- one period production is represented by

$$(\text{time } t-1) \ xA \rightarrow xB \ (\text{time } t)$$

- y_j is a nonnegative price of good j, normalized so that

$$y \geq 0 \text{ and } ey = 1,$$

  where $e = (1, \ldots, 1) \in R^n$.

- one period change in prices is represented by

$$(\text{time } t-1)\ Ay \to By\ (\text{time } t),$$

where the components of Ay give the values of the inputs, and the components of By give the values of the outputs.
- An interest rate b from which the *interest factor*

$$\beta = 1 + \frac{b}{100}$$

is derived.
- An expansion rate a from which the *expansion factor*

$$\alpha = 1 + \frac{a}{100}$$

is derived.

The Axioms of EEM:

Axiom 1: $xB \geq \alpha xA$
i.e., the inputs cannot exceed the outputs from the preceeding period.
Axiom 2: $By \leq \beta Ay$
i.e., the value of outputs must not exceed the value of the inputs
Axiom 3: $x(B - \alpha A)y = 0$
i.e., overproduced goods become free goods, so that prices must be zero.
Axiom 4: $x(B - \beta A)y = 0$
i.e., unprofitable processes must not be used, so that of intensity zero.
Axiom 5: $xBy > 0$
i.e., total values of all goods produced must be positive.

Assumption 5.1. $A + B > 0$

Therefore, every process either uses as an input or produces as an output some amount of every good.

Theorem 5.1. *Under these axioms and the assumption, there exists a solution* (x, y) *and a unique value* α *and* β *with* $\alpha = \beta$.

Thompson [43] gives an LP formulation of the solution of EEM as follows. Let

$$M_\alpha = B - \alpha A$$

and let E be the $m \times n$ matrix with all entries 1. Then:

$$\begin{array}{ll} \min xf & \max ey \\ \text{s.t. } x(M_\alpha + E) \geq e & \text{s.t. } (M_\alpha + E)y \leq f \\ x \geq 0 & y \geq 0 \end{array}$$

It is easy to see that the matrix game M_α has a value zero iff $xf = ey = 1$, and the value of the game M_α is zero iff (x, y, α, β) satisfies these axioms. Therefore, finding the solution of EEM reduces to the problem of finding the parameter α for which the solution of the LP problem yields $xf = ey = 1$.

5.2 Champernowne's critique

Champernowne published a critique in [5] that can be summarized as follows.

(1) That $A+B > 0$ implies that every good must be an input or an output of every process. Hence, the good expanding at the lowest rate determines the overall rate of expansion, which is unnatural.
(2) In the model, the workers' consumption are confined to subsistence level, and the processes must be operating with zero profits, the properties class save all their income and the working class consume all of theirs.
(3) The condition that excess production leads to free goods is unnatural.
(4) That there is no resource constraints is not a justifiable assumption.

Taking the Champernowne's criticizm seriously, J.G. Kemeny, Morgenstern and Thompson [12], and Morgenstern and Thompson [22] have remedied and generalized the EEM.

5.3 Von Neumann's lemma and Kakutani's fixed point theorem

To prove the existence of an equilibrium, von Neumann provided a lemma, which was to be reformulated by Sizuo Kakutani as a famous fixed point theorem [11]. To quote von Neumann from the Introduction in [30]:

> The Mathematical proof is possible only by means of a generalization of Brouwer's Fix-Point Theorem, i.e., by the use of very fundamental *topological* facts. This generalized fix-point theorem (the "lemma" of paragraph 7) is also interesting in itself.

Von Neumann also pointed out in the footnote on page 5 that the minimax theorem can be proved in a *new way* from this lemma.

We shall state this lemma as faithfully to the original as possible to get a flavor of the genious's way of presentation.

> Let R^m be the m dimensional space of all points $x = (x_1, \ldots, x_m)$, R^n the n dimensional space of all points $y = (y_1, \ldots, y_n)$, R^{m+n} the $m + n$ dimensional space of all points $(x, y) = (x_1, \ldots, x_m, y_1, \ldots, y_n)$.
>
> A set (in R^m or R^n or R^{m+n}) which is *not empty, convex closed and bounded* we call a set C.

Let S°, T° be sets C in R^m and R^n respectively, and let $S^\circ \times T^\circ$ be the set of all (x, y) in R^{m+n} where the range of x is S° and the range of y is T°. Let V, W be two closed subsets of $S^\circ \times T^\circ$. For every x in S° let the set $Q(x)$ of all y with (x, y) in V be a set C; for each y in T° let the set $P(y)$ of all x with (x, y) in W be a set C. Then the following lemma applies.

Lemma 5.1 (Von Neumann 1932 at Princeton).
Under the above assumptions, V, W have (at least) one point in common.

Our problem follows by putting $S^\circ = S$, $T^\circ = T$ and $V =$ the set of all $(x, y) = (x_1, \ldots, x_m, y_1, \ldots, y_n)$ fulfilling Axiom 1, $W =$ the set of all $(x, y) = (x_1, \ldots, x_m, y_1, \ldots, y_n)$ fulfilling Axiom 2. It can be easily seen that V, W are closed and that the sets $S^\circ = S$, $T^\circ = T$, $Q(x)$, $P(y)$ are all simplices, i.e., sets C. The common points of these V, W are, of course, our required solutions $(x, y) = (x_1, \ldots, x_m, y_1, \ldots, y_n)$.

Theorem 5.2 (Kakutani's fixed point theorem 1941). *Let X be a compact convex subset of R^n and let $f\colon X \to X$ be a set-valued function for which*

- *for all $x \in X$ the set $f(x)$ is nonempty and convex*
- *the graph of f is closed, i.e.,*

$$x_n \to x,\ y_n \to y \text{ and } \forall n\ y_n \in f(x_n) \Rightarrow y \in f(x).$$

Then there exists $x^* \in X$ such that $x^* \in f(x^*)$.

To see that the Kakutani's fixed point theorem is a generalization of the above lemma of von Neumann, let us define the correspondence

$$F\colon S^\circ \times T^\circ \to S^\circ \times T^\circ$$

by

$$F(x, y) = P(y) \times Q(x), \qquad \forall (x, y) \in S^\circ \times T^\circ.$$

By assumption $S^\circ \times T^\circ$ is nonempty, convex and compact. F is nonempty, convex-valued by assumption, and closed because V and W are closed subsets of $S^\circ \times T^\circ$, and

$$P(y) = \{x \mid (x, y) \in W\} \quad \text{and} \quad Q(x) = \{y \mid (x, y) \in V\}.$$

6. Influences of von Neumann on economics

The minimax theorem and the solution to EEM are both related to the linear programming (LP) model. The *symplex method* for computing the solution of an LP model was established by George Dantzig in 1951 [6], who was a student of *Albert Tucker*. But, the first statement of the *duality principle* of LP was given by von Neumann's mimeograph in 1947. The LP model influenced Dorfman, Samuelson and Solow to write a book [8] in 1958.

Thompson [43] tries to measure the von Neumann's influences on economics by examining the work of Nobel laureates in economics: included are Arrow, Debreu, Kantrovich, Koopmans, Samuelson and Solow. We must add to this list John Forbes Nash and the most recent, Robert J. Aumann.

Also, his influence is seen in the fields of Operations Resaerch, Management Sciences, Statistics (Abraham Wald's contribution [45]), computer sciences or even in biology. Thompson [43] calls the new (for the time) economics based on mathematical programming and computation, the mathematical programming economics, and call von Neumann the initiator of this field.

7. N-person cooperative games

7.1 Coalitional games

In this monumental book [31], von Neumann and Morgenstern developed the theory of two-person zero-sum games together with an elementary proof of the minimax theorem, and the theory of n-person cooperative games. The essential difference arisen when considering n-person situations is, to them, the possibility of forming coalitions. Cooperation is described by a coalition of players.

Let $N = \{1, 2, \ldots, n\}$ be the set of players. Then any nonempty subset S of N is called a coalition. The basic apparatus in their cooperative game theory is the *characteristic function* v that describes for each coalition S the 'worth' or 'power' $v(S)$ the coalition acquires as the minimax value of the two-person zero-sum game between the coalition S and its complementary coalition $N \setminus S$. In this way, a *constant-sum* n-person cooperative game (N, v) can be defined, and this was later extended to be non constant-sum.

As the solution of the cooperative game, they defined the *stable sets*, which is a set of payoffs to the players with appropriate stability. They interpreted a stable set as a *standard of behavior* that is logically consistent with rational behavior. This is a solution concept quite unfamiliar in its form in the history of mathematics as reviewed below.

7.2 Stable sets

Given a cooperative game (N, v), the vector $x = (x_1, \ldots, x_n) \in R^n$ is called *an imputation* if it satisfies

total rationality: $\sum_{i \in N} x_i = v(N)$
individual rationality: $x_i \geq v(\{i\}), \quad \forall i \in N$

Let A be the set of imputations. For any x, $y \in A$ and $S \subseteq N$, we define consecutively as follows:

(1) $x \operatorname{dom}_S y \iff \sum_{i \in N} x_i \leq v(S)$, and $x_i > y_i \quad \forall i \in S$.
(2) $\operatorname{Dom}_S x = \{y \mid y \in A,\ x \operatorname{dom}_S y\}$
(3) $\operatorname{Dom} x = \bigcup_{S \subseteq N} \operatorname{Dom}_S x$
(4) For $K \subseteq A$,
  a) $\operatorname{Dom}_S K = \bigcup_{x \in K} \operatorname{Dom}_S x$
  b) $\operatorname{Dom} K = \bigcup_{S \subseteq N} \operatorname{Dom}_S K$

Definition 7.1. *$K \subseteq A$ is called a stable set if*

$$K = A \setminus \operatorname{Dom} K.$$

Thus, a stable set K is the set of all imputations which are not dominated by any imputation in K.

Remark 7.1. K is a stable set $\iff$

internal stability: x, $y \in K \Rightarrow \neg[x \operatorname{dom} y]$
external stability: $z \notin K \Rightarrow \exists x \in K\ [x \operatorname{dom} z]$

Definition 7.2. *The set $C = \{x \in A \mid \nexists z \in A\ [z \operatorname{dom} x]\}$ is called the core of a game.*

Remark 7.2. $C \subseteq K$ for all stable sets K.

The word *core* was not used in the book, though the core is the central solution concept in the cooperative game theory today. It might be true that since the core is frequently empty, von Neumann as a mathematician avoided to take the risk that a solution may not exist. However, 25 years later, William F. Lucas presented in 1969 a ten-person game without stable sets [17].

7.3 Stable sets of zero-sum three person games

As an example, they computed the stable sets in a game called a *majority game* with three players.

$$v(\{1,2,3\}) = v(\{1,2\}) = v(\{1,3\}) = v(\{2,3\}) = 1;$$
$$v(\{i\}) = 0, \qquad i \in \{1,2,3\}$$

objective solution: $K = \{(\frac{1}{2}, \frac{1}{2}, 0), (\frac{1}{2}, 0, \frac{1}{2}), (0, \frac{1}{2}, \frac{1}{2})\}$
discriminatory solution: $K_i(c)$, for $0 \leq c < \frac{1}{2}$ and $i = 1, 2, 3$, where

$$K_i(c) = \{x \in A \mid x_i = c,\ x_j + x_k = 1 - c\},$$

and $\{i, j, k\} = \{1, 2, 3\}$.

The discriminatory solution describes the situation in which one player is assigned a payoff less than $1/2$, and the other two players divide the rest in any way they wish. Being a standard of behavior, such a discrimination is consistent with a rational social behavior. Note that the discriminatory solution is a continuum, and the number of discriminatory solutions are also uncountable.

Von Neumann was quite impressed by the social meaning the stable set may have in spite of the fact that it is defined solely by the mathematical consideration. Martin Shubik notes, on the train from New York to Princeton in 1952, that when he asked von Neumann as to the noncooperative game by Nash, "He (von Neumann) indicated ... that a cooperative theory made more social sense" [38].

7.4 One seller and two buyers

The next example is an economic application of stable sets presented for the first time in the history of economics, describing not only competitive trades but also a collusive behavior of buyers in order to reduce the price.

- player A: the seller of a house with value a
- player B: buyer with evaluation b
- player C: buyer with evaluation c
- Assumption: $0 < a < b \leq c$

$v(\{A\}) = a$; $v(\{B\}) = v(\{C\}) = 0$; $v(\{A, B\}) = b$; $v(\{A, C\}) = c$; $v(\{B, C\}) = 0$; $v(\{A, B, C\}) = c$.

A typical stable set K is given as follows.

$$K = \{(p, 0, c - p) \mid b \leq p \leq c\}$$
$$\cup \{(p, d(p), c - p - d(p)) \mid a \leq p \leq b,\ d(p) = 0 \text{ if } p = b\},$$

where the curve DYE with points $(p, d(p), c - p - d(p))$ go down within 30 degrees relative to the vertical direction. Note that point Y is dominated by points z or z′, but these points are in turn dominated by point w on the curve, which shows the external stability.

The payoff $d(p)$ is a compensation paid from player C to B with which player B ceases to be a competitor of player C. Note that the segment

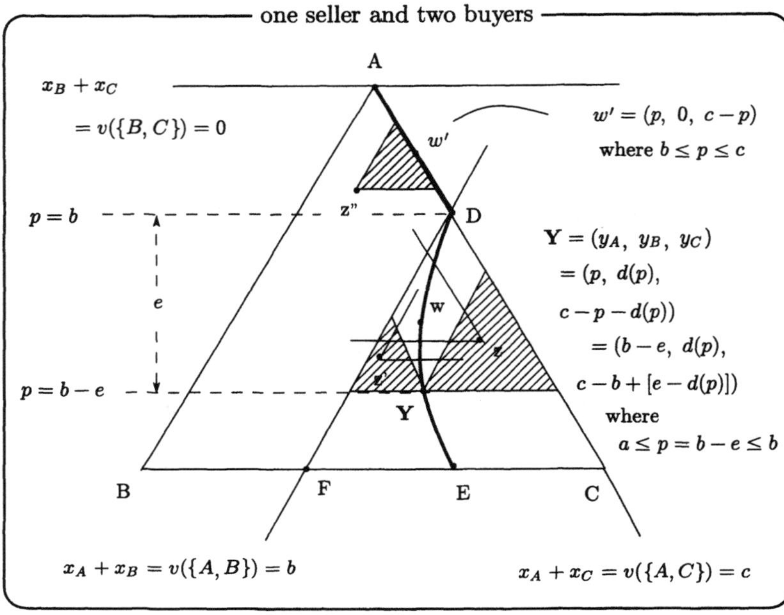

AD $= [(c, 0, 0), (b, 0, c - b)]$ is the core of the game and contained in every one of infinite number of stable sets.

The competitive trade is a usual economic behavior that every solution should describe. But no economic solution was known at that time that would describe both the competitive and collusive trade as a coherent result of rational behavior.

This analysis does not lose its relevance even today when viewing the trade as one between the public agency and two construction companies. Collusion is in fact a 'standard' of behavior[4].

7.5 A missing axiom?

Implicit in the theory of cooperative games is an assumption that players can make a *binding agreement*. Due to this assumption, any coalition can be formed once players agree to do so. Von Neumann and Morgenstern clearly recognized the necessity of this assumption and an axiom to obtain the binding agreement as a rule of a game [31]:

> Two players who wish to collaborate must get together on this subject before the play, i.e., outside game. The player who lives up

[4] Hiroshi Okuda, the president of Nippon Keidanren spoke in TV that collusion is a part of culture.

> to his agreement must possess the conviction that the partner too will do likewise. As long as we are concerned only with the rules of the game, we are in no position to judge what the basis for such a conviction may be. In other words what, if anything, enforces the "sanctity" of such agreements? ... On a later occasion we propose to investigate what theoretical structures are required in order to eliminate these concepts. (I.e., auxiliary concepts such as "agreements", "understandings", etc.)

As stated in the quote, von Neumann and Morgenstern promised to propose "what theoretical structures are required in order to eliminate these concepts." However, this promise was not fulfilled at least in the book [31].

It may be due to this lack of structures that cooperative game theory today is still not a major analytical tool for economics compared to noncooperative game theory initiated by John F. Nash.

8. John F. Nash and the noncooperative game theory

Before 1950, game theory was meant by the two-person zero-sum game and the n-person cooperative game established in the book *Theory of Games and Economic Behavior* [31]. But, by May of 1950, there appeared the theory of games with n players acting independently; that is, the theory of *noncooperative games* submitted by John Nash to Princeton University as a doctoral thesis. In this theory, players do not form coalitions, and the payoff to each player is explicitly dependent of strategies of all the players. The solution of the game is a profile of strategies of all players such that the payoff to each player does not increase by a unilateral change of the strategy. The solution, now called the *Nash equilibrium*, is not only a generalization of the solution to the two-person zero-sum game, but also has become an indispensable tool in recent economic analyses. The Nobel prize of 1994 no doubt implies the contribution to economics of the theory of noncooperative games founded by Nash.

Owing to the Nobel prize, there are several excellent commentaries on Nash's work beginning from "The Work of John Nash in Game Theory" in *Journal of Economic Theory* vol.69 (1996), Myerson's paper [19], Introduction by Binmore [27] or more recent book "the essential JOHN NASH" edited by H.W. Kuhn and S. Nasar [14], and so on. Therefore, we shall review only briefly including the idea of evolutionary approach to equilibrium.

8.1 Bargaining problem, noncoopertive games and two-person cooperative games

The first academic publication is

- The Bargaining Problem, *Econometrica* **18**, 155–162 (1950),

in which a unique solution to the two-person bargaining problem including the bilateral monopoly as a special case is proposed. The solution is sometimes called the "Nash product maximization" because it maximizes the product of the payoff to each player measured from the given *threat point*. The game form is not in strategic form, nor in the characteristic function form, but presented in the axiomatic approach just like the utility theory of von Neumann and Morgenstern in [31]. This is the work when Nash was still in his teens, and is the first solution to the problem of bilateral monopoly studied unsuccessfully by famous economists such as Hicks and Edgeworth.

The theory of *noncooperative games* was introduced in the doctoral thesis mentioned above and published as

- Equilibrium Points in N-Person Games, *Proceedings of the National Academy of Sciences* **36**, 48–49 (1950).
- Non-cooperative Games, *Annals of Mathematics* **54(2)**, 286–295 (1951).

The former is only of 1 page long, and basic concepts of noncooperative games are stated informally but rigorously including the existence proof of the equilibrium point by Kakutani's fixed point theorem. In the latter, the noncooperative game is defined formally, and the equilibrium existence proof is presented by using Brouwer's fixed point theorem, which is much more ellegant and transparent than the original PhD's version.

The third category of games that Nash presented is the two-person cooperative game that von Neumann and Morgenstern only insufficiently dealt with.

- Two-Person Cooperative Games, *Econometrica* **21**, 128–140 (1953).

In this paper, the bargaining problem is reformulated as a two-stage game in a strategic form consisting of the "threat stage" and the subsequent "demand stage," thereby obtaining the solution corresponding to the Nash product maximization as a unique equilibrium point of the game possessing the saddle point property. Thus, this is a beautiful generalization of the minimax theorem. Moreover, this work is not just a reformulation of the bargaining problem, but is an illustration of his proposal that a cooperative game should be formulated as a strategic noncooperative game and the solution be analyzed by its equilibrium point. This doctrine is now well known as the *Nash Program*, and it can be said that the Nobel prize in 1994 is awarded to the Nash program initiated by Nash and promoted by Reinhard Selten and John C. Harsanyi.

8.2 Evolutionary views of the equilibrium point

The PhD thesis contains an interpretation of Nash equilibria in terms of bounded rational plays of the game. To quote from the Introduction by Binmore [27]:

> We shall now take up the 'mass-action' interpretation of equilibrium points. .... It is unnecessary to assume that the participants have full knowledge of the total structure of the game, or the ability and inclination to go through any complex reasoning processes. But the participants are supposed to accumulate empirical information on the relative advantages of the various pure strategies at their disposal.

With these boundedly rational players, Nash develops the idea that each of the n players is randomly chosen from each of n populations, and by learning the empirical distribution of each n tuple of pure strategies, i.e., by learning a mixed strategy, each player may choose a pure strategy best replying the mixed strategy. This argument is now known as the 'fictitious play,' that is originally used as a heuristic algorithm to compute Nash equilibria. Incidentally, the paper by Robinson [34] which is just after the Nash's paper in the *Annals of Mathematics* dealt with the fictious play computation of the saddle point of two-person zero-sum games.

Another point that would be related to evolutionary argument is the mapping he constructed in proving the existence of equilibrium points by Brouwer's fixed point theorem. For any $s = (p, q) \in S_1 \times S_2$ the mapping from $S_1 \times S_2$ to itself is given by

$$p'_i = \frac{p_i + c_i(s)}{1 + \sum_{k=1}^{m} c_k(s)}, \quad q'_j = \frac{q_j + d_j(s)}{1 + \sum_{k=1}^{n} d_k(s)}$$

where

$$\begin{aligned} c_i(s) &= \max(A_i.q^T - pAq^T, 0), && i = 1, \ldots, m; \\ d_j(s) &= \max(pB._j - pBq^T, 0), && j = 1, \ldots, n. \end{aligned}$$

Here, $c_i(s)$ describes pure strategy i's relative advantage over the current mixed strategy p against the opponent's mixed strategy q. If this advantage is positive, then the mapping may increase the probability for the pure strategy i. This is quite reminiscent ofthe *replicator dynamic* with respect to which strict Nash equilibria can be asymptotically stable.

8.3 Nash's comments on the experiment

In the early 1950s, Melvin Dresher and Merrill Flood conducted an experiment to examine whether or not people do play the Nash equilibrium in the game given below.

	d	c
c	$-1,\ 2$	$0.5,\ 1$
d	$0,\ 0.5$	$1,\ -1$

This game is the original form of what we now know as the *Prisoners' Dilemma* being named by Albert W. Tucker. The Nash equilibrium is of course (d, d). However, the result of the experiment seemed to disprove the Nash equilibrium in that the average payoff in 100 times repetition was 0.4 for player 1 and 0.65 for player 2. They concluded therefore that people may behave to 'split the difference' in such a situation.

Being asked to comment on the result, Nash replied essentially as follows (see A. Roth's paper [36]):

(1) Repetition makes the game different from the original one-shot game, so that the test is inadequate.
(2) In the repeated game, the result is better approximated by the strategy what we now know as the *trigger strategy.*
(3) 100 times repetition is a situation that is difficult to apply the *backward induction.*
(4) If the experiment was conducted with randomly chosen pair of players and without any information of what actions were taken by the opponent, some intereting result would obtain.

Each of these comments is still quite interesting today. It is not clear whether or not the theory of repeated games was already established when these comments were made. Nevertheless, the first comment is correct, and the second comment would suggest that Nash knew the result of what we now know as *Folk Theorem.* The third comment points out that real players are of bounded rationality, so that it should be interesting if the game is played under the condition of what we now call evolutionary. Such an experiment was in fact conducted 30 years or more later by Robert Axelrod [3] as the computer tournament of the Prisoner's Dilemma.

In view of these comments and the interpretation of equilibrium points, the initiator of the noncooperative game theory not only initiate the theory, but from the outset saw the direction of the theory that in fact has evolved until today.

9. Concluding remarks

We have seen that famous mathematicians like Émile Borel and Hugo Steinhaus had studied a two-person game theory before the minimax theorem. Around 1928, von Neumann himself engaged also in the work of formalizing the seemingly chaotic quantum mechanics, the papers on which were to be synthesized into the 'Bible,' *Mathematische Grundlagen der Quantenmechanik* in 1932.

While Borel and Steinhaus had strong interest in applying mathematics to military or social problems, von Neumann's aim was not just applying mathematics, but mathematizing the basis of social sciences paralleled by the above project on physics. The book, *Theory of Games and Economic Behavior* [31] published in 1944 resulted by the collaboration with Oskar Morgenstern therefore should be viewed as an attempt to formalize the social science.

In view of the state of economic theory today, von Neumann's 'program' to formalize social sciences appears to have been partially fulfilled, but not directly by his own theory. We may therefore wish to expect the Robert Aumann's winning the Nobel prize to be the beginning of formalization by the full game theory; that is, by cooperative game theory as well as noncooperative game theory.

References

[1] Aumann, R.J.: Markets with a continuum of traders. Econometrica **32**, 39-50 (1964)

[2] Aumann, R.J.: Lectures on Game Theory. Westview Press 1989

[3] Axelrod, R.: The Evolution of Cooperation. Basic Books 1984

[4] Borel, É.: La théorie du jeu et les équations intégrales à noyau symétrique. Comptes Rendus Hebdomadaires des Séances de l'Academie des Sciences **173**, 1304-1308 (1921). English Translation (Savage, L.J.): The theory of play and integral equations with skew symmetric kernels. Econometrica **21**, 97-100 (1953)

[5] Champernowne, D.G.: A note on J. von Neumann's article. Review of Economic Studies **13**, 10-18 (1945-6)

[6] Dantzig, G.B.: Programming of interdependent activities II. mathematical model. Econometrica **17**, 200-211 (1951)

[7] Dantzig, G.B.: Constructive proof of the mini-max theorem. Pacific Journal of Mathematics **6**, 25-33 (1956)

[8] Dorfman, R., Samuelson, P.A., Solow, R.M.: Linear Programming and Economic Analysis. McGraw-Hill 1958

[9] Fréchet, M.: Émile Borel, Initiator of the theory of psychological games and its application. Econometrica **21**, 95-99, 118-24 (1953)

[10] Gamow, G., Stern, M.: Puzzle-Math. The Viking Press, USA 1958. Japanese Translation (Yura, T.): Kazu ha Majutsu-shi. Hakuyosha 1958

[11] Kakutani, S.: A generalization of Brouwer's fixed point theorem. Duke Mathematical Journal **8**, 457-459 (1941)

[12] Kemeny, J.G., Morgenstern, O., Thompson, G.L.: A generalization of von Neumann's model of an expanding economy. Econometrica **24**, 115-135 (1956)

[13] Kuhn, H.W.: On games of fair division. In: Essays in Mathematical Economics in Honor of Oskar Morgenstern (Shubik, M. ed.). Princeton University Press 1967

[14] Kuhn, H.W., Nasar, S.: The Essential John Nash. Princeton University Press 2002

[15] Leonard, R.J.: Creating a context for game theory. In: Toward a History of Game Theory (Weintraub, E.R. ed.). Duke University Press 1992

[16] Loomis, L.H.: On a theorem of von Neumann. Proceedings of the National Academy of Sciences **32**, 213-215 (1946)

[17] Lucas, W.F.: The proof that a game may not have a solution. Transactions of the American Mathematical Society **137**, 219-229 (1969)

[18] Mirowski, P.: What were von Neumann and Morgenstern trying to accomplish? In: Toward a History of Game Theory (Weintraub, E.R. ed.). Duke University Press, 1992
[19] Myerson, R.B.: Nash equilibrium and the history of economic theory. Journal of Economic Literature **37**, 1067-1082 (1999)
[20] Morgenstern, O.: Wirtschaftsprognose: Eine Untersuchung ihrer Voraussetzungen und Möglichkeiten. Julius Springer, Wien 1928
[21] Morgenstern, O.: The collaboration between Oskar Morgenstern and John von Neumann on the theory of games. Journal of Economic Literature **14**, 805-816 (1976)
[22] Morgenstern, O., Thompson, G.L.: Mathematical Theory of Expanding and Contracting Economies. Heath-Lexington, Boston 1976
[23] Nash, J.F.: The Bargaining Problem. Econometrica **18**, 155-162 (1950)
[24] Nash, J.F.: Equilibrium points in n-person games. Proceedings of the National Academy of Sciences **36**, 48-49 (1950)
[25] Nash, J.F.: Non-cooperative games. Annals of Mathematics **54**, 286-295 (1951)
[26] Nash, J.F.: Two-Person Cooperative Games. Econometrica **21**, 128-140 (1953)
[27] Nash, J.F.: Esseys on Game Theory (introduced by K. Binmore). Edward Elgar, UK 1996
[28] von Neumann, J.: Zur theorie der gesellschaftsspiele. Mathematische Annalen **100**, 295-320 (1928). English translation: In: Contributions to the Theory of Games IV (Tucker, A.W. et al. eds.). Annals of Mathematics Studies **40**, 1959
[29] von Neumann, J.: Mathematische Grundlagen der Quantenmechanik. Springer-Verlag, Berlin 1932
[30] von Neumann, J.: Über ein ökonomisches gleichungssystem und ein verallgemeinerung des Brouwerschen fixpunktsatzes. Ergebnisse eines Mathematischen Kolloquiums **8**, 1937. English translation: A model of general equilibrium. Review of Economic Studies **13**, 1-9 (1945)
[31] von Neumann, J., Morgenstern, O.: Theory of Games and Economic Behavior. Princeton University Press 1944
[32] von Neumann, J.: Communications on the Borel Notes. Econometrica **21**, 124-125 (1953)
[33] Punzo, L.F.: Von Neumann and Karl Menger's mathematical colloquium. In: John von Neumann and Modern Economics (Dore, M. et al. eds.). Oxford University Press 1989
[34] Robinson, J.: An iterative method of solving a game. Annals of Mathematics **54**, 296-301 (1951)
[35] Samuelson, P.A.: A revisionist view of von Neumann's growth model. In: John von Neumann and Modern Economics (Dore, M. et al. eds.). Oxford University Press 1989
[36] Roth, A.E.: The early history of experimental economics. Journal of the History of Economic Thought **15**, 184-209 (1993)
[37] Schwalbe, U., Walker, P.P.: Zermelo and the early history of game theory. Games and Economic Behavior **34**, 123-137 (2001)
[38] Shubik, M.: Game theory at Princeton, 1949-1955: a personal peminiscence. In: Toward a History of Game Theory (Weintraub, E.R. ed.). Duke University Press 1992
[39] Steinhaus, H.: Definitions for a theory of games and pursuit. Mysl Akademicka **1**, 13-14 (1925). English translation (Kuhn, H.): In: Naval Research Logistics Quarterly **7.2**, 105-108 (1959)

[40] Steinhaus, H.: Sur la division pragmatique. Econometrica **17** (supplement), 315-319 (1949)
[41] Steinhaus, H. Mathematical Snapshots, 2nd edition. Oxford University Press, New York 1960
[42] Suzuki, M.: Introduction to Game Theory (in Japanese). Kyouritsu Shuppan 1981
[43] Thompson, G.: Jonn von Neumann's contributions to mathematical programming economics. In: John von Neumann and Modern Economics (Dore, M. et al. eds.). Oxford University Press, 1989
[44] Ville, J.: Sur la théorie générale des jeux où intervient l'habilité des joueurs. In: Traité du Calcul des Probabilités et ses Applications Volume IV, (Borel, É. et al. eds.). pp.105-113, Gautier-Villars, Paris 1938
[45] Wald, A.: Statistical Decision Functions. John Wiley & Sons, New York 1950
[46] Zermelo, E.: Über eine anwendung der mengenlehre auf die theorie des schachspiels. Proceedings of the Fifth International Congress of Mathematicians **2**, 501-504 (1913)

Adv. Math. Econ. 9, 99–107 (2006)

Advances in
MATHEMATICAL
ECONOMICS

Approximation of excess demand on the boundary and equilibrium price set*

Manabu Toda†

School of Social Sciences, Waseda University, 169-8050, Tokyo, Japan.
(e-mail: mtoda@waseda.jp)

Received: December 1, 2004
Revised: January 6, 2005

JEL classification: D50

Mathematics Subject Classification (2000): 91B50

Abstract. When preferences may not be homothetic but satisfy other regularity conditions such as monotonicity, the market excess demand function is characterized by continuity and Walras' law on almost entire region of the price simplex. In particular, Mas-Colell (1977) shows that for a continuous function f defined on the interior of the price simplex satisfying Walras' law and the boundary condition, there exists an exchange economy $\mathscr{E}$ whose excess demand function is approximately equal to f and the equilibrium price set of $\mathscr{E}$ is exactly equal to the one of f. This paper shows that if f may be finite on the boundary of the price simplex, $\mathscr{E}$ can be chosen so that the equilibrium price set of $\mathscr{E}$ is approximately equal to the one of f. Theorem 3 in Wong (1997), showing the equivalence between Brouwer's fixed-point theorem and Arrow-Debreu's equilibrium existence theorem, follows from this result.

Key words: excess demand, decomposition theorem, fixed-point theorem

1. Introduction

The classical theorem of Eisenberg (1961) shows that when preferences are homothetic and the income distribution is independent of prices, the market excess demand function behaves like an individual excess demand function.

* This research is financially supported by Waseda University 21COE-GLOPE and Grant-in-Aid for Scientific Research #15530125 from JSPS.

† The author thanks Professors Kazuya Kamiya and Akira Yamazaki for their useful comments on an earlier version. He is also benefited from the comments and suggestions of two anonymous referees and a co-editor of the journal. Any remaining errors are independent.

Then, a natural question arises; when preferences may not be homothetic but satisfy other regularity conditions such as monotonicity, which properties of an individual excess demand function are inherited by the community excess demand function? The answer is the following. The market excess demand function may be arbitrary on almost entire region of the price simplex as far as it satisfies continuity and Walras' law. Since the seminal papers of Sonnenschein (1973a), (1973b), a number of (approximate) characterization theorems of market excess demand functions have been obtained.[1]

For instance, Debreu (1974) shows that a continuous function f on the closed price simplex satisfying Walras' law coincides with a market excess demand function of monotonic consumers if prices are away from the boundary by an arbitrarily small distance. In his result, it may be the case that f has an equilibrium price on the boundary, while the associated economy has no boundary equilibrium. Mas-Colell (1977) obtains a similar approximate coincidence for a continuous function f defined on the interior of the price simplex satisfying Walras' law and the standard boundary condition. He observes that the equilibrium prices of f coincide with the equilibrium prices of the associated economy.

In this paper, we consider a continuous function f defined on a part of the price simplex including the (relative) interior satisfying Walras' law and a boundary condition similar to Mas-Colell (1977). We demonstrate the existence of a sequence of exchange economies with monotonic preferences whose market excess demand functions become arbitrarily close to f and the equilibrium price sets of the economies are approximately equal to the one of f. Since our result is based on Mas-Colell (1977), this paper clarifies the implications of his results as well as the results of Debreu (1974).

Because the continuity assumption implies the boundedness of demand for a free good, Arrow and Hahn (1971) argue that the non-satiation hypothesis that underlies Walras' law is at least partly inconsistent with satiation in any single good. On the other hand, Wong (1997) shows that a continuous function on the closed price simplex satisfying Walras' law is generated by an exchange economy with non-satiated consumers. The present paper is on the same line. Our main theorem indicates that a continuous function on the closed price simplex satisfying Walras' law is approximated by a community excess demand function of monotonic consumers.

Our result also implies that any compact subset of the closed price simplex is a topological limit of equilibrium prices of exchange economies. This strengthens the observation of Mas-Colell (1977); any compact subset of the interior of the price simplex is the equilibrium price set of an exchange economy.

[1] For a comprehensive survey of the literature, the reader is referred to Shafer and Sonnenschein (1982).

Our result has another implication. Uzawa (1962) shows that Brouwer's fixed-point theorem is equivalent to the equilibrium existence for an excess demand function on the closed price simplex. As pointed out by Wong (1997), Uzawa's result together with the theorems of Debreu (1974) and Mas-Colell (1977) may not provide an immediate answer to the question how an equilibrium for an excess demand function on the closed price simplex relates to an equilibrium for economies and this question has remained open until the paper of Wong (1997). In his paper, Wong (1997) shows that Brouwer's fixed-point theorem is equivalent to the equilibrium existence for exchange economies with non-satiated consumers. On the other hand, our theorem implies the equivalence between Brouwer's fixed-point theorem and the equilibrium existence for exchange economies with monotonic consumers. Since the equilibrium existence for non-satiated economies implies the equilibrium existence for monotonic economies, the equivalence theorem of Wong (1997) follows from the result of this paper.

The next section gives our main theorems and some corollaries together with their proofs. The final section contains some concluding remarks.

2. Statement of results

The ℓ-dimensional Euclidean space $\mathbb{R}^\ell$ is the commodity space. For each commodity bundle $x \in \mathbb{R}^\ell$, $\|x\|$ is the Euclidean norm of x. Let P denote the open price simplex $\{p \in \mathbb{R}^\ell_{++} \mid \sum_{i=1}^\ell p_i = 1\}$. The closure and the relative boundary of P are denoted by $\overline{P}$ and ∂P, respectively. For each $\varepsilon > 0$, let

$$\overline{P}_\varepsilon = \{p \in P \mid p_i \geq \varepsilon \ \text{ for each } \ i = 1, \ldots, \ell\},$$
$$P_\varepsilon = \{p \in P \mid p_i > \varepsilon \ \text{ for each } \ i = 1, \ldots, \ell\}.$$

For a sequence $\{E^n\}$ of subsets of $\overline{P}$, $\mathsf{L_i}(E^n)$ and $\mathsf{L_s}(E^n)$ denote the topological limes inferior and superior, respectively. For the definitions, see Hildenbrand (1974).

Let $P \subseteq S \subseteq \overline{P}$. A continuous function $f\colon S \to \mathbb{R}^\ell$ is *an excess demand function* if the following three conditions are satisfied.

(1) For each $p \in S$, $p \cdot f(p) = 0$.
(2) There exists $\kappa \in \mathbb{R}^\ell$ such that $f(p) \geq \kappa$ for each $p \in S$.
(3) If $p^n \to p \in \partial P \setminus S$, then $\|f(p^n)\| \to +\infty$.

For an excess demand function f, *the equilibrium price set of f* is

$$E_f = \{p \in S \mid f(p) \leq 0\}.$$

An exchange economy, denoted $\mathscr{E} = \{(u^i, \omega^i)\}_{i=1}^m$, is a finite collection of consumers each characterized by a continuous, strictly monotonic, and strictly quasi-concave utility function u^i on $\mathbb{R}^\ell_+$ and an initial endowment vector $\omega^i > 0$. For each $i = 1, \ldots, m$ and each $p \in P$, let $x^i(p)$ be the maximizer of u^i over the budget set $B^i(p) = \{x \in \mathbb{R}^\ell_+ \mid p \cdot x \leq p \cdot \omega^i\}$. We define $f_{\mathscr{E}} \colon P \to \mathbb{R}^\ell$ by

$$f_{\mathscr{E}}(p) = \sum_{i=1}^{m} x^i(p) - \omega^i.$$

The equilibrium price set $E_{\mathscr{E}}$ of exchange economy $\mathscr{E}$ is $\{p \in P \mid f_{\mathscr{E}}(p) = 0\}$.

Our first result is as follows.

Theorem 2.1. *Let $P \subseteq S \subseteq \overline{P}$ and $f \colon S \to \mathbb{R}^\ell$ an excess demand function. For each sequence $\{\varepsilon_n\}$ of positive numbers converging to 0, there exists a sequence $\{\mathscr{E}_n\}$ of exchange economies such that $f(p) = f_{\mathscr{E}_n}(p)$ for each $p \in \overline{P}_{\varepsilon_n}$ and $\mathsf{L_s}(E_{\mathscr{E}_n}) \subset E_f$.*

Proof. Let g be an excess demand function defined on P and let $\{\varepsilon'_n\}$ be a sequence of positive numbers such that $\varepsilon'_n < \varepsilon_n$ for each n. By H.4.2. in p. 41 of Mas-Colell (1985), there exists a continuous function $\alpha^n \colon P \to [0,1]$ such that $\alpha^n(p) = 0$ for $p \in \overline{P}_{\varepsilon'_n}$ and $\alpha^n(p) = 1$ for $p \in P \setminus \overline{P}_{\varepsilon'_n}$. For each n, we define function $h^n \colon P \to \mathbb{R}^\ell$ by

$$h^n(p) = f(p) + \alpha^n(p) \cdot g(p).$$

Since h^n is an excess demand function on P, by the theorem of Mas-Colell (1977), there exist $\eta_n \in (0, \varepsilon_n)$ and an exchange economy $\mathscr{E}_n$ such that,

$$h^n(p) = f_{\mathscr{E}_n}(p)$$

for each $p \in \overline{P}_{\eta_n}$ and

$$E_{h^n} = E_{\mathscr{E}_n} \subset P_{\eta_n}$$

Note that $f \equiv f_{\mathscr{E}_n}$ on $\overline{P}_{\varepsilon_n}$ for each n. Let $\overline{p} \in \mathsf{L_s}(E_{\mathscr{E}_n})$. Then, there exists a sequence $\{\overline{p}^n\}$ converging to $\overline{p}$ such that $\overline{p}^n \in E_{\mathscr{E}_n}$ for each n. By definition,

$$h^n(\overline{p}^n) = f(\overline{p}^n) + \alpha^n(\overline{p}^n) \cdot g(\overline{p}^n) = 0$$

for each n. By way of contradiction, suppose that $\overline{p} \notin S$. Then, for some j, $f_j(\overline{p}^n) \to +\infty$. On the other hand, since $\alpha^n(\overline{p}^n) \leq 1$,

$$f_j(\overline{p}^n) = -\alpha^n(\overline{p}^n) \cdot g_j(\overline{p}^n) \leq -\alpha^n(\overline{p}^n) \cdot \kappa \leq -\kappa$$

where κ is a lower bound of g which may be assumed to be negative. This is a contradiction. Therefore, $\overline{p} \in S$. If $\overline{p} \in P$, then it is easy to see that $\overline{p} \in E_f$. Otherwise, it suffices to consider the case of $f(\overline{p}) \neq 0$. Hence, $\|f(\overline{p}^n)\| > 0$ for sufficiently large n. Therefore,

$$\frac{f(\overline{p}^n)}{\|f(\overline{p}^n)\|} = -\frac{\alpha^n(\overline{p}^n)\cdot g(\overline{p}^n)}{\|\alpha^n(\overline{p}^n)\cdot g(\overline{p}^n)\|} = -\frac{g(\overline{p}^n)}{\|g(\overline{p}^n)\|} \leq -\frac{\kappa}{\|g(\overline{p}^n)\|}.$$

Because f is continuous at $\overline{p}$, the left hand side of the above inequality converges to $\frac{f(\overline{p})}{\|f(\overline{p})\|}$. On the other hand, the right hand side converges to 0 for $\|g(\overline{p}^n)\| \to +\infty$. Hence, we may conclude that $\frac{f(\overline{p})}{\|f(\overline{p})\|} \leq 0$, implying $f(\overline{p}) \leq 0$ so that $\overline{p} \in E_f$. □

Corollary 2.1. *For any excess demand function f on S, $E_f \neq \emptyset$.*

Proof. It is well-known that $E_{\mathscr{E}} \neq \emptyset$ for each exchange economy $\mathscr{E}$. Then, in Theorem 2.1, $E_{\mathscr{E}_n} \neq \emptyset$ for each n. Therefore, $\emptyset \neq \mathsf{L_s}(E_{\mathscr{E}_n}) \subset E_f$.

Theorem 2.1 fully justifies the use of fixed-point theorem in proving the existence of an equilibrium in an exchange economy composed of monotonic consumers. To see this, let us remind Uzawa's equivalence. Uzawa (1962) shows that for a continuous excess demand function on $\overline{P}$ satisfying Walras' law, the equilibrium existence is equivalent to Brouwer's fixed point theorem. However, as pointed out by Wong (1997), we may not immediately conclude from Uzawa's result and the theorems of Debreu (1974) or of Mas-Colell (1977) that Brouwer's theorem is indispensable for the equilibrium existence in an exchange economy. Wong (1997) applies his decomposition theorem to obtain the equivalence between Brouwer's theorem and the equilibrium existence for exchange economies with non-satiated consumers. We may also apply Theorem 2.1 to obtain a similar equivalence under the assumption of monotonic preferences.

Corollary 2.2 (Shinotsuka and Toda 1994). *The equilibrium existence in an exchange economy with monotonic consumers is 'equivalent' to Brouwer's fixed-point theorem.*

Proof. It is obvious that the equilibrium existence in an exchange economy with monotonic consumers follows from Brouwer's theorem. Conversely, in Corollary 2.1, let $S = \overline{P}$. Then, the equilibrium existence in an exchange economy with monotonic consumers implies the existence of equilibrium prices for a continuous function on $\overline{P}$ satisfying Walras' law. By Uzawa (1962), this implies Brouwer's fixed point theorem. □

Remark 2.1. Corollary 2.2 is originally due to Shinotsuka and Toda (1994). Since the equilibrium existence in an exchange economy with non-satiated consumers implies the equilibrium existence in an exchange economy with monotonic consumers, Corollary 2.2 provides an alternative proof of Theorem 3 in Wong (1997).

Theorem 2.1 shows that for an excess demand function f which has a finite value on a part of the boundary of the price simplex, there exists a sequence of exchange economies whose equilibrium prices converge to an equilibrium price of f. It does not guarantee that all of the equilibrium prices of f can be approximated by equilibrium prices of exchange economies. The next theorem, which is the main result of this paper, shows this.

Theorem 2.2. *Let $P \subseteq S \subseteq \overline{P}$ and $f\colon S \to \mathbb{R}^\ell$ an excess demand function. Then for any sequence $\{\varepsilon_n\}$ of positive numbers converging to 0, there exists a sequence $\{\mathscr{E}_n\}$ of exchange economies such that*

$$f(p) = f_{\mathscr{E}_n}(p) \text{ for each } p \in \overline{P}_{\varepsilon_n},$$

and

$$\mathsf{L}_\mathsf{i}(E_{\mathscr{E}_n}) = \mathsf{L}_\mathsf{s}(E_{\mathscr{E}_n}) = E_f.$$

Corollary 2.3. *For any compact set $K \subset \overline{P}$, there is a sequence $\{\mathscr{E}_n\}$ of exchange economies such that*

$$K = \mathsf{L}_\mathsf{i}(E_{\mathscr{E}_n}) = \mathsf{L}_\mathsf{s}(E_{\mathscr{E}_n}).$$

Proof of Corollary 2.3. Let $\overline{p} \in K$ and $h(p) = \overline{p} - \frac{\overline{p}\cdot p}{p\cdot p}p$ for each $p \in \overline{P}$. For each $p \in \overline{P}$, let $\alpha(p) = \min\{\|p - z\| \mid z \in K\}$. Define a function $f\colon \overline{P} \to \mathbb{R}^\ell$ by $f(p) = \alpha(p)\cdot h(p)$. Then, f is an excess demand function on $\overline{P}$ and $E_f = K$. By Theorem 2.2, there exists a desired sequence of exchange economies. □

Remark 2.2. Corollary 2.3 is in fact a direct consequence of Corollary 1 in Mas-Colell (1977). Indeed, for any compact set $K \subset \overline{P}$, there exists a sequence $\{K_n\}$ of compact subsets of P such that $K = \mathsf{L}_\mathsf{i}(K_n) = \mathsf{L}_\mathsf{s}(K_n)$. Corollary 1 in Mas-Colell (1977) shows that for each n, there exists an exchange economy $\mathscr{E}_n$ such that $K_n = E_{\mathscr{E}_n}$. Therefore, it is straightforward to show that for each excess demand function, there exists a sequence of exchange economies satisfying the second requirement in Theorem 2.2. The first requirement in Theorem 2.2 complicates the arguments.

Proof of Theorem 2.2. Let $\{\varepsilon'_n\}$ be a sequence such that $0 < \varepsilon'_n < \varepsilon_n$ for each n. For each n, define a function φ^n on $\overline{P}$ by

$$\varphi^n(p) = \big((1 - \ell\varepsilon'_n)p_1 + \varepsilon'_n, \ldots, (1 - \ell\varepsilon'_n)p_\ell + \varepsilon'_n\big).$$

For sufficiently large n, $\varphi^n(p) \in \overline{P}_{\varepsilon'_n}$ for each $p \in \overline{P}$. Let us define $E^n = \varphi^n(E_f)$. Because E_f is compact and φ^n is continuous, E^n is compact. By construction, $\mathsf{L}_\mathsf{i}(E^n) = \mathsf{L}_\mathsf{s}(E^n) = E_f$. For each n, define $\rho^n(p) = \min\{\|p - z\| \mid z \in E^n\}$ for $p \in P$. It is obvious that ρ^n is well-defined, continuous and bounded on P. We define function $g\colon P \to \mathbb{R}^\ell$ by

$$g(p) = \left(\frac{1}{\ell p_1} - 1, \ldots, \frac{1}{\ell p_\ell} - 1\right).$$

Moreover, define $g^n \colon P \to \mathbb{R}^\ell$ by $g^n(p) = \rho^n(p) \cdot g(p)$ for each n. Then, g^n is an excess demand function on P.

Let $\alpha^n \colon P \to [0,1]$ be the function defined in the proof of Theorem 2.1 and let

$$h^n(p) = (1 - \alpha^n(p))f(p) + \alpha^n(p)g^n(p),$$

which is an excess demand function on P.

For each $\overline{p} \in E_f$, if $\overline{p} \in P$, then for sufficiently large n, $\overline{p} \in \overline{P}_{\varepsilon_n}$. Therefore, $\alpha^n(\overline{p}) = 0$ and hence $h^n(\overline{p}) = f(\overline{p}) = 0$ for sufficiently large n. That is, $\overline{p} \in E_{h^n}$ for sufficiently large n, hence $\overline{p} \in \mathsf{L_i}(E_{h^n})$. On the other hand, if $\overline{p} \in \partial P$, then let $\overline{p}^n = \varphi^n(\overline{p})$. It is obvious that $\overline{p}^n \to \overline{p}$. By construction, $\alpha^n(\overline{p}^n) = 1$ and $g^n(\overline{p}^n) = 0$ for each n. Hence, $h^n(\overline{p}^n) = 0$ for each n. This shows that $\overline{p} \in \mathsf{L_i}(E_{h^n})$. Therefore, $E_f \subset \mathsf{L_i}(E_{h^n}) \subset \mathsf{L_s}(E_{h^n})$.

Conversely, let $\overline{p} \in \mathsf{L_s}(E_{h^n})$. There exists a sequence $\{\overline{p}^n\}$ such that $\overline{p}^n \in E_{h^n}$ and $\overline{p}^n \to \overline{p}$. By way of contradiction, suppose that $\overline{p} \notin S$. If $\alpha^n(\overline{p}^n) = 1$ for infinitely many n, then along a subsequence,

$$h^n(\overline{p}^n) = g^n(\overline{p}^n) = 0$$

for each n. Then, $\overline{p}^n \in E^n$ for each n, which implies $\overline{p} \in E_f$. This contradicts $\overline{p} \notin S$. If $\alpha^n(\overline{p}^n) = 0$ for infinitely many n, then along a subsequence,

$$h^n(\overline{p}^n) = f(\overline{p}^n) = 0$$

for each n. This contradicts the fact that $\|f(\overline{p}^n)\| \to +\infty$.

Therefore, we may assume that $0 < \alpha^n(\overline{p}^n) < 1$ for every sufficiently large n. Since $\rho^n(\overline{p}^n)$ is bounded, we may also assume that $\rho^n(\overline{p}^n) \to \overline{\rho}$ for some $\overline{\rho} \geq 0$. If $\overline{\rho} = 0$, then

$$\lim_{n\to\infty} \min\{\|\overline{p}^n - z\| \mid z \in E^n\} = 0.$$

Then, there exists a sequence $\{z^n\}$ such that $z^n \in E^n$ and $\|\overline{p}^n - z^n\| \to 0$. Thus, $\|\overline{p} - z^n\| = \|\overline{p} - \overline{p}^n + \overline{p}^n - z\| \leq \|\overline{p} - \overline{p}^n\| + \|\overline{p}^n - z^n\| \to 0$. Therefore, $\lim_{n\to\infty} z^n = \overline{p}$. Since $\mathsf{L_s}(E^n) = E_f$, $\overline{p} \in E_f$. This contradicts $\overline{p} \notin S$. Then, $\overline{\rho} > 0$. Furthermore, we may assume that $\alpha^n(\overline{p}^n) \to \overline{\alpha} \in [0,1]$.

Let us first consider the case of $0 < \overline{\alpha} \leq 1$. Because $\|g(\overline{p}^n)\| \to +\infty$, there exists $j \in \{1, \ldots, \ell\}$ such that $g_j(\overline{p}^n) \to +\infty$. Since $\alpha^n(\overline{p}^n)g_j^n(\overline{p}^n) = \alpha^n(\overline{p}^n)\rho^n(\overline{p}^n)g_j(\overline{p}^n) = -(1 - \alpha^n(\overline{p}^n))f_j(\overline{p}^n)$ for each n, we have

$$g_j(\overline{p}^n) = -\left(\frac{1 - \alpha^n(\overline{p}^n)}{\alpha^n(\overline{p}^n)\rho^n(\overline{p}^n)}\right) f_j(\overline{p}^n) \leq -\left(\frac{1 - \alpha^n(\overline{p}^n)}{\alpha^n(\overline{p}^n)\rho^n(\overline{p}^n)}\right)\kappa.$$

Since the right hand side of the above inequality is convergent, $\{g_j(\overline{p}^n)\}$ is also convergent, which is a contradiction.

Next, consider the case of $\overline{\alpha} = 0$. Because $\|f(\overline{p}^n)\| \to +\infty$, there exists $j \in \{1, \dots, \ell\}$ such that $f_j(\overline{p}^n) \to +\infty$. Since $(1 - \alpha^n(\overline{p}^n))f_j(\overline{p}^n) = -\alpha^n(\overline{p}^n)\rho^n(\overline{p}^n)g_j(\overline{p}^n)$ for each n,

$$f_j(\overline{p}^n) = -\left(\frac{\alpha^n(\overline{p}^n)\rho^n(\overline{p}^n)}{1 - \alpha^n(\overline{p}^n)}\right)g_j(\overline{p}^n) \leq \frac{\alpha^n(\overline{p}^n)\rho^n(\overline{p}^n)}{1 - \alpha^n(\overline{p}^n)}.$$

The right hand side of the above inequality converges to 0, which is a contradiction. Then, we may conclude that $\overline{p} \in S$.

If $\overline{p} \in P$, then $\overline{p}^n \in P$ for sufficiently large n. Therefore, $\alpha^n(\overline{p}^n) = 0$ for sufficiently large n. Then, $h^n(\overline{p}^n) = f(\overline{p}^n) = 0$ for sufficiently large n because h^n satisfies the boundary condition. Since $\overline{p} \in P \subset S$ and f is continuous on S, $f(\overline{p}) = 0$. Therefore, $\overline{p} \in E_f$.

Finally, let us consider the case of $\overline{p} \in \partial P \cap S$. If $\alpha^n(\overline{p}^n) = 0$ for infinitely many n, then along a subsequence of $\{\overline{p}^n\}$, still denoted by itself, $h^n(\overline{p}^n) = f(\overline{p}^n) = 0$ for each n. Because a subsequence of $\{\overline{p}^n\}$ converges to $\overline{p}$ and f is continuous at $\overline{p}$, $f(\overline{p}) = 0$ and hence $\overline{p} \in E_f$.

If $\alpha^n(\overline{p}^n) = 1$ for infinitely many n, by the same argument, $h^n(\overline{p}^n) = g^n(\overline{p}^n) = 0$ for each n. Hence, $\overline{p}^n \in E^n$ for each n. Because $\mathsf{L_i}(E^n) = \mathsf{L_s}(E^n) = E_f, \overline{p} \in E_f$.

Suppose that $0 < \alpha^n(\overline{p}^n) < 1$ for sufficiently large n. Since

$$h^n(\overline{p}^n) = (1 - \alpha^n(\overline{p}^n))f(\overline{p}^n) + \alpha^n(\overline{p}^n)g^n(\overline{p}^n) = 0,$$

letting $\beta^n(\overline{p}^n) = \frac{\alpha^n(\overline{p}^n)}{1-\alpha^n(\overline{p}^n)}$, $f(\overline{p}^n) = -\beta^n(\overline{p}^n)g^n(\overline{p}^n)$.

If $f(\overline{p}) = 0$, then it is trivial that $\overline{p} \in E_f$. Suppose that $f(\overline{p}) \neq 0$. Then, $\|f(\overline{p}^n)\| \neq 0$ for sufficiently large n. Therefore,

$$\begin{aligned}\frac{f(\overline{p}^n)}{\|f(\overline{p}^n)\|} &= \frac{-\beta^n(\overline{p}^n)g^n(\overline{p}^n)}{\|\beta^n(\overline{p}^n)\cdot g^n(\overline{p}^n)\|} = -\frac{g^n(\overline{p}^n)}{\|g^n(\overline{p}^n)\|}\\ &= -\frac{\rho^n(\overline{p}^n)g(\overline{p}^n)}{\|\rho^n(\overline{p}^n)g(\overline{p}^n)\|} = -\frac{g(\overline{p}^n)}{\|g(\overline{p}^n)\|} \leq \frac{1}{\|g(\overline{p}^n)\|}e\end{aligned}$$

where $e = (1, \dots, 1) \in \mathbb{R}^\ell$. Since f is continuous at $\overline{p}$, $\frac{f(\overline{p}^n)}{\|f(\overline{p}^n)\|} \to \frac{f(\overline{p})}{\|f(\overline{p})\|}$. On the other hand, since $\|g(\overline{p}^n)\| \to +\infty$, $\frac{e}{\|g(\overline{p}^n)\|} \to 0$. Therefore, $\frac{f(\overline{p})}{\|f(\overline{p})\|} \leq 0$, hence $f(\overline{p}) \leq 0$, which implies $\overline{p} \in E_f$. Therefore, it has been demonstrated that

$$\mathsf{L_i}(E_{h^n}) = \mathsf{L_s}(E_{h^n}) = E_f.$$

By Mas-Colell (1977), for each n, there exist $\eta_n \in (0, \varepsilon_n)$ and an economy $\mathscr{E}_n$ such that $f_{\mathscr{E}_n}(p) = h^n(p)$ for each $p \in \overline{P}_{\eta_n}$ and $E_{\mathscr{E}_n} = E_{h^n} \subset \overline{P}_{\eta_n}$. Since $h^n(p) = f(p)$ for each $p \in \overline{P}_{\varepsilon_n}$ and $\mathsf{L_i}(E_{h^n}) = \mathsf{L_s}(E_{h^n}) = E_f$, the sequence $\{\mathscr{E}_n\}$ satisfies the desired properties. □

3. Concluding remarks

If we take $S = \overline{P}$, then Theorem 2.2 is reduced to the theorem of Debreu (1974). It also gives an alternative form of the result of Mas-Colell (1977). He shows that for each excess demand function f on P and for each $\varepsilon > 0$, there exist an exchange economy $\mathscr{E}$ and $\eta \in (0, \varepsilon)$ such that $f(p) = f_{\mathscr{E}}(p)$ for each $p \in \overline{P}_\eta$ and $E_f = E_{\mathscr{E}} \subset \overline{P}_\eta$. If we take $S = P$ in Theorem 2.2, then $E_f \subset \overline{P}_{\varepsilon_n} \subset P$ and hence $E_f \subset E_{\mathscr{E}_n}$ for sufficiently large n. Suppose that for infinitely many n, there exists $p^n \in E_{\mathscr{E}_n}$ such that $p^n \notin E_f$. Since $f(p) = f_{\mathscr{E}_n}(p)$ for each $p \in \overline{P}_{\varepsilon_n}$, $p^n \notin \overline{P}_{\varepsilon_n}$. Along a subsequence, we may assume that $p^n \to \overline{p} \in \partial P$. By theorem 2.2, $\overline{p} \in E_f$, which contradicts $E_f \subset P$. Therefore, $E_{\mathscr{E}_n} \subset E_f$ for sufficiently large n. Then, we may conclude that $E_f = E_{\mathscr{E}_n}$ for sufficiently large n. This is exactly what he shows.

Furthermore, Mas-Colell (1977) shows that for each compact $K \subset P$, there exists an exchange economy $\mathscr{E}$ such that $K = E_{\mathscr{E}}$. Since $K \subset \overline{P}_{\varepsilon_n}$ for sufficiently large n, by the same kind of argument as above, it follows from Corollary 2.3 that $K = E_{\mathscr{E}_n}$ for sufficiently large n.

References

[1] Arrow, K.J., Hahn. F.H.: General Competitive Analysis. Holden Day, San Francisco 1971

[2] Debreu, G.: Excess demand functions. J. Math. Econ. **1**, 15-21 (1974)

[3] Eisenberg, B.: Aggregation of utility functions. Manage. Sci. **7**, 337-350 (1961)

[4] Hildenbrand, W.: Core and Equilibria of a Large Economy. Princeton University Press, Princeton 1974

[5] Mas-Colell, A.: On the equilibrium price set of an exchange economy. J. Math. Econ. **4**, 117-126 (1977)

[6] Mas-Colell, A.: The Theory of General Economic Equilibrium, A Differentiable Approach. Cambridge University Press, Cambridge 1985

[7] Shafer, W., Sonnenschein. H.: Market demand and excess demand functions, In: Handbook of Mathematical Economics, volume II (Arrow, K.J. et al. eds.). pp. 671-693 North Holland, New York, Amsterdam 1982

[8] Shinotsuka T., Toda. M.: Equilibrium Existence and Fixed Point Theorems: Equivalence Theorems, unpublished (1994)

[9] Sonnenschein, H.: Do Walras' identity and continuity characterize the class of community excess demand functions? J. Econ. Theory **6**, 345-354 (1972a)

[10] Sonnenschein, H.: The utility hypothesis and market demand theory. Western Econ. J. **11**, 404-410 (1972b)

[11] Uzawa, H.: Walras' existence and Brouwer's fixed point theorem. Econ. Stud. Quart. **13**, 59-62 (1962)

[12] Wong, K.-C.: Excess demand functions, equilibrium prices, and existence of equilibrium. Econ. Theory **10**, 39-54 (1997)

Adv. Math. Econ. 9, 109–116 (2006)

Advances in
MATHEMATICAL
ECONOMICS

The minimal risk of hedging with a convex risk measure*

Yuji Umezawa

Graduate School of Mathematical Sciences, The University of Tokyo
3-8-1 Komaba, Meguro-ku, Tokyo 153-8914, Japan
(e-mail: yume_love@mbn.nifty.com)

Received: July 28, 2005
Revised: December 20, 2005

JEL classification: D81

Mathematics Subject Classification (2000): 91B30

Abstract. We study the minimal hedging risk for a bounded European contingent claim when we use a convex risk measure. We find the infimum of hedging risk by using a kind of min-max theorem. Also we show that this infimum is again regarded as a convex risk measure.

Key words: risk measure, hedging

1. Introduction

Let $(\Omega, \mathcal{F}, P)$ be a probability space. For $1 \leq q \leq \infty$, We denote $L^q(\Omega, \mathcal{F}, P)$ by L^q, and its norm by $\| \cdot \|_q$. Let $\mathcal{P}$ be the set of probability measures on $(\Omega, \mathcal{F})$ that are absolutely continuous with respect to P. Föllmer and Schied [3] introduce the following notation.

Definition 1. *We say that a mapping* $\rho\colon L^\infty \to \mathbf{R}$ *is a convex risk measure, if the following three conditions are satisfied:*
(1) $X \geq Y \Longrightarrow \rho(X) \leq \rho(Y)$,
(2) $\rho(\lambda X + (1-\lambda)Y) \leq \lambda\rho(X) + (1-\lambda)\rho(Y), \quad \lambda \in (0,1)$,
(3) $\rho(X + c) = \rho(X) - c, \quad c \in \mathbf{R}$.

* This research is supported by the 21 century COE program at Graduate School of Mathematical Sciences, the University of Tokyo.

For a convex risk measure ρ, $\tilde{\rho}\colon L^\infty \to \mathbf{R}$, $\tilde{\rho}(X) = \rho(X) - \rho(0)$ is also a convex risk measure, and $\tilde{\rho}(0) = 0$. So we may assume $\rho(0) = 0$ in the following discussions.

Föllmer and Schied [4] proved the following.

Theorem 1. *For a convex risk measure $\rho\colon L^\infty \to \mathbf{R}$, the following properties are equivalent.*
(1) There exists a penalty function $\alpha\colon \mathcal{P} \to \mathbf{R}\cup\{+\infty\}$, which is bounded from below such that $\rho(X) = \sup_{Q\in\mathcal{P}}(E^Q[-X] - \alpha(Q))$.
(2) (Fatou Property) $\rho(X) \leq \liminf_{n\to\infty} \rho(X_n)$ holds for any sequence $(X_n)_{n\in\mathbf{N}}$ of random variable which is uniformly bounded by 1 and converges to $X \in L^\infty$ in probability.
(3) ρ is continuous from above, i.e., if a sequence $(X_n)_{n\in\mathbf{N}}$ of random variable in L^∞ decreases to $X \in L^\infty$ a.s., then $\rho(X_n)$ converges to $\rho(X)$.

Let $\alpha_{min}(Q) = \sup_{Y\in\mathcal{A}_\rho} E^Q[-Y]$, where $\mathcal{A}_\rho = \{X \in L^\infty \mid \rho(X) \leq 0\}$. Then we have $\alpha_{min}(Q) \leq \alpha(Q)$, $Q \in \mathcal{P}$ for any penalty function α satisfying the equation in (1). Note that $\alpha_{min}(Q) \geq 0$ for $Q \in \mathcal{P}$ by the assumption $\rho(0) = 0$.

Now we state our main theorem. Let $\mathcal{C} \subset L^\infty$ be a nonempty convex subset, and $\mathcal{M}(\mathcal{C}) = \left\{Q \in \mathcal{P} \,\middle|\, \sup_{Z\in\mathcal{C}} E^Q[Z] < \infty\right\}$.

Theorem 2. *Let $\rho\colon L^\infty \to \mathbf{R}$ be a convex risk measure which is continuous from above. Suppose that ρ is continuous from below, i.e., if a sequence $(X_n)_{n\in\mathbf{N}}$ of random variable in L^∞ increases to $X \in L^\infty$ a.s., then $\rho(X_n)$ converges to $\rho(X)$. Then we have*

$$\inf_{Z\in\mathcal{C}} \rho(Z + H) = \sup_{Q\in\mathcal{P}} (E^Q[-H] - \tilde{\alpha}(Q)), \tag{1}$$

for any $H \in L^\infty$, where

$$\tilde{\alpha}(Q) = \alpha_{min}(Q) + \sup_{Z\in\mathcal{C}} E^Q[Z], \qquad Q \in \mathcal{P}. \tag{2}$$

Remark 1. This theorem had already been shown in [1]. We give another proof by a kind of min-max theorem.

Our proof is given in Section 3.

Now let us consider the following mathematical financial market model. Let $(\Omega, \mathcal{F}, P; \{\mathcal{F}(t)\}_{t\in[0,T]})$ be a filtered probability space. We assume that the filtration $\{\mathcal{F}(t)\}_{t\in[0,T]}$ satisfies the usual conditions, i.e., $\{\mathcal{F}(t)\}_{t\in[0,T]}$ is right-continuous and $\mathcal{F}(0)$ contains all P-negligible sets in $\mathcal{F}$. We also assume that $\mathcal{F}(0)$ is trivial and $\mathcal{F}(T) = \mathcal{F}$. Let $S(t) = (S^i(t))$, $1 \leq i \leq d$, be an $\{\mathcal{F}(t)\}$-adapted, RCLL, and locally bounded d dimensional process. This process is interpreted as the discount price processes of d risky assets.

We say that a d dimensional process $\xi(t) = (\xi^i(t))$, $1 \le i \le d$ is a strategy if ξ is $\{\mathcal{F}(t)\}$-predictable and S-integrable. We define an appropriate class $\mathcal{A}d$ of strategies by the following.

$$\mathcal{A}d = \left\{ \xi = (\xi^i) \,\middle|\, \xi \ \ \textit{is a strategy and} \ \int_0^{\cdot} \xi(u)\, dS(u) \ \ \textit{is bounded.} \right\}. \qquad (3)$$

For a pair (v, ξ), $v \ge 0$, $\xi \in \mathcal{A}d$, we define a process $\{V(t)\}_{t\in[0,T]}$ by

$$V(t) = V(t; (v, \xi)) = v + \int_0^t \xi(u)\, dS(u), \qquad t \in [0, T]. \qquad (4)$$

This process $V(t; (v, \xi))$ is interpreted as the value of self-financing portfolio strategy (v, ξ) at time $t \in [0, T]$.

We denote by $\mathcal{M}(S)$ the set of probability measures $Q \in \mathcal{P}$ such that the components $S^i(t)$, $1 \le i \le d$ are local martingales under Q. We assume that $\mathcal{M}(S) \ne \phi$. Then we have the following.

Corollary 1. *Let ρ: $L^\infty \to \mathbf{R}$ be a convex risk measure which is continuous from above and below. Then we have*

$$\inf_{\xi\in\mathcal{A}d} \rho(V(T; (0, \xi)) + H) = \inf_{Q\in\mathcal{P}} (E^Q[-H] - \tilde{\alpha}(Q)), \qquad (5)$$

for $H \in L^\infty$, where

$$\tilde{\alpha}(Q) = \begin{cases} \alpha_{min}(Q), & Q \in \mathcal{M}(S) \cap \{Q \in \mathcal{P} \mid \alpha_{min}(Q) < \infty\}, \\ +\infty, & \textit{otherwise.} \end{cases} \qquad (6)$$

Remark 2. Delbaen [2] showed this result in the case where ρ is a coherent risk measure and $H = 0$.

2. Remarks on a convex risk measure

We prove the following in this section.

Theorem 3. *For a convex risk measure ρ which is continuous from above, the following properties are equivalent.*
(1) ρ is continuous from below.
(2) For arbitrary $c > 0$, the set $\{Q \in \mathcal{P} \mid \alpha_{min}(Q) \le c\}$ is $L^1(P)$-weakly compact convex subset.

We make some preparation. Let $\rho\colon L^\infty \to \mathbf{R}$ be a convex risk measure which is continuous from above. Let Λ_c and Λ_∞ denote

$$\begin{aligned} \Lambda_c &= \{Q \in \mathcal{P} \mid \alpha_{min}(Q) \le c\} \qquad c > 0, \\ \Lambda_\infty &= \{Q \in \mathcal{P} \mid \alpha_{min}(Q) < \infty\}. \end{aligned} \tag{7}$$

We note that

$$\rho(X) = \sup_{Q\in\mathcal{Q}} (E^Q[-X] - \alpha_{min}(Q)), \qquad \mathcal{Q} \supset \Lambda_\infty,\ X \in L^\infty. \tag{8}$$

Lemma 1. *We have* $\rho(X) = \sup_{Q\in\Lambda_c} (E^Q[-X] - \alpha_{min}(Q))$ *for* $X \in L^\infty$ *and* $c > 2\|X\|_\infty$.

Proof. $\rho(X) \ge \sup_{Q\in\Lambda_c} (E^Q[-X] - \alpha_{min}(Q))$ is obvious. We show the inverse inequality. For each $n \in \mathbf{N}$, there exists $Q_n \in \mathcal{P}$ such that $\rho(X) - 1/n \le E^{Q_n}[-X] - \alpha_{min}(Q_n)$. We can easily see that $\rho(X) \ge -\|X\|_\infty$ by the monotonicity of ρ. Then for $n \ge 1/(c - 2\|X\|_\infty)$ we see that

$$\alpha_{min}(Q_n) \le E^{Q_n}[-X] - \rho(X) + 1/n \le 2\|X\|_\infty + (c - 2\|X\|_\infty) = c. \tag{9}$$

And so $Q_n \in \Lambda_c$. This implies that

$$\rho(X) - 1/n \le E^{Q_n}[-X] - \alpha_{min}(Q_n) \le \sup_{Q\in\Lambda_c} (E^Q[-X] - \alpha_{min}(Q)). \tag{10}$$

Letting $n \to \infty$, we have $\rho(X) \le \sup_{Q\in\Lambda_c} (E^Q[-X] - \alpha_{min}(Q))$. This completes the proof.

Now we prove Theorem 3. Assume that the assertion (1) holds. Since the mapping $Q \mapsto E^Q[-Y]$ is continuous for any $Y \in L^\infty$, we can immediately see that $\alpha_{min}\colon Q \mapsto \sup_{Y\in\mathcal{A}_\rho} E^Q[-Y]$ is lower semicontinuous with respect to L^1-weak topology. Hence Λ_c is closed for $c > 0$.

Let $(B_n)_{n\in\mathbf{N}}$ be a decreasing sequence of measurable sets such that $\bigcap_n B_n = \phi$. Take $Q \in \Lambda_c$. Then we have $c \ge \alpha_{min}(Q) \ge E^Q[-\lambda 1_{B_n^c}] - \rho(\lambda 1_{B_n^c})$ for $\lambda > 0$, and so $c/\lambda + \rho(\lambda 1_{B_n^c})/\lambda + 1 \ge Q[B_n]$. Since $\rho(\lambda 1_{B_n^c}) \to -\lambda$ by the assumption, we have

$$c/\lambda \ge \lim_{n\to\infty} \sup_{Q\in\Lambda_c} Q[B_n], \qquad \lambda > 0. \tag{11}$$

Letting $\lambda \to \infty$, we have $\lim_{n\to\infty} \sup_{Q\in\Lambda_c} Q[B_n] = 0$ for any $c > 0$, and this implies that the set Λ_c is uniformly P-integrable. Hence we obtain the assertion (2) by Dunford-Pettis theorem.

Assume that the assertion (2) holds. Let $\{X_n\}_{n\in\mathbf{N}}$ be random variables in L^∞ such that X_n increases to X as $n \to \infty$. Then there exists a positive number $M > 0$ such that $\|X_n\|_\infty \le M$, $n \in \mathbf{N}$ and $\|X\|_\infty \le M$. We have

$$\begin{aligned} \rho(X_n) &= \sup_{Q\in\Lambda_{2M+1}} (E^Q[-X_n] - \alpha_{min}(Q)), \qquad n \in \mathbf{N}, \\ \rho(X) &= \sup_{Q\in\Lambda_{2M+1}} (E^Q[-X] - \alpha_{min}(Q)). \end{aligned} \tag{12}$$

by Lemma 1. Since Λ_{2M+1} is L^1-weakly compact by assumption, Dini's theorem implies that

$$\left|(E^Q[-X_n] - \alpha_{min}(Q)) - (E^Q[-X] - \alpha_{min}(Q))\right| = \left|E^Q[X] - E^Q[X_n]\right| \tag{13}$$

converges to 0 uniformly in $Q \in \Lambda_{2M+1}$ as $n \to \infty$. Hence we have the assertion (1). This completes the proof.

3. Proof of our main theorem

Before we start our proof, we prepare a version of minimax theorem due to Kim [5]. For convenience, we set the conditions a little stronger than that of the original.

Lemma 2. *Let $\mathcal{X}$ be a nonempty convex subset of some locally convex linear topological space, $\mathcal{Y}$ be a non-empty subset of a vector space (not necessarily topologized), and f be a real-valued function on $\mathcal{X} \times \mathcal{Y}$ such that*
(1) $x \mapsto f(x, y)$ is convex and lower semicontinuous for any $y \in \mathcal{Y}$,
(2) there exists $y_0 \in \mathcal{Y}$ such that $(1-\lambda)f(x, y_1) + \lambda f(x, y_2) \le f(x, y_0)$, $x \in \mathcal{X}$ for any y_1, $y_2 \in \mathcal{Y}$ and $\lambda \in [0, 1]$,
(3) the mapping $\lambda \in [0, 1] \mapsto f(x, \lambda y_1 + (1-\lambda)y_2)$ is continuous for any $x \in \mathcal{X}$ and y_1, $y_2 \in \mathcal{Y}$,
and
(4) there exists a non-empty compact subset C_F of $\mathcal{X}$ such that

$$\inf_{x\in\mathcal{X}\setminus C_F} f(x, y_0) \ge \max\Big\{\inf_{x\in C_F} f(x, y_0),\ \inf_{x\in\mathcal{X}} \sup_{y\in\mathcal{Y}} f(x, y)\Big\}, \quad y_0 \in co(F), \tag{14}$$

for any non-empty finite set F of Y, where $co(F)$ is the minimal convex set which contains all elements of F. Then we have

$$\sup_{y\in\mathcal{Y}} \inf_{x\in\mathcal{X}} f(x, y) \ge \inf_{x\in\mathcal{X}} \sup_{y\in\mathcal{Y}} f(x, y). \tag{15}$$

Now we prove Theorem 2.

Step 1. First we consider the case where $\mathcal{M}(\mathcal{C}) \cap \{Q \in \mathcal{P} \mid \alpha_{min}(Q) < \infty\} \neq \phi$. We can easily see that

$$\begin{aligned} \inf_{Z \in \mathcal{C}} \rho(Z+H) &= \inf_{Z \in \mathcal{C}} \sup_{Q \in \mathcal{P}} (E^Q[-Z-H] - \alpha_{min}(Q)) \\ &\geq \sup_{Q \in \mathcal{P}} \inf_{Z \in \mathcal{C}} (E^Q[-Z-H] - \alpha_{min}(Q)) \\ &= \sup_{Q \in \mathcal{P}} (E^Q[-H] - \tilde{\alpha}(Q)). \end{aligned} \tag{16}$$

We show the inverse inequality. We apply Lemma 2 for $\mathcal{X} = \mathcal{P}$, $\mathcal{Y} = \mathcal{C}$. To show the inverse inequality, it is sufficient that the mapping

$$f\colon\ (Q, Z) \mapsto E^Q[Z+H] + \alpha_{min}(Q) \tag{17}$$

satisfies the conditions in Lemma 2. Clearly the conditions (1), (2), (3) are satisfied (It is already shown in the proof of Theorem 3 that the mapping $Q \mapsto \alpha_{min}(Q)$ is lower semicontinuous with respect to L^1-weak topology). We verify that f satisfies Condition (4). Let $F = \{Z_1, Z_2, \ldots, Z_m\}$, $m < \infty$, $Z_0 \in co(F)$, and

$$M = \max_{1 \leq i \leq m} \|Z_i\|_\infty \vee \left\{ \inf_{Q \in \Lambda_\infty \cap \mathcal{M}(\mathcal{C})} \left(\alpha_{min}(Q) + \sup_{Z \in \mathcal{C}} E^Q[Z] \right) + 2\|H\|_\infty \right\}. \tag{18}$$

We show that $C_F = \Lambda_{2M+1}$ satisfies Condition (4). We see that

$$\begin{aligned} &\inf_{Q \in \Lambda_{2M+1}} (E^Q[Z_0+H] + \alpha_{min}(Q)) \\ &\quad = \inf_{Q \in \mathcal{P}} (E^Q[Z_0+H] + \alpha_{min}(Q)) \\ &\quad \leq \inf_{Q \in \mathcal{P} \setminus \Lambda_{2M+1}} (E^Q[Z_0+H] + \alpha_{min}(Q)). \end{aligned} \tag{19}$$

by Lemma 1. And we see that

$$\begin{aligned} &E^Q[Z_0+H] + \alpha_{min}(Q) \\ &\quad \geq -\|Z_0\|_\infty - \|H\|_\infty + 2M + 1 \\ &\quad \geq -\|H\|_\infty + M + 1 \\ &\quad \geq \|H\|_\infty + \inf_{Q \in \Lambda_\infty \cap \mathcal{M}(\mathcal{C})} \left(\alpha_{min}(Q) + \sup_{Z \in \mathcal{C}} E^Q[Z] \right) \\ &\quad \geq \inf_{Q \in \mathcal{P}} \sup_{Z \in \mathcal{C}} (E^Q[Z+H] + \alpha_{min}(Q)). \end{aligned} \tag{20}$$

for $Q \in \mathcal{P} \setminus \Lambda_{2M+1}$. Hence we have

$$\inf_{Q\in\mathcal{P}}\sup_{Z\in\mathcal{C}}(E^Q[Z+H]+\alpha_{min}(Q))$$
$$\leq \inf_{Q\in\mathcal{P}\setminus\Lambda_{2M+1}}(E^Q[Z+H]+\alpha_{min}(Q)). \tag{21}$$

So we verify that f satisfies Condition (4).

Step 2. We consider the case where $\mathcal{M}(\mathcal{C})\cap\{Q\in\mathcal{P}\mid\alpha_{min}(Q)<\infty\}=\phi$. In this case, it is sufficient to show that $\inf_{Z\in\mathcal{C}}\rho(Z+H)=-\infty$. Let $\mathcal{C}_n=\{Z\in\mathcal{C}\mid\|Z\|_\infty\leq n\}$ for each $n\in\mathbf{N}$. We can easily see that $\mathcal{C}_n$ is convex and

$$\mathcal{M}(\mathcal{C}_n)\cap\{Q\in\mathcal{P}\mid\alpha_{min}(Q)<\infty\}=\{Q\in\mathcal{P}\mid\alpha_{min}(Q)<\infty\}\neq\phi. \tag{22}$$

Then using the result of Step 1 we have

$$\inf_{Z\in\mathcal{C}_n}\rho(Z+H)=\sup_{Q\in\mathcal{P}}\Big\{E^Q[-H]-\Big(\alpha_{min}(Q)+\sup_{Z\in\mathcal{C}_n}E^Q[Z]\Big)\Big\}. \tag{23}$$

Assume that $\inf_{Z\in\mathcal{C}}\rho(Z+H)=\gamma>-\infty$. Since $\inf_{Z\in\mathcal{C}_n}\rho(Z+H)\downarrow\gamma$ as $n\to\infty$, there exists $Q_n\in\mathcal{P}$ such that

$$\gamma-1/n\leq E^{Q_n}[-H]-\Big(\alpha_{min}(Q_n)+\sup_{Z\in\mathcal{C}_n}E^{Q_n}[Z]\Big) \tag{24}$$

for $n\in\mathbf{N}$. Then we see that

$$\begin{aligned}\alpha_{min}(Q_n)&\leq E^{Q_n}[-H]-\gamma+1/n-\sup_{Z\in\mathcal{C}_n}E^{Q_n}[Z]\\&\leq\|H\|_\infty-\gamma+1-\sup_{Z\in\mathcal{C}_1}E^{Q_n}[Z]\\&\leq(\|H\|_\infty-\gamma+2)\vee 1.\end{aligned} \tag{25}$$

Since the set $\{Q\in\mathcal{P}\mid\alpha_{min}(Q)\leq(\|H\|_\infty-\gamma+2)\vee 1\}$ is L^1-weakly compact by Theorem 3, there exists a subsequence $\{Q_{n_k}\}$ of $\{Q_n\}_{n\in\mathbf{N}}$ and $\bar{Q}\in\{Q\in\mathcal{P}\mid\alpha_{min}(Q)\leq(\|H\|_\infty-\gamma+2)\vee 1\}$ such that $Q_k\to\bar{Q}$ as $k\to\infty$.

We note that $Q\mapsto\sup_{Z\in\mathcal{C}_m}E^Q[Z]$ is lower semicontinuous for fixed $m\in\mathbf{N}$. Then we see that

$$\begin{aligned}\sup_{Z\in\mathcal{C}_m}E^{\bar{Q}}[Z]&\leq\alpha_{min}(\bar{Q})+\sup_{Z\in\mathcal{C}_m}E^{\bar{Q}}[Z]\\&\leq\liminf_{k\to\infty}\alpha_{min}(Q_{n_k})+\liminf_{k\to\infty}\sup_{Z\in\mathcal{C}_m}E^{Q_{n_k}}[Z]\\&\leq\liminf_{k\to\infty}(\alpha_{min}(Q_{n_k})+\sup_{Z\in\mathcal{C}_{n_k}}E^{Q_{n_k}}[Z])\\&\leq\liminf_{k\to\infty}(E^{Q_{n_k}}[-H]-\gamma+1/n_k)\\&\leq\|H\|_\infty-\gamma.\end{aligned} \tag{26}$$

for $n_k \geq m$. Letting $m \to \infty$, we have $\sup_{Z \in \mathcal{C}} E^{\bar{Q}}[Z] \leq \|H\|_\infty - \gamma < \infty$. Then we have $\bar{Q} \in \mathcal{M}(\mathcal{C}) \cap \{Q \in \mathcal{P} \mid \alpha_{min}(Q) < \infty\}$. This is a contradiction. Hence we have $\inf_{Z \in \mathcal{C}} \rho(Z + H) = -\infty$. This completes the proof.

We can prove Corollary 1 by applying Theorem 2 for $\mathcal{C} = \{V(T; (0, \xi)) \mid \xi \in \mathcal{A}d\}$, since we can easily see that $\mathcal{M}(\mathcal{C}) = \mathcal{M}(S)$.

Acknowledgement. The author would like to thank Professor Shigeo Kusuoka for his useful advices.

References

[1] Barrieu, P., El Karoui, N.: Inf-convolution of risk measures and optimal risk transfer. Finance Stochast. **9**, 269-298 (2005)
[2] Delbaen, F.: Coherent risk measures. Lecture notes, Pisa 2001
[3] Föllmer, H., Schied, A.: Robust preferences and convex measures of risk. In: Advances in Finance and Stochastics. Essays in Honour of Dieter Sondermann. pp.39-56 Springer-Verlag 2002
[4] Föllmer, H., Schied, A.: Stochastic Finance. Walter de Gruyter 2002
[5] Kim, W.K.: A non-compact generalization of Horvath's intersection theorem. Bull. Korean. Math. Soc. **32**, 153-162 (1995)

Adv. Math. Econ. 9, 117–126 (2006)

Advances in
MATHEMATICAL
ECONOMICS

The distribution of firm size

Na Zhang

Graduate School of Mathematical Sciences, The University of Tokyo,
3-8-1 Komaba, Meguro-ku, Tokyo, 153-8914, Japan
(e-mail: cutyzn@yahoo.com)

Received: January 20, 2005
Revised: September 5, 2005

JEL classification: C0

Mathematics Subject Classification (2000): 60E07, 60F99

Abstract. In this paper, we study the distribution of firm size by using a model based on Sato's paper in 1970, and proved the static distribution of firm size satisfies Pareto distribution in its upper tail.

Key words: firm size, Pareto distribution, Yule distribution

1. Introduction

Studies on empirical size distributions have a long history and attracted many scientists' interest in the past years, since these distributions were frequently used to describe sociological, biological and economic phenomena (e.g. [4]). These empirical size distributions include (1) distributions of incomes by size, (2) distributions of words in prose samples by their frequency of occurrence, (3) distributions of scientists by number of papers published, (4) distributions of cities by population, (5) distributions of biological gene by number of species, and (6) distributions of firms by size.

More than one hundred years ago, Pareto [2] reported three forms of size distributions. Let i denote the size of a variable which has discrete integer values. Consider a lot of members with size i, $f(i)$ is the frequency distribution of i. The Pareto distributions are given by

(1). $f(i) = Ai^{-\rho-1}, \rho > 1.$
(2). $f(i) = A(i-c)^{-\rho-1}, \rho > 1, c > 0.$
(3). $f(i) = A(i-c)^{-\rho-1} \exp^{-ri}(\rho + r(i-c)), \rho > 1, r > 0, c > 0.$

In 1924, Yule [5] constructed a probability model with $f(i) = cB(i, \rho + 1)$ as its limiting distribution, in order to explain the distributions of biological genera by numbers of species, where B is the Beta function and c is a constant. This distribution is called Yule distribution. Actually, Yule distribution can be approximated in its upper tail by Pareto distribution. In 1955, Simon [4] constructed a stochastic model to describe the distribution of words by their frequency of occurrence and obtained Yule distribution as the stationary solution of the stochastic process. In his model, he supposed that the probability of absolute growth of a variable is proportional to its size, and relative growth or the growth rate is stochastically independent of size. It is called the law of Proportional Effect. In 1970, Sato [3] studied the size distributions which follow the law of nonproportional effect. Sato derived steady-state distributions for a few specific forms of the size-growth relation.

In the present paper, Sato's model is introduced and used to describe the growth of firms size. The empirical results are proved by using a strict mathematical method.

2. Stochastic model and main result

Let $(\Omega, \mathscr{F}, P; \{\mathscr{F}_n\}_{n=1}^{\infty})$ be a filtered probability space. Let $\alpha \in (0,1)$, $a \in \left(0, \dfrac{1}{1-\alpha}\right)$ and $b = \dfrac{1-a}{\alpha}$. Note that $a + b > 0$. Let N_n, $S_{n,i}$, $i = 1, 2, \ldots, N_n$, be $\mathscr{F}_n$-measurable random variables, for each $n = 1, 2, \ldots$, satisfying the following assumptions.

(A-1) $P(N_{n+1} = N_n,\ S_{n+1,i} = S_{n,i} + 1,\ S_{n+1,j} = S_{n,j},\ j \neq i \mid \mathscr{F}_n) = (1-\alpha)\dfrac{aS_{n,i} + b}{\sum_{k=1}^{N_n}(aS_{n,k} + b)},\ i = 1, 2, \ldots, N_n.$

(A-2) $P(N_{n+1} = N_n + 1,\ S_{n+1,N_{n+1}} = 1,\ S_{n+1,m} = S_{n,m},\ m = 1, 2, \ldots, N_n \mid \mathscr{F}_n) = \alpha.$

(A-3) $N_1 = 1$, $S_{1,1} = 1$.

This model can be used to explain a system of developing firms, as described in Figure 1.

At time 1, there is only one firm with size 1. Let N_n, $n = 1, 2, \ldots$, denote the total number of firms at time n, and $S_{n,i}$ be the size of the i-th firm at time n, $1 \leq i \leq N_n$. For all n, N_n and $S_{n,i}$ satisfy the above assumptions. Actually the above assumptions indicate the following. When the total size of the firms increases 1, the size of i-th firm increase 1 at time $n+1$, with probability $(1-\alpha)(aS_{n,i} + b) \Big/ \left(\sum_{k=1}^{N_n} aS_{n,k} + b\right)$, and a new firm is created with size of 1 with probability α.

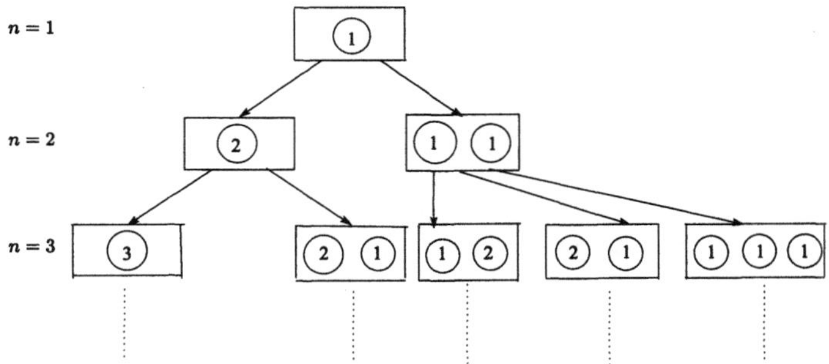

Fig. 1. The schematic of size increase in developing firms.

Let $f_{n,k}$ be the number of the firms with size of k at time n, that is, $f_{n,k}$ is the cardinal number of the set $\{i; S_{n,i} = k,\ i = 1, 2, \ldots, N_n\}$. $f_{n,k} = 0$ when $k > n$. Our main result is the following,

Theorem 1. *Let c_k, $k = 1, 2, \ldots$, be defined by*

$$c_k = \frac{\alpha}{1 + (a+b)(1-\alpha)} \frac{B(k + \frac{b}{a}, 1+\gamma)}{B(1 + \frac{b}{a}, 1+\gamma)},$$

where $B(x, y)$ is Beta function, $\gamma = \frac{1}{a(1-\alpha)}$. Then, $n^{-\frac{1}{2}+\varepsilon}(f_{n,k} - nc_k) \to 0$, almost surely, as $n \to \infty$, for any $\varepsilon > 0$ and $k \geq 1$.

In particular $\dfrac{f_{n,k}}{n} \to c_k$, almost surely, as $n \to \infty$, for any $k \geq 1$.

Remark 2. (1) The limit distribution of firm sizes satisfies Pareto distribution of second kind, i.e. here $\gamma = \frac{1}{a(1-\alpha)}$ is Pareto coefficient.
(2) When $a = 1$, $b = 0$, Sato's model is simplified into Simon's model. In this case, the probability that the size of i-th firm increases 1 at time $n+1$ is $(1-\alpha)S_{n,i}/n$, when the total size of the firms increases 1. Also $c_k = \dfrac{\alpha}{2-\alpha} B\Big(k, 1 + \dfrac{1}{1-\alpha}\Big)$, and the Pareto coefficient is $\dfrac{1}{1-\alpha}$.

3. Some analysis about the model

Let us make some preparations.

Lemma 3. *For any $n \geq 1$ and $k \geq 1$, we have the following.*

(1) $P(f_{n+1,k+1} = f_{n,k+1} + 1,\ f_{n+1,k} = f_{n,k} - 1,\ f_{n+1,j} = f_{n,j},\ j \neq k,$
$N_{n+1} = N_n \mid \mathscr{F}_n) = \dfrac{f_{n,k}(ak+b)(1-\alpha)}{an + bN_n}.$

(2) $P(f_{n+1,1} = f_{n,1} + 1,\ f_{n+1,k} = f_{n,k},\ k = 2, \ldots, n,\ N_{n+1} = N_n + 1 \mid \mathscr{F}_n) = \alpha$.

Proof. By Assumption 1, we have

$$\begin{aligned}
&P(f_{n+1,k+1} = f_{n,k+1} + 1,\ f_{n+1,k} = f_{n,k} - 1,\ f_{n+1,j} = f_{n,j}\ j \neq q,\\
&\quad N_{n+1} = N_n \mid \mathscr{F}_n)\\
&\quad = P(\{\exists i, S_{n,i} = k,\ S_{n+1,i} = S_{n,i} + 1\} \mid \mathscr{F}_n)\\
&\quad = E(f_{n,k}\, 1_{\{S_{n,i}=k,\ S_{n+1,i}=S_{n,i}+1,\ N_{n+1}=N_n\}} \mid \mathscr{F}_n)\\
&\quad = f_{n,k} P(S_{n,i} = k,\ S_{n+1,i} = S_{n,i} + 1,\ N_{n+1} = N_n \mid \mathscr{F}_n)\\
&\quad = \frac{(ak+b)(1-\alpha)}{an + bN_n} f_{n,k}.
\end{aligned}$$

So we have the assertion (1).

The assertion (2) follows from (A-2). □

Proposition 4. *Suppose that X_n, $n = 1, 2, \ldots$, are random variables which satisfy*

$$E\left[\max_{1 \le k \le n} |X_k|^2\right] \le C n^{\delta}, \qquad n = 1, 2, \ldots, \tag{1}$$

for some constants $C > 0$ and $\delta > 0$. Then $n^{-\frac{\delta}{2}-\varepsilon} X_n \to 0$ a.s. for any $\varepsilon > 0$.

Proof. For any $l \in \mathbb{N}$, we have

$$E\left[\max_{2^l \le k \le 2^{l+1}} \left(\frac{|X_k|}{k^{\frac{\delta}{2}+\varepsilon}}\right)^2\right] \le 2^{-l(\frac{\delta}{2}+\varepsilon)} E\left[\max_{2^l \le k \le 2^{l+1}} X_k^2\right] \le C\, 2^{\delta - 2l\varepsilon}.$$

So we have

$$E\left[\sum_{l=1}^{\infty} \max_{2^l \le k \le 2^{l+1}} \left(\frac{|X_k|}{k^{\frac{\delta}{2}+\varepsilon}}\right)^2\right] \le C \sum_{l=1}^{\infty} 2^{\delta - 2l\varepsilon} < \infty,$$

which implies that $\displaystyle\max_{2^l \le k \le 2^{l+1}} \frac{|X_k|}{k^{\frac{\delta}{2}+\varepsilon}} \to 0$ a.s., as $l \to \infty$.

This completes the proof. □

Using this proposition, we get the evaluation about N_n, $n = 1, 2, \ldots$.

Lemma 5. $\displaystyle\frac{1}{n^{\frac{1}{2}+\varepsilon}} |N_n - n\alpha| \to 0$, *a.s. as $n \to \infty$, for any $\varepsilon > 0$.*

Proof. Notice that N_n satisfies

$$P(N_{n+1} = N_n + 1 \mid \mathscr{F}_n) = \alpha,$$
$$P(N_{n+1} = N_n \mid \mathscr{F}_n) = 1 - \alpha.$$

Therefore we have,

$$E\left[\max_{1 \le k \le n} (N_k - k\alpha)^2\right] \le 4E\left[(N_n - n\alpha)^2\right] = 4\left[n(\alpha - \alpha^2) + 2\alpha^2 - 3\alpha + 1\right].$$

By Proposition 4, we have our assertion. □

4. Proof of the main result

For $n,\ k \ge 1$, let $X_{n,k} = f_{n,k} - nc_k$, $d_{n,k} = X_{n,k} - E[X_{n,k} \mid \mathscr{F}_{n-1}]$, $C_{n,k} = \begin{cases} \dfrac{(ak+b)(1-\alpha)}{an+bN_n}, & n \ge k, \\ 0, & n < k, \end{cases}$ and $u_k = \dfrac{(ak+b)(1-\alpha)}{a+b\alpha}$. Note that $f_{n,k} = 0$ for $n \le k-1$, then by the Lemma 3, we have, for any k and $n \ge 1$,

$$E[f_{n+1,k} \mid \mathscr{F}_n] = f_{n,k} + C_{n,k-1} f_{n,k-1} - C_{n,k} f_{n,k}, \qquad k \ge 2, \tag{2}$$
$$E[f_{n+1,1} \mid \mathscr{F}_n] = f_{n,1} + \alpha - C_{n,1} f_{n,1}. \tag{3}$$

Following Equations (2) and (3), we have

$$E[X_{n+1,k} \mid \mathscr{F}_n] = (1 - C_{n,k})X_{n,k} + C_{n,k-1} f_{n,k-1} - c_k - C_{n,k} nc_k, \tag{4}$$
$$E[X_{n+1,1} \mid \mathscr{F}_n] = (1 - C_{n,1})X_{n,1} + \alpha - nc_1 C_{n,1} - c_1. \tag{5}$$

For each integer $n \ge 1$ and $k \ge 1$, we denote $\gamma_{n,k} = 1 - C_{n,k}$. Let $\varepsilon_{n,1} = \alpha - nc_1 C_{n,1} - c_1$ and $\varepsilon_{n,k} = C_{n,k-1} f_{n,k-1} - c_k - C_{n,k} nc_k$, $k \ge 2$. Then we have, $X_{n+1,k} = d_{n+1,k} + \gamma_{n,k} X_{n,k} + \varepsilon_{n,k}$.

We see that

$$\left(\prod_{j=1}^{n-1} \gamma_{j,k}\right)^{-1} X_{n,k} = M_{n,k} + A_{n,k},$$

where $M_{n,k} = \displaystyle\sum_{l=1}^{n-1} \left(\prod_{j=1}^{l} \gamma_{j,k}\right)^{-1} d_{l+1,k}$ is a martingale in n and $A_{n,k} = \displaystyle\sum_{l=1}^{n-1} \left(\prod_{j=1}^{l} \gamma_{j,k}\right)^{-1} \varepsilon_{l,k}$.

Lemma 6. *Let* $c = \min\{a, a+b\}$. *Then for each* $k \ge 1$, *there are constants* r_k *and* s_k *such that*

(1) $$\left(\prod_{j=1}^{n}\gamma_{j,k}\right)^{-1}\leq r_k\exp\left(\frac{u_k|b|}{c}\sum_{j=1}^{n}\frac{1}{j}\left|\alpha-\frac{N_j}{j}\right|\right)n^{u_k},\qquad n\geq 1.$$

(2) $$\left(\prod_{j=1}^{n}\gamma_{j,k}\right)^{-1}\geq s_k\exp\left(-\frac{u_k|b|}{c}\sum_{j=1}^{n}\frac{1}{j}\left|\alpha-\frac{N_j}{j}\right|\right)n^{u_k},\qquad n\geq 1.$$

Proof. For each $k\geq 1$, let $i_k=\min\left\{n\geq 1,\ \frac{(ak+b)(1-\alpha)}{cn}<1\right\}\vee k$. Then we have

$$\log\left(\left(\prod_{j=i_k}^{n}\gamma_{j,k}\right)^{-1}\right)=-\sum_{j=i_k}^{n}\log(\gamma_{j,k})$$
$$=-\sum_{j=i_k}^{n}\log(1-C_{j,k})=I_1+I_2,\qquad n>i_k,$$

where $I_1=\sum_{j=i_k}^{n}C_{j,k}$ and $I_2=\sum_{j=i_k}^{n}\sum_{l=2}^{\infty}\frac{1}{l}(C_{j,k})^l$. Then we have

$$I_1=\sum_{j=i_k}^{n}\frac{1}{j}u_k+\sum_{j=i_k}^{n}\left(C_{j,k}-\frac{1}{j}u_k\right)\leq u_k(1+\log n)+\frac{u_k|b|}{c}\sum_{j=i_k}^{n}\frac{1}{j}\left|\alpha-\frac{N_j}{j}\right|,$$

and

$$\begin{aligned}I_2&=\sum_{m=2}^{\infty}\frac{1}{m}\sum_{j=i_k}^{n}\frac{1}{j^2}\left(\frac{(ak+b)(1-\alpha)}{a+b\frac{N_j}{j}}\right)^2(C_{j,k})^{m-2}\\&\leq\sum_{m=2}^{\infty}\frac{1}{m}\left(\frac{(ak+b)(1-\alpha)}{c}\right)^2\left(\frac{(ak+b)(1-\alpha)}{i_kc}\right)^{m-2}\sum_{j=i_k}^{n}\frac{1}{j^2}\\&\leq\sum_{m=1}^{\infty}\frac{2i_k^2}{m}\left(\frac{(ak+b)(1-\alpha)}{i_kc}\right)^m\\&\leq 2i_k^2\log\left(1-\frac{(ak+b)(1-\alpha)}{i_kc}\right).\end{aligned}$$

So we have

$$\left(\prod_{j=i_k}^{n}\gamma_{j,k}\right)^{-1}\leq\left(1-\frac{(ak+b)(1-\alpha)}{i_kc}\right)^{2i_k^2}$$
$$\times\exp\left(u_k+\frac{u_k|b|}{c}\sum_{j=i_k}^{n}\frac{1}{j}\left|\alpha-\frac{N_j}{j}\right|\right)n^{u_k}.$$

On the other hand,

$$\log\left(\left(\prod_{j=i_k}^{n}\gamma_{j,k}\right)^{-1}\right)\geq I_1\geq u_k\log n-\sum_{j=1}^{i_k}\frac{1}{j}u_k-\frac{u_k|b|}{c}\sum_{j=i_k}^{n}\frac{1}{j}\left|\alpha-\frac{N_j}{j}\right|,$$

and so,

$$\left(\prod_{j=i_k}^{n}\gamma_{j,k}\right)^{-1}\geq\exp\left(-\sum_{j=1}^{i_k}\frac{1}{j}u_k-\frac{u_k|b|}{c}\sum_{j=i_k}^{n}\frac{1}{j}\left|\alpha-\frac{N_j}{j}\right|\right)n^{u_k}.$$

Since $\alpha\leq\gamma_{n,k}\leq 1$, then we have our assertion. □

Next, we evaluate martingale $\{M_{n,k}\}_{n=1}^{\infty}$ and the remain part $\{A_{n,k}\}_{n=1}^{\infty}$. Let $\tau=\tau_t$ be the stopping time defined by $\tau=\inf\{n,|N_n-n\alpha|\geq tn^{\frac{3}{4}}\}$, $t>0$. Then we have $|N_{\tau\wedge n}-(\tau\wedge n)\alpha|\leq t(\tau\wedge n)^{\frac{3}{4}}+1\leq(t+1)(\tau\wedge n)^{\frac{3}{4}}$.

Proposition 7. *For each $k\in\mathbb{N}$ and $t>0$, there exist some constant $\tilde{C}_{t,k}$ such that $E\left[\max_{1\leq m\leq n}(M_{m\wedge\tau,k})^2\right]\leq\tilde{C}_{t,k}n^{2u_k+1}$, $n>1$.*

Proof. Note that

$$|d_{n,k}|=\left|X_{n,k}-X_{n-1,k}-E[X_{n,k}-X_{n-1,k}\mid\mathscr{F}_{n-1}]\right|\leq 2(1+c_k).\quad(6)$$

Therefore we have,

$$E\left[\max_{1\leq m\leq n}M_{m\wedge\tau,k}^2\right]\leq 4E\left[|M_{n\wedge\tau,k}|^2\right]\leq 8E\left[\sum_{l=1}^{(n-1)\wedge\tau}\left(\prod_{j=1}^{l}\gamma_{j,k}\right)^{-2}d_{l+1,k}^2\right]$$
$$\leq 32(1+c_k)^2\sum_{l=1}^{n-1}r_k^2\exp\left(\frac{2u_k|b|}{c}\sum_{j=1}^{l}\frac{t+1}{j^{\frac{5}{4}}}\right)l^{2u_k}.\quad(7)$$

So letting $\tilde{C}_{t,k}=32(1+c_k)^2r_k^2\exp\left(\frac{2u_k|b|}{c}\sum_{j=1}^{\infty}\frac{t+1}{j^{\frac{5}{4}}}\right)$, we have the assertion. □

Proposition 8. *There exist some constants $\hat{C}_{t,k}$, for each $k\in\mathbb{N}$ and $t>0$, such that $E\left[|A_{n\wedge\tau,k}|^2\right]\leq\hat{C}_{t,k}n^{2u_k+1}$, $n>1$.*

Proof. We prove this proposition by induction in k.
Step 1. We consider the case that $k=1$. Notice that

$$
\begin{aligned}
|\varepsilon_{n,1}| &= \left|\alpha - c_1 - \frac{(a+b)(1-\alpha)}{a+b\frac{N_n}{n}} c_1\right| \\
&= \left|\frac{(a+b)(1-\alpha)}{a+b\alpha} c_1 - \frac{(a+b)(1-\alpha)}{a+b\frac{N_n}{n}} c_1\right| \\
&\leq \frac{(a+b)(1-\alpha)|b|c_1}{c^2}\left|\frac{N_n - n\alpha}{n}\right|. \qquad (8)
\end{aligned}
$$

By the definition of $A_{n,k}$ and Lemma 5 we have

$$
\begin{aligned}
E\big[|A_{n\wedge\tau,1}|^2\big] &\leq nE\left[\sum_{l=1}^{(n-1)\wedge\tau}\left(\prod_{j=1}^{l}\gamma_{j,1}\right)^{-2}|\varepsilon_{l,1}|^2\right] \\
&\leq n\sum_{l=1}^{n-1}\left\{r_1^2\exp\left(\frac{2u_1|b|}{c}\sum_{j=1}^{l}\frac{t}{j^{\frac{5}{4}}}\right)l^{2u_1}\frac{(u_1|b|c_1)^2}{c^2}E\left[\frac{(N_l-l\alpha)^2}{l^2}\right]\right\} \\
&\leq 4r_1^2\exp\left(\frac{2u_1|b|}{c}\sum_{j=1}^{\infty}\frac{t+1}{j^{\frac{5}{4}}}\right)\frac{(u_1|b|c_1)^2}{c^2}n \\
&\quad\times\sum_{l=1}^{n-1}\{(\alpha-\alpha^2)l^{2u_1-1}+(2\alpha^2-3\alpha+1)l^{2u_1-2}\}.
\end{aligned}
$$

Letting $\hat{C}_{t,1} = 8r_1^2\frac{(u_1|b|c_1)^2}{c^2}\exp\left(\frac{2u_1|b|}{c}\sum_{j=1}^{\infty}\frac{t+1}{j^{\frac{5}{4}}}\right)$, then we have our assertion for $k=1$.

Step 2. Suppose that our assertion is valid for k. Because $\left(\prod_{j=1}^{n-1}\gamma_{j,k}\right)^{-1}X_{n,k} = M_{n,k} + A_{n,k}$, by the assumption for k and Proposition 7, we have $E\left[\max_{1\leq m\leq n}\left(\prod_{j=1}^{(m-1)\wedge\tau}\gamma_{j,k}\right)^{-2}X^2_{m\wedge\tau,k}\right] \leq 2(\tilde{C}_{t,k}+\hat{C}_{t,k})n^{2u_k+1}$, $n\geq 1$. Note that

$$
\begin{aligned}
|\varepsilon_{n,k+1}| &= |C_{n,k}f_{n,k} - c_k + 1 - C_{n,k+1}nc_{k+1}| \\
&\leq |C_{n,k}(f_{n,k}-nc_k)| + |nC_{n,k}-u_k|c_k + |nC_{n,k+1}-u_{k+1}|c_{k+1} \\
&\leq \frac{(ak+b)(1-\alpha)}{c}\left|\frac{X_{n,k}}{n}\right| + \frac{b}{c}(u_kc_k+u_{k+1}c_{k+1})\left|\alpha-\frac{N_n}{n}\right|. \qquad (9)
\end{aligned}
$$

If $n\leq\tau$,

$$
\left(\prod_{j=1}^{n}\gamma_{j,k+1}\right)^{-1}X_{n,k} = (\gamma_{n,k+1})^{-1}\left(\prod_{j=1}^{n-1}\gamma_{j,k+1}\right)^{-1}X_{n,k}
$$

$$= \gamma_{n,k+1}^{-1} \frac{\left(\prod_{j=1}^{n-1} \gamma_{j,k+1}\right)^{-1}}{\left(\prod_{j=1}^{n-1} \gamma_{j,k}\right)^{-1}} \max_{1 \le m \le n} \left(\prod_{j=1}^{m-1} \gamma_{j,k} \right)^{-1} X_{m,k}$$

$$\le \alpha^{-1} \frac{r_{k+1}}{s_k} \exp\left(\frac{|b|(u_{k+1} + u_k)}{c} \sum_{j=1}^{n-1} \frac{t+1}{j^{\frac{5}{4}}} \right) (n-1)^{u_{k+1} - u_k}$$

$$\times \max_{1 \le m \le n} \left(\prod_{j=1}^{m-1} \gamma_{j,k} \right)^{-1} X_{m,k}.$$

By Lemma 6, we have

$$E\big[(A_{n\wedge\tau,k+1})^2\big] \le E\left[n \sum_{h=1}^{(n-1)\wedge\tau} \left(\prod_{j=1}^{h} \gamma_{j,k+1} \right)^{-2} \varepsilon_{h,k+1}^2 \right]$$

$$= n \sum_{h=1}^{n-1} E\left[\left(\prod_{j=1}^{h} \gamma_{j,k+1} \right)^{-2} \varepsilon_{h,k+1}^2,\ h \le \tau \right]$$

$$\le 2n \frac{(ak+b)^2(1-\alpha)^2}{c^2} \sum_{h=1}^{n-1} E\left[\left(\prod_{j=1}^{h} \gamma_{j,k+1} \right)^{-2} \frac{X_{h,k}^2}{h^2},\ h \le \tau \right]$$

$$+ 2n \left(\frac{b}{c} (u_k c_k + u_{k+1} c_{k+1}) \right)^2 \sum_{h=1}^{n-1} E\left[\left(\prod_{j=1}^{h} \gamma_{j,k+1} \right)^{-2} \frac{(N_h - h\alpha)^2}{h^2},\ h \le \tau \right]$$

$$\le 2n \frac{(ak+b)^2(1-\alpha)^2}{c^2} \sum_{h=1}^{n-1} \alpha^{-2} \frac{r_{k+1}^2}{s_k^2} \exp\left(\frac{2|b|(u_{k+1} + u_k)}{c} \sum_{j=1}^{n-1} \frac{t+1}{j^{\frac{5}{4}}} \right)$$

$$\times h^{2u_{k+1} - 2u_k - 2} E\left[\max_{1 \le m \le h} \left(\prod_{j=1}^{m-1} \gamma_{j,k} \right)^{-1} X_{m,k},\ h \le \tau \right]$$

$$+ 4n \left(\frac{b}{c} (u_k c_k + u_{k+1} c_{k+1}) \right)^2 r_{k+1}^2 \sum_{h=1}^{n-1} \exp\left(\frac{2u_{k+1}|b|}{c} \sum_{j=1}^{h} \frac{t+1}{j^{\frac{5}{4}}} \right) h^{2u_{k+1} - 1}$$

$$\le 2n \frac{(ak+b)^2(1-\alpha)^2}{c^2}$$

$$\times \sum_{h=1}^{n-1} 2(\tilde{C}_{t,k} + \hat{C}_{t,k}) h^{2u_{k+1} - 1} \frac{r_{k+1}^2}{s_k^2} \exp\left(\frac{2|b|(u_{k+1} + u_k)}{c} \sum_{j=1}^{h} \frac{t+1}{j^{\frac{5}{4}}} \right)$$

$$+ 4n \left(\frac{b}{c} (u_k c_k + u_{k+1} c_{k+1}) \right)^2 r_{k+1}^2 \exp\left(\frac{2u_{k+1}|b|}{c} \sum_{j=1}^{\infty} \frac{t+1}{j^{\frac{5}{4}}} \right) h^{2u_{k+1}}.$$

So there exists a constant $\hat{C}_{t,k+1}$ such that $E\big[(A_{n\wedge\tau,k+1})^2\big] \leq \hat{C}_{t,k+1}n^{2u_{k+1}+1}$. This completes our assertion. □

Now let us prove Theorem 1. By Propositions 7 and 8 we have $E\left[\max_{1\leq m\leq n}\left(\prod_{j=1}^{m\wedge\tau-1}\gamma_{j,k}\right)^{-2}X_{m\wedge\tau,k}^2\right] \leq 2(\tilde{C}_{t,k}+\hat{C}_{t,k})n^{2u_k+1}$, $n \geq 1$. By assertion (2) in *Lemma 6*, we have for every $\omega \in \{\tau = \infty\}$, $\left(\prod_{j=1}^{m}\gamma_{j,k}\right)^{-2} \geq s_k^2\exp\left(-\frac{2u_k|b|}{c}\sum_{j=1}^{m}\frac{t}{j^{\frac{5}{4}}}\right)m^{2u_k}$. Let $v = s_k^2\exp\left(-\frac{2u_k|b|}{c}\sum_{j=1}^{\infty}\frac{t}{j^{\frac{5}{4}}}\right)$. So we see that

$$
\begin{aligned}
&E\left[\max_{1\leq m\leq n} vm^{2u_k}1_{\{\tau=\infty\}}(X_{m\wedge\tau,k})^2\right]\\
&\leq E\left[\max_{1\leq m\leq n}\left(\prod_{j=1}^{m}\gamma_{j,k}\right)^{-2}X_{m,k}^2,\ \tau=\infty\right]\\
&\leq 2(\tilde{C}_{t,k}+\hat{C}_{t,k})\left(1-\frac{(ak+b)(1-\alpha)}{c}\right)^{-2}n^{2u_k+1}.
\end{aligned}
$$

According to the Proposition 4 we get that $\frac{X_{n,k}1_{\{\tau=\infty\}}}{n^{\frac{1}{2}+\varepsilon}}$ converges to 0 almost surely. Notice that $P(\tau_t = \infty) \to 1$, as $t \to \infty$. So $\frac{X_{n,k}}{n^{\frac{1}{2}+\varepsilon}}$ converges to 0 almost surely.

References

[1] Durrett, R.: Probability Theory and Examples. Wadsworth & Brooks, Califonia 1991
[2] Pareto, V.: Le Cours d'Economie Politique. Macmillan, London 1896-1897
[3] Sato, K.: Size, growth and the Pareto curve. Discussion Paper No.145, State University of New York at Buffalo (1970)
[4] Simon, H.A.: On a Class of Skew Distribution. Biometrica **42**, 425-440 (1955)
[5] Yule, G.U.: A mathematical theory of evolution. F.R.S. Phil. Trans. B **213**, 21

Subject Index

Instructions for Authors

A. General

1. Papers submitted for publication will be considered only if they have not been and will not be published elsewhere without permission from the publisher and the Research Center for Mathematical Economics.

2. Every submitted paper will be subject to review. The names of reviewers will not be disclosed to the authors or to anybody not involved in the editorial process.

3. The authors are asked to transfer the copyright to their articles to Springer-Verlag if and when these are accepted for publication.

The copyright covers the exclusive and unlimited rights to reproduce and distribute the article in any form of reproduction. It also covers translation rights for all languages and countries.

4. Manuscript must be written in English. One original and 3 sets of photocopies should be submitted to the following address.

Professor Toru Maruyama
Department of Economics
Keio University
2-15-45 Mita, Minato-ku, Tokyo
108-8345 Japan

5. **Offprints**: Twenty-five (25) **offprints** of each paper will be supplied free of charge. Additional offprints can be ordered at cost price.

B. Preparation of Manuscript

1. Manuscripts must be double-spaced (not 1.5), with wide margins (at least 25 mm), and large type (at least 12 point) on one side of A4 paper. Any manuscript that does not meet these requirements will be returned to the author immediately for retyping.

2. All manuscripts would finally be composed using our Springer LaTeX macro package. The Springer macros use standard LaTeX packages - if you do not have these packages refer to `http://www.ctan.org` or `http://www.dante.de/tex`. If authors make manuscripts by word-processing software other than TeX, please follow our styles as possible. For authors who prepare their manuscripts by TeX, we strongly recommend to visit our homepage, `http://www.springeronline.com/economics/`. You can download all the necessary macro packages with instructions for LaTeX2e from `ftp://ftp.springer.de/pub/tex/latex/svjour/global/`. For support, please contact `texhelp@springer.de`.

3. **The title page** must include: title; short (running) title of up to 60/85 characters; first names and surnames of all coauthors with superscript numerals indicating their affiliations; full street addresses of all affiliations; address to which proofs should be sent; fax number; and any footnotes referring to the title (indicated by asterisks*).

4. **Summary/abstract**: Each paper must be preceded by a summary/an abstract, which should not exceed 100 words.

5. **The Journal of Economic Literature index number (JEL classification)** should be indicated and the statement of the **2000 Mathematics Subject Classification (MSC) numbers** is desirable. You can check JEL classification with Internet at `http://ideas.repec.org/JEL/` as well as 2000 MSC numbers at `http://www.ams.org/msc`.

6. **Main text**: All tables and figures must be cited in the text and numbered consecutively with Arabic numerals according to the sequence in

which they are cited. Please mark the desired position of tables and figures in the left margin of the manuscript.

Do not italicize, underscore, or use boldface for headings and subheadings. Words that are to be italicized should be underscored in pencil.

Abbreviations must be spelled out at first mention in summary/abstract and main text. Abbreviations should also be spelled out at first mention in figure legends and table footnotes.

Short equations can be run in with the text. Equations that are displayed on a separate line should be numbered.

7. **References**: The list of references should be in alphabetical order and include the names and initials of all authors (see examples below). Whenever possible, please update all references to papers accepted for publication, preprints or technical reports, giving the exact name of the journal, as well as the volume, first and last page numbers and year, if the article has already been published or accepted for publication.

When styling the references, the following examples should be observed:

Journal article:
1. or [F-M] Freed, D.S., Melrose, R.B.: A mod *k* index theorem. Invent. Math. **107**, 283-299 (1992)

Complete book:
2. or [C-S] Conway, J.H., Sloane, N.J.: Sphere packings, lattices, and groups (Grundlehren Math. Wiss. Bd. 290) Berlin Heidelberg New York: Springer 1988

Single contribution in a book:
3. or [B] Border, K.C.: Functional analytic tools for expected utility theory. In: Aliprantis, C.D. et al. (eds.): Positive operators, Riesz spaces and economics. Berlin Heidelberg New York: Springer 1991, pp. 69-88

8. **Citations in the text** should be either by numbers in square brackets, e.g. [1], referring to an alphabetically ordered and numbered list, or by the author's initials in square brackets, e.g. [F-M], or by author and year in parentheses, e.g. Freed and Melrose (1992). Any of these styles is acceptable if used consistently throughout the paper. In the third system, if a work with more than two authors is cited, only the first author's name plus "et al." need be given and if there is more than one reference by the same author or team of authors in the same year, then a, b, c should be added after the year both in the text and in the list of references.

9. **Tables** are to be numbered separately from the illustrations. Each table should have a brief and informative title. All abbreviations used in a table must be defined in a table footnote on first use, even if already defined in the text. In subsequent tables abbreviations need not be redefined. Individual footnotes should be indicated by superscript lowercase a, b, c, etc. Permission forms must be provided for any tables from previously published sources (same procedure as with figures; see below).

10. **Figures**: If you have access to suitable software, you can design your figures directly on a computer, but creation by other means is of course also possible. In any case the originals should be pasted into the camera-ready copy at the appropriate places and with the correct orientation. If necessary, the figures may be drawn overscale, but in this case suitably reduced copies should be pasted into the script.

If a figure has been published previously, acknowledge its source and submit written permission signed by author and publisher. The source must be included in the reference list. If a permission fee is required, it must be paid by the author. Responsibility for meeting this requirement lies entirely with the author.

MIX
Papier aus verantwortungsvollen Quellen
Paper from responsible sources
FSC® C105338

If you have any concerns about our products,
you can contact us on
ProductSafety@springernature.com

In case Publisher is established outside the EU,
the EU authorized representative is:
Springer Nature Customer Service Center GmbH
Europaplatz 3, 69115 Heidelberg, Germany

Printed by Libri Plureos GmbH
in Hamburg, Germany